THE BALFOUR DECLARATION

THE BALFOUR DECLARATION

SIXTY-SEVEN WORDS

100 YEARS OF CONFLICT

Elliot Jager

gefen
publishing house בית הוצאה לאור גפן Est. 1981
JERUSALEM ● NEW YORK

Scripture quotations are from the King James Bible.

COVER DESIGN: Leah Ben Avraham/Noonin Graphics
TYPESETTING: Benjie Herskowitz, Etc Studios

ISBN: 978-965-229-924-6

1 3 5 7 9 8 6 4 2

Gefen Publishing House Ltd.   Gefen Books
6 Hatzvi Street   516-593-1234
Jerusalem 94386, Israel   orders@gefenpublishing.com
972-2-538-0247
orders@gefenpublishing.com

www.gefenpublishing.com

Printed in Israel

Library of Congress Cataloging-in-Publication Data

Names: Jager, Elliot, author.
Title: The Balfour Declaration : sixty-seven words - 100 years of conflict :
    a concise account of the players, their motivations, and the setting for
    one of the most consequential letters of modern history / by Elliot Jager.
Description: Jerusalem, Israel : Gefen Publishing House Ltd., [2017]
Identifiers: LCCN 2017021488 | ISBN 9789652299246
Subjects: LCSH: Balfour Declaration. | Palestine--History. | Zionism--Great
    Britain. | Great Britain--Foreign relations--Middle East. | Middle
    East--Foreign relations--Great Britain.
Classification: LCC DS125.5 .J34 2017 | DDC 956.94/04--dc23 LC record available
at https://lccn.loc.gov/2017021488

For Lisa

CONTENTS

Introduction

NEVER ENDING WAR

The year 2017 marks the centenary of the Balfour Declaration. I thought I had a pretty good idea about what the Balfour Declaration was – until I began working on this book.[1]

As most people who keep up with Arab-Israel affairs know, the Balfour Declaration was a letter from British Foreign Secretary Arthur James Balfour to Lord Rothschild, a leader of British Jewry, that began a process by which the international community, the League of Nations, and later, the United Nations came to embrace the idea of the establishment in Palestine of a national home for the Jewish people.

The more research I did, the clearer it became that the Balfour Declaration is the alpha and omega of the Arab-Israel conflict, it gets to the crux of why the conflict has dragged on for a hundred years, and it illuminates why on July 25, 2016, Mahmoud Abbas sent a letter to the twenty-two-member Arab League asking for help in taking legal action against Britain for issuing the Balfour Declaration in the first place.

An octogenarian, Abbas is chairman of the Palestine Liberation Organization (PLO), president of the Palestinian Authority (PA) – and with normative international legal standards for statehood cast aside – "president of the state of Palestine," or so say 136 countries. In that capacity, from 2009 through 2017, he has refused to negotiate with Israel.[2]

---

1   I was disabused of the notion that I really knew enough about the declaration when, in my capacity as editorial director of www.balfour100.com, I began immersing myself in the subject.

2   As Abbas explains, his hands were tied. "It was [President Barack] Obama who suggested a full settlement freeze [as a prerequisite for negotiations]. I said OK, I accept. We both went up the tree. After that, he came down with a ladder and he removed the ladder and said to me, jump." "Palestinian Leader Mahmoud Abbas's Frustration with Obama," *Newsweek*, April 24, 2011, http://www.newsweek.com/palestinian-leader-mahmoud-abbass-frustration-obama-66509. That's partly true, but what Abbas and his people want (for now, anyway) is for the UN to force Israel back to the 1949 armistice lines without concessions from his camp.

Since 2007, when Hamas (officially known as the Islamic Resistance Movement), a competing Palestinian faction, ousted the PLO from the Gaza Strip, Abbas's influence has waned even in the West Bank where he is headquartered.

The PLO's opposition to the Balfour Declaration is nothing new, having been enshrined in Article 20 of the 1968 PLO covenant:

> The Balfour Declaration, the Mandate for Palestine, and everything that has been based upon them, are deemed null and void. Claims of historical or religious ties of Jews with Palestine are incompatible with the facts of history and the true conception of what constitutes statehood. Judaism, being a religion, is not an independent nationality. Nor do Jews constitute a single nation with an identity of its own; they are citizens of the states to which they belong.[3]

The Hamas covenant of 1988 takes essentially the same anti-Balfour line – with an openly anti-Semitic twist – in its Article 22:

> You may speak as much as you want about regional and world wars. They [the Jews] were behind World War I, when they were able to destroy the Islamic Caliphate, making financial gains and controlling resources. They obtained the Balfour Declaration, formed the League of Nations through which they could rule the world. They were behind World War II, through which they made huge financial gains by trading in armaments, and paved the way for the establishment of their state. It was they who instigated the replacement of the League of Nations with the United Nations and the Security Council to enable them to rule the world through them. There is no war going on anywhere, without having their finger in it.[4]

Both the militant Hamas and the comparatively moderate PLO oppose a national home for the Jewish people. They say Judaism is a religion and as such the Jews don't deserve a state.

Of course, Islam is also a religion and there are fifty-six countries that

---

3   The Avalon Project – Documents in Law, History and Diplomacy, "The Palestinian National Charter: Resolutions of the Palestine National Council July 1–17, 1968," http://avalon.law.yale.edu/20th_century/plocov.asp.

4   The Avalon Project, "Hamas Covenant 1988," accessed June 14, 2017, http://avalon.law.yale.edu/20th_century/hamas.asp.

identify as Muslim and hold membership in the Organization of Islamic Cooperation. In other words, Islamic civilization and the Muslim religion merit dozens of states, but Jewish civilization and the Jewish religion do not merit a single country.

The 1993 Oslo Accords notwithstanding,[5] the PLO covenant – with its denunciation of the Balfour Declaration – has never been legally amended, and for good reason. The problem Palestinian Arabs have with Israel is its existence – not "settlements," "occupied" territory or the security barrier.[6]

Abbas has consistently made the point that the Palestinians won't recognize or accept Israel as a Jewish state.[7] That would acknowledge the *legitimacy* of a Jewish national home and doing so would basically end the conflict. Granted that Arabs and Jews would still need to negotiate boundaries and such, but that would hardly be insurmountable once the Arabs genuinely renounced their obsession with wiping Israel off the face of the earth.

Setting out his reasoning for the proposed lawsuit, Abbas paints a grossly distorted account of the Arab-Israel conflict – one that holds Britain and the Jewish people solely responsible for the misfortunes that have befallen the Palestinian Arabs. He indicts the Balfour Declaration for having had catastrophic consequences for the Palestinian Arabs: it is to blame for their dispersion, and it has blocked them from creating their own Arab state of Palestine. The Palestinian Arabs will never "forgive those who conspired against" them and will remain faithful to their covenant while "working hard to end the occupation of our land and our holy places," Abbas wrote the League.[8]

---

5 The accords signed by the government of Yitzhak Rabin and PLO leader Yasser Arafat established the Palestinian Authority. The agreement cited UN Security Council Resolution 242, which called for the withdrawal of Israeli armed forces from territories captured in the 1967 Arab-Israel war. The accords made no commitment for the establishment of a sovereign Palestinian Arab state. Rabin made clear in the final campaign debate (https://youtu.be/uvwc6ULGes4) with Yitzhak Shamir that he opposed the establishment of a Palestinian state. In his last Knesset speech before he was assassinated by Yigal Amir, a Jewish fanatic, he stated that he opposed dividing Israel's capital Jerusalem (https://youtu.be/6JhxG9Iu4t4).

6 The first West Bank settlement was established strategically at Kfar Etzion, at the southern entrance to Jerusalem, in 1967. The West Bank and Gaza were occupied between 1949 and 1967 by Jordan and Egypt respectively and captured by Israel in the Six-Day War. The security fence was erected, starting in 2003, to block suicide bombers from being driven into Israel during the second intifada.

7 Isabel Kershner, "Abbas Rejects Calling Israel a Jewish State," *New York Times*, April 27, 2009, http://www.nytimes.com/2009/04/28/world/middleeast/28mideast.html.

8 "Palestinian Leader Slams Balfour Declaration in Summit Speech," text of report by Palestinian presidency-controlled news agency Wafa website, July 25, 2016. BBC Worldwide Monitoring, July 27, 2016, accessed via LexisNexis June 14, 2017, http://www.monitor.bbc.co.uk/.

Abbas makes plain that the "occupation" began with the establishment of the Jewish state in 1948 and only got worse after the 1967 Six-Day War. He predictably blames Israel for that war, which resulted in the Jewish state taking control of "the *remaining* lands of historic Palestine in the West Bank, including eastern Jerusalem, and the Gaza Strip."[9]

He demands that the international community compel Israel to withdraw to the 1949 armistice lines so that Palestine can be created in the West Bank, "East" Jerusalem,[10] and Gaza. Of course, when the Arabs held those territories (1949–1967) they did not establish a Palestinian state. But since 1974, in the wake of the Yom Kippur War the previous year, the PLO decided on a change in strategy – it would accept an "independent combatant national authority" over any territory that was "liberated" from Israel.[11]

Recognizing that it could not wipe out Israel in one fell swoop, Palestinian leaders accepted that Israel's destruction would have to be achieved in stages. Beginning in the late 1980s, this strategy was further adapted to allow for a potent cocktail – violence, negotiations, lawfare[12] and suasion or imploring the international community to bring Israel to its knees.

Sure enough, in one resolution after another the UN Security Council has basically adopted the Palestinian Arab narrative that eastern Jerusalem is occupied territory and that Jews have no claim – neither historic nor strategic – to Judea and Samaria.[13]

To reiterate, the conflict is not about "occupied" territory or settlements. The late Palestinian leader Yasser Arafat[14] said plainly that his signing of the 1993 Oslo Peace Accords with Israel was a purely tactical move. On May 10, 1994, speaking at a Johannesburg, South African mosque, Arafat explained,

---

9   Ibid.
10 Jerusalem, a city built on hills, is wedged into the West Bank with Samaria to the north and Judea to the south. In 1967, Israel captured the northern, southern, and eastern sectors of Jerusalem that had been held by Jordan.
11 "Palestine Liberation Organization: Ten Point Plan (June 8, 1974)," Jewish Virtual Library, accessed June 14, 2017, http://www.jewishvirtuallibrary.org/ten-point-plan-of-the-plo-june-1974.
12 Robert Nicholson, "Should Israel Fear Palestinian Lawfare?" *Mosaic*, January 9, 2015, https://mosaicmagazine.com/picks/2015/01/should-israel-fear-palestinian-lawfare/.
13 United Nations Security Council Online, Security Council Resolutions, accessed June 14, 2017, http://www.un.org/en/sc/documents/resolutions/. See, for example, resolutions 446 (1979), 452 (1979), 465 (1980), 476 (1980), 478 (1980), 1397 (2002), 1515 (2003), 1850 (2008), and 2334 (2016) all of which were passed with at least tacit support from successive US administrations.
14 Cairo-born Yasser Arafat (1929–2004) was the longtime leader of the Palestine Liberation Organization and chief of its main Fatah faction. See Jim Hoagland, "Arafat's Loose Lips," *Washington Post*, May 26, 1994, https://www.washingtonpost.com/archive/opinions/1994/05/26/arafats-loose-lips/ffd735a8-fe5f-4172-87fa-a77b4261c820/?utm_term=.e531b9972848.

"This agreement, I am not considering it more than the agreement which had been signed between our prophet Mohammed and Koraish, and you remember the Caliph Omar had refused this agreement and [considered] it a despicable truce."[15]

In the Palestinian Muslim lexicon, what Arafat was signaling is that like the prophet's deal with the Koraish tribe in Arabia, the Oslo accords would also be abrogated when the time was ripe.

The Arab-Israel conflict is an all-or-nothing (zero-sum) clash, because that is the way the Arabs are playing it. If tomorrow the PLO and Hamas recognized Israel's right to exist as a Jewish state and agreed to a demilitarized West Bank and Gaza, Israel would help facilitate the establishment of a Palestinian Arab state. Alternately, if tomorrow the Palestinian polity agreed to political confederation with Jordan (whose population is overwhelmingly Palestinian), recognized Israel's right to exist as a Jewish state, and accepted demilitarization of the West Bank and Gaza, no Israeli government would stand in its way. There would still be plenty of nitty-gritty details to work out, about strategic settlement blocs, for example, but none which are insurmountable.

This brings us back to the Balfour Declaration. Besides marking the 100th anniversary of the declaration, 2017 is the 120th anniversary of the First Zionist Congress, the 70th anniversary of the UN General Assembly Partition Resolution, the 50th anniversary of the Six-Day War, the 40th anniversary of Anwar Sadat's visit to Jerusalem, and the 30th anniversary of the first intifada.

Let me say here that the Balfour Declaration was not a plot against the Arabs. The more you understand how the declaration came to be and how it played out between 1917 (when it was issued) and 1948 (when Israel was born), the more evident it becomes that so much of the calamity that has befallen the Palestinian Arabs has been self-inflicted. Regrettably, the Arabs have a history of "never having lost a chance to miss an opportunity," in the words of the late Israeli statesman Abba Eban.[16]

In the pages ahead you will see how for WWI-era British policymakers, the Balfour Declaration was *foremost* a matter of wartime national interest.

15 Ibid.
16 See Marc D. Charney, "Abba Eban, Eloquent Defender and Voice of Israel, Is Dead at 87," *New York Times*, November 18, 2002, http://www.nytimes.com/2002/11/18/world/abba-eban-eloquent-defender-and-voice-of-israel-is-dead-at-87.html.

For the Jewish people, it represented *foremost* the beginning of the end of two thousand years of statelessness.

And for its Arab enemies – and their enablers – the Balfour Declaration was and remains the West's never-expiated "original sin" – because it made it possible for a non-Muslim people to have sovereignty over a sliver of the "Arab and Muslim Middle East."

This vast Middle East has been Muslim since 638 when the Arabs came up from Arabia and conquered Jerusalem.[17] The Arabs' evolving response to the Balfour Declaration demonstrated that they could not get their head around the idea of sharing even a tiny slice of the region with the Jewish people.

Still, I can understand why the Arabs would reject the Balfour Declaration. I do not say their antagonism is illegitimate or unfounded. I do not claim that justice is exclusively on the side of Zionism. And although this book ends more or less in 1949, I do not assert that as a polity today's Israel is never in the wrong. However, I do contend that continued Arab rejection of the Balfour Declaration one hundred years on makes any compromise leading to a genuine conflict resolution impossible.

So, the purpose of this book is to put in plain words what the declaration was, how it came to be, who was involved, and to show how utterly relentless the Arabs have been in rejecting the Jewish homeland idea.

Elliot Jager
August 2017
Jerusalem, Israel

---

17 Thereby supplanting the Byzantine Christian empire.

Chapter 1

A WORLD TORN ASUNDER

Here is where the world stood on Friday morning, November 2, 1917:

A world war, which had begun in the summer of 1914, was still pitting the Central Powers – including Germany, Austria-Hungary, and the Ottoman Empire (Turkey) – against the Allies led by France, Britain, and Russia. Only seven months earlier, on April 6, the United States had reluctantly abandoned neutrality and entered the fray on the side of the Allies.

In addressing the US Congress, President Woodrow Wilson said: "It is a fearful thing to lead this great peaceful people into war, into the most terrible and disastrous of all wars, civilization itself seeming to be in the balance."[1]

Now, the first American soldiers were in France, at the front.

The world had been torn asunder.

That morning, the newspapers reported – incorrectly it transpired – that Austro-German forces had captured 60,000 Italian Allied prisoners. Also reported was heavy artillery fire on the western front at Flanders, near German-occupied Belgium.

In Russia, where Tsar Nicholas II had been overthrown in March, the government of the liberal Alexander Kerensky had just done well in local elections. But the country's resolve to stay in the war was shattered; within one week, on November 7, the Bolsheviks (or communists), led by Vladimir Lenin, would overthrow Kerensky and Russia would pull out of the war.

The war had devastated Britain. Nevertheless, the British Empire would fight on for another full year until November 11, 1918, when the Central Powers capitulated. By then, well over 700,000 British troops from every stratum of society had been killed in the war.

---

1   Woodrow Wilson, "Address to a Joint Session of Congress Requesting a Declaration of War Against Germany," April 2, 1917. Online by Gerhard Peters and John T. Woolley, The American Presidency Project, http://www.presidency.ucsb.edu/ws/?pid=65366.

Also, on that Friday morning in November, the newspapers reported that Beersheba,[2] a desert town in Ottoman-controlled Palestine, had been captured by British forces. The British Army, headquartered in Egypt, would soon take control of Palestine's Gaza coastal strip.

But one piece of momentous news came too late to make it into the morning newspapers that day. British Foreign Secretary Arthur James Balfour (1848–1930) – Conservative member of a wartime coalition government led by Liberal Party prime minister David Lloyd George (1863–1945) – had written to Lionel Walter Rothschild (1868–1937), a leader of the Jewish community. The letter, now known as the Balfour Declaration, read:

Dear Lord Rothschild,

I have much pleasure in conveying to you, on behalf of His Majesty's Government, the following declaration of sympathy with Jewish Zionist aspirations which has been submitted to, and approved by, the Cabinet.

"His Majesty's Government view with favour the establishment in Palestine of a national home for the Jewish people, and will use their best endeavours to facilitate the achievement of this object, it being clearly understood that nothing shall be done which may prejudice the civil and religious rights of existing non-Jewish communities in Palestine, or the rights and political status enjoyed by Jews in any other country".

I should be grateful if you would bring this declaration to the knowledge of the Zionist Federation.

Yours,

Arthur James Balfour[3]

---

2   The capture of Beersheba was pivotal to ousting the Turks from Palestine and troops from Australia and also New Zealand played a major role.

3   The Avalon Project, "Balfour Declaration 1917," accessed June 14, 2017, http://avalon.law.yale. edu/20th_century/balfour.asp. The letter was banged out on a typewriter that must have been old-fashioned even for its time. "Yours" and "Arthur Balfour" were scribbled in longhand. The "s" in "yours" is smudged. Rothschild turned over the letter to the British Museum. It is now at the British Library.

A full week later, on November 9, 1917, a terse dispatch on the declaration headlined "Britain Favors Zionism" appeared in the *New York Times*. The newspaper and its German Jewish owners were unsympathetic to the Zionist cause. Citing Balfour's letter, the newspaper referred without comment to a London *Jewish Chronicle* commentary that spoke of an end to Jewish exile.

In Britain, the *Daily Express* – then owned by Lord Beaverbrook – ran the story (also on November 9) under the more expansive headline: "A State for the Jews."

That same November 9, 1917, the *Times* of London headlined its brief report: "Palestine for the Jews. Official sympathy."

Many other newspapers also carried the story:

- The *Daily Chronicle* opined that "one has to go back to Cyrus for a parallel," referring to Babylon's Cyrus the Great who had allowed the Jews to return to Palestine circa 458 BCE. Nebuchadnezzar, a previous ruler of Babylon had expelled the Jews and destroyed their temple in 586 BCE. In lauding the declaration, the *Chronicle* said it would bolster the British Empire's hold on the strategic Suez Canal.

- The *Irish Times* – "It would be a great gain that the Jews become a nation and not a hyphenation"

- The *Globe* – "It is indeed a victory for the Jews, but equally a British triumph"

- The *Manchester Guardian* – "This extraordinary people"

- The *Scotsman* – "Next Year in Jerusalem"[4]

First, though, there was the matter of completing the liberation of Palestine from the crumbling Ottoman Empire.

Toward the end of January and beginning of February 1915, an Ottoman attempt to capture the strategic Suez Canal in British-controlled Egypt had been pushed back by the British Army in a key attack now known as the Battle of the Suez Canal.

As they contemplated the inevitable post-war colonial competition with France and other powers, British strategists – among them T. E. Lawrence

---

4   For a compendium of press reactions see Nahum Sokolow, A. J. Balfour and Arthur Hertzberg, *History of Zionism 1600–1916* (New York: Ktav, 1969), 84–99. See, too, Leonard Stein, *The Balfour Declaration* (London: Vallentine Mitchell, 1961), 562.

("Lawrence of Arabia") – had sought, with dubious results beyond the Arabian Peninsula, to mobilize Arab chieftains in the Allied war against the Ottoman Turks.

Thus, in talks between the British high commissioner in Egypt, Sir Henry McMahon, and Hussein bin Ali, the Hashemite ruler who had declared himself Sharif of Mecca, Britain promised on October 24, 1915, to back Arab independence in Arabia. Crucially, no reference was made to Palestine.[5]

The Arab Revolt started in June 1916 with attacks on Ottoman garrisons in Arabia.

Keep in mind that at the post-WWI Paris Peace Conference – also known as the Versailles Peace Conference – in 1919 Hussein and his son Feisal did not so much as suggest that McMahon had promised Palestine for the Arabs.

McMahon himself wrote in the *Times* in 1937: "I feel it my duty to state, and I do so definitely and emphatically, that it was not intended by me in giving this pledge to King Hussein to include Palestine in the area in which Arab independence was promised. I had also every reason to believe at the time that the fact that Palestine was not included in my pledge was well understood by King Hussein."[6]

In May 1916, Sir Mark Sykes (1879–1919) of Britain and François Georges-Picot (1870–1951) of France had, without informing either the Zionists or the Arabs, broadly arranged how the powers would divide the Mideast once Ottoman Turkey was defeated.

Much of Palestine was to come under international control. The secret Sykes-Picot Agreement (also approved in principle by Tsarist Russia) would later be made public by Lenin's Russia. When they learned of the accord, both Zionists and Arabs were dismayed.

This is a good point at which to pause and note that the Balfour Declaration was an outlier in the sense that it was not a secret; there was no subterfuge. The secret negotiations over how to divide the Ottoman Empire

---

5   On the matter of Palestine being excluded, see Stein, *Balfour Declaration*, 225. Besides the title of Sharif, Hussein bin Ali was also known as the Emir Hussein and King Hussein. "Sherif Hussein bin Ali," *Wikipedia*, modified July 20, 2017, https://en.wikipedia.org/wiki/Hussein_bin_Ali,_Sharif_of_ Mecca.

6   Henry McMahon, "Letter to the Times," July 23, 1937. See, too, "The McMahon Correspondence of 1915–16," *Bulletin of International News* 16, no. 5 (1939): 6–13.

after its expected fall were driven by the needs of war; hence, the desire to elevate Hussein as an alternative caliph to the Turkish sultan.

The map drawing and memo writing by Britain, France, Russia, and also Greece and Italy made sense only because of the war; the cartography didn't actually create genuine boundaries, but served as expressions of zones of interests. The ubiquitous backdrop was what was happening on the battlefield – the British failure of the Dardanelles Campaign on the Gallipoli Peninsula, for instance, weakened its negotiating stance with Hussein. And far from seeing himself as a pawn of British imperialism, Hussein sought to exploit British desperation. He would be the landlord, and the British his tenants. The British already had analogous relationships with other Arabian Gulf emirs.[7] Nation state sovereignty, it should be noted, was a construct of Western international law. Ottoman Turkey claimed to be a Muslim caliphate; the sultan was its supreme leader, his political power legitimized by religion.

The loyalty of ordinary Arabs, Turks, Persians, Berbers, and Kurds was first and foremost to their immediate family, then to clan and tribe. The Ottomans had ruled over the Middle East since 1299, and from the Maghreb (or North Africa) to the Mashriq (the Arab world east of Egypt) there were no sovereign Arab states.

The first glimmers of Arab nationalism in opposition to the Ottoman Turks might be traceable to Negib Azouri (1870–1916), a Lebanese Maronite Christian who, writing in Paris in 1905, proposed the creation of a pan-Arab state – rooted in race and language not Islam – to stretch from the "Tigris and the Euphrates to the Suez and from the Mediterranean to the Arabian Sea."[8]

Azouri would have excluded Egypt from his pan-Arab state because, he wrote, "the Egyptians do not belong to the Arab race; they are of the African Berber family and the language which they spoke before Islam bears no similarity to Arabic."[9]

On December 11, 1917, General Edmund Allenby demonstratively en-

---

7   I owe these insights to a Van Leer Institute (Jerusalem) lecture by Eugene Rogan of St. Anthony's College, Oxford, presented on November 7, 2016. Let me hasten to add that these are my personal take-aways and not necessarily a rendition of his views.

8   Walter Laqueur and Dan Schueftan, *The Israel-Arab Reader: A Documentary History of the Middle East Conflict* (New York: Penguin Books, 2016), 10.

9   Sylvia Kedourie, *Arab Nationalism: An Anthology* (Berkeley: University of California Press, 1976), 81.

tered Jerusalem's Old City on foot, through the Jaffa Gate, signifying the capture of the city. In London, Prime Minister David Lloyd George heralded the city's capture as "a Christmas present for the British people."[10]

The rest of Palestine and the Mideast followed in due course. In Iraq, Baghdad fell to British forces in March 1918. By September-October 1918, the Ottomans had been utterly defeated and driven back to Anatolia (today's Turkey).

The Palestine that the British took charge of was parched and terribly neglected: Jerusalem had few pavements, no sewer system, and no electricity. Wartime blockades had contributed to food shortages; locusts had ruined what little could be grown. Not much seemed to have changed since the American writer Mark Twain (1835–1910) had visited in 1867 and described the country as dreary, desolate, and unlovely. "Palestine sits in sackcloth and ashes. Over it broods the spell of a curse that has withered its fields and fettered its energies."[11]

10 David B. Green, "1917: General Allenby Shows How a 'Moral Man' Conquers Jerusalem." *Haaretz*, December 11, 2014, http://www.haaretz.com/jewish/features/.premium-1.630999.

11 Mark Twain, *The Innocents Abroad, or the New Pilgrims' Progress: Being Some Account of the Steamship Quaker City's Pleasure Excursion to Europe and the Holy Land,* vol. 2 (New York: Harper and Brothers, 1911), 358.

Chapter 2

THE MISSING MAN:
THEODOR HERZL AND
MODERN POLITICAL ZIONISM

There is a prequel to our account of the Balfour Declaration and it involves Theodor Herzl.

His was an abbreviated, extraordinary, and heartbreaking life. Herzl (1860–1904) was the architect of modern political Zionism, the visionary who, harking back to the biblical and historic covenant of the Jewish people concerning the Land of Israel, developed a blueprint for reestablishing the Jewish commonwealth.

Elegant and aristocratic in demeanor, Herzl became the founding diplomat and chief statesman of the Zionist movement who tirelessly lobbied presidents, kings, and popes to secure support for the idea of a Jewish homeland.

He was born in 1860, into a comfortable, acculturated, German-speaking Jewish family in Budapest. In the milieu of the Austro-Hungarian Empire, he moved to Vienna, the Empire's second capital, when he was about eighteen. In 1884, at the age of twenty-four, he graduated with a doctorate in law from the University of Vienna.

Herzl was drawn to writing and soon established a name for himself as a "feuilletonist" and literary essayist.[1] He was also a playwright and a journalist. Beginning in 1891, he worked for the Viennese *Neue Freie Presse* as its Paris correspondent.

Far bigger than the Austro-Hungarian Empire was the Russian Empire, which included Ukraine, most of Lithuania, Estonia, Latvia, and Poland,

---

1   A feuilleton was the part of a European newspaper devoted to light fiction, sketches, reviews, and general entertainment articles.

where hatred and persecution of the Jews was institutionalized and regime-fueled.

Elsewhere in Europe, Jews had ostensibly been emancipated, namely, been given all the rights of citizenship. Yet, even in enlightened Vienna, Herzl himself encountered anti-Semitism in the university student union. He quit the union in protest, and the experience started him thinking about how to solve "the Jewish problem."

What if the Jews converted to Christianity en masse, he wondered? Would that put an end to the Jew as "the other?" In 1894, Herzl wrote a play, *The New Ghetto*, which showed he had come to accept that neither conversion nor assimilation would be a solution.

Herzl's defining moment came around January 1895, while he was covering the trial of Captain Alfred Dreyfus, an assimilated French Jew, who was facing court-martial on trumped up charges of espionage. Dreyfus was about as un-Jewish and ostentatiously French as one could imagine; yet, as Herzl had come to understand, that did not stop the crowds outside the courtroom from baying "Down with the Jews!"[2]

Consequently, Herzl explored an array of options for solving the Jewish problem. He secured a meeting with Baron Maurice de Hirsch (1831–1896), railroad magnate and leading German Jewish philanthropist, to talk about his inchoate idea of Zionism. While that discussion, on June 2, 1895, came to nothing, it prompted Herzl to refine his Zionist idea in notes and in the diary he kept whose first entry began:

"For some time past I have been occupied with a work of infinite grandeur. At the moment I do not know whether I shall carry it through. It looks like a mighty dream. But for days and weeks it has possessed me beyond the limits of consciousness," he wrote in 1895.[3] That work was a seminal pamphlet of Zionism, entitled *Der Judenstaat* or *The Jewish State*.

Its target was affluent western European Jewish benefactors who, Herzl hoped, would bankroll a Jewish exodus from inhospitable eastern Europe. But those who read the draft told Herzl that the scheme was mad – literally. So, he put the idea aside and returned to Vienna to become his newspaper's literary editor.

---

2 For a compelling novelistic treatment of the affair, see Robert Harris, *An Officer and a Spy* (New York: Vintage, 2014).

3 Theodor Herzl and Raphael Patai, *The Complete Diaries of Theodor Herzl* (New York: Herzl Press, 1960).

Nevertheless, Herzl showed his pamphlet to Jewish notables in Vienna and during his trips to Paris and London. He managed to win over one crucial acolyte, Max Nordau (1849–1923), a physician and social activist. "If you are insane," Nordau wrote to Herzl, "we are insane together. Count me in!"[4]

Encouraged, Herzl redrafted his pamphlet for a popular audience and had it published in Vienna on February 14, 1896. It was soon translated into half a dozen European languages.

Having dismissed both assimilation and conversion as solutions to "the Jewish problem," Herzl proposed in his pamphlet the creation of an independent state sponsored by one or more of the major world powers.

"Let sovereignty be granted to us over a portion of the globe adequate to meet our rightful national requirements; we will attend to the rest," he wrote. A Jewish company would be established to handle financing and logistics. Emigration would be voluntary and incremental.[5]

Having laid out his idea of a Jewish homeland, Herzl would spend the remaining years of his life promoting the scheme to anyone who could positively influence events – Jewish philanthropists, the Muslim sultan of Turkey, the Italian king, the German Kaiser, the Russian interior minister, and the Catholic pope. He piqued the interest of some, though most thought his ideas fanciful. Others rejected the notion of Jewish sovereignty as sacrilegious.

To label Herzl as the founder of modern political Zionism, as a movement, does not mean that he was the first Zionist of the nineteenth century.

I mentioned the 1895 trial of Dreyfus, so it is worth offering some context on the connection between modernity and Zionism. An important catalyst for Herzl's political Zionism was the French Revolution (1789–1799) and the subsequent Emancipation of the Jews (1814) in that country.

This led to Jews being permitted to move to urban areas and to embrace a secular lifestyle. Jewish identity could now be national, and not solely religious: one could now be a French Jew, and not only a Jew who lived in France. Secularism and tolerance opened up opportunities, including citizenship. Yet, it also created dilemmas. Did Jews have to sacrifice their identity to gain acceptance? And what about those who did sublimate their heritage and were nonetheless met with rejection?

---

4   Paul Johnson, *A History of the Jews* (New York: Harper and Row, 1987), 398.

5   Theodor Herzl, "The Jewish Question," chap. 2 in *The Jewish State* (New York: American Zionist Emergency Council, 1946).

Over in eastern Europe in 1881, fifteen years before Herzl's *The Jewish State*, grassroots groups called Hovevei Zion ("Lovers of Zion") had begun to organize in the Russian Empire. The intellectual groundwork had been laid by theoreticians such as Rabbi Yehudah Alkalai (1798–1878); Rabbi Zvi Hirsch Kalischer (1795–1874); the socialist Moses Hess (1812–1875), who recognized that Emancipation was not solving the Jewish problem; Eliezer Ben-Yehuda (1858–1922), who took it upon himself to transform biblical Hebrew into a living language; and Leo Pinsker (1821–1891), a medical doctor who figured that "Judeophobia" was a consequence of the Jews being foreigners everywhere.

But Herzl was uniquely gifted, possessing that rare combination of being a visionary, public relations mastermind, intellectual, and community organizer. Still, generating support for political Zionism within the Jewish world was not easy. Wealthy Jews, for the most part, had little sympathy for political Zionism as opposed to providing philanthropic support for Jewish life in Palestine.

Well, if the elite would not get on board, then Herzl would push his idea from the bottom up. It helped that the Hovevei Zion associations came under his leadership and were incorporated into the Zionist movement.

The situation for Jews in 1897 was mixed. In Turkey proper there was an ambience of tolerance, and Jews were permitted to work in virtually any field. For Jews in the Ottoman Empire's Arab, Kurdish, and Persian areas, life could sometimes be grim. In greater Tripolitania (present-day western Libya), Arab mobs destroyed the synagogue in 1897. In general, Jews were treated as dhimmi or second-class citizens, and many communities lived in fear for their security. They faced harassment and knew that local authorities would turn a blind eye even when Jews were killed in the streets.[6]

---

6   Historically, Islamic civilization regarded Christians and Jews as "People of the Book." Islamic tradition holds that both Jews and Christians broke their covenant with God and corrupted His Scripture. Therefore, they believe only Allah's covenant with Muhammad is true and complete. While Jews and Christians were granted dhimmi or protective second-class status under Islam, Jews often had to pay tribute or a special poll tax; they were forbidden to carry arms. They often had to wear special clothes to distinguish them from the majority population. They had to show deference to Muslims. But within those parameters, and in contrast to European Christian civilization, Jews did have religio-legal recourse. Indeed, though there were also dark times, there were golden periods of Jewish life in Muslim civilization. So long as Jews or Christians submitted to Muslim sovereignty, they could be tolerated and even thrive. These realities were in place when political Zionism came on the scene. And all this helps explain why the idea of a sovereign Jewish state in the Middle East is anathema. It implies a challenge to Muslim religious preeminence. None of the twenty-two member states of the Arab League or the fifty-seven member states of the Organization of

Elsewhere, throughout the immense Tsarist Empire – which included Russia's vast expanse, Ukraine, most of Lithuania, Estonia, Latvia, and Poland – Christian hatred and persecution of the Jews was institutionalized and regime-fueled.

In western Europe, Jews had been ostensibly emancipated and given the rights of citizenship. In France, for example, Jews were given equal rights in 1791. In practice, even in countries where Jews were permitted to acculturate and blend in, they faced continued anti-Semitism, as demonstrated by the Dreyfus Affair (1894–1906).

That was the context in which Herzl founded a weekly Zionist newspaper called *Die Welt* (The World) in June 1897, and more momentously on August 29, 1897, convened the First Zionist Congress in Basel, Switzerland.

Herzl wanted to create an ambiance of respectability and solemnity. This was, after all, a unique and historic gathering about reestablishing a Jewish homeland after 2,000 years of exile. Delegates were thus instructed to wear formal dress befitting the occasion. The Congress issued the following mission statement: "Zionism aims at establishing for the Jewish people a publicly and legally assured home in Palestine."[7]

And this is what Herzl wrote in his diary on September 3, 1897: "Were I to sum up the Basel Congress in a word – which I shall guard against pronouncing publicly – it would be this: At Basel I founded the Jewish state. If I said this out loud today, I would be answered by universal laughter. Perhaps in five years, and certainly in fifty, everyone will know it."[8]

The congress established the World Zionist Organization and elected Herzl as its president. It paved the way for the institutions that were required to raise both funds and consciousness for the return of the Jewish people to Palestine.

The First Zionist Congress was a precursor to the rationale behind the Balfour Declaration because it sought to secure an international declaration approving the idea of a Jewish homeland. Herzl didn't live to see the Balfour Declaration, but it was more or less what he had hoped for – a pronounce-

Islamic Cooperation has recognized Israel's right to exist as a Jewish state. To do that would imply permanent acceptance of a non-Muslim polity in Dar al-Islam – literally, "the home of Islam," or the Middle East. Treaties and truces, however, are permitted. See Martin Gilbert, *In Ishmael's House: A History of Jews in Muslim Lands* (New Haven: Yale, 2010) and Bernard Lewis, *The Jews of Islam* (Princeton, NJ: Princeton University Press, 2014).

7   Basel Program," Jewish Encyclopedia, accessed August 6, 2017, http://www.jewishencyclopedia.com/articles/2612-basel-program.

8   Herzl and Patai, *Diaries of Theodor Herzl*, vol. 2, 581.

ment by a superpower that would gain the imprimatur of the international community, thereby bolstering the practical and legal efforts initiated by the Jews themselves to reconstitute their homeland in Palestine.

In 1898, the Second Zionist Congress set up a bank in London (established Jewish bankers had distanced themselves from the Zionist enterprise). In 1901, the Jewish National Fund was set up, also in London. In June 1902, Herzl testified before the Royal Commission on Alien Immigration to lobby Britain to allow Jews from Russia to find haven in England.

In late 1898, Herzl made his first trip to Eretz Yisrael (Land of Israel), then under Ottoman rule. On the way, in Turkey, he met with German kaiser Wilhelm II on October 18, and received a promise that the emperor would lobby for the Zionist idea with Sultan Abdul Hamid II.[9]

Herzl's efforts, starting in June 19, 1896, to persuade the sultan to back the Zionist enterprise came to nothing – though as late as 1915, Turkey reportedly flirted with the idea of selling some of Palestine to the Zionist movement for the creation of a Jewish homeland.[10]

Back in 1855, philanthropist Sir Moses Montefiore (1784–1885), a leader of British Jews, had already bought land to enable the resettlement of a small number of Jews. In 1891, Arab and Muslim leaders petitioned Sultan Abdul Hamid II to stop Jewish immigration and forbid the sale of land – even wasteland – to Jewish people. Anti-Zionist societies and newspapers were created in Cairo, Jerusalem, and other places. Newly established Jewish communities – or settlements – were attacked by Arab bands starting in 1886. The Ottomans also deported many Jews.

Herzl met with the kaiser again at Mikveh Israel, the first Jewish agricultural school in what would later become Holon (today part of metropolitan Tel Aviv). They met a third time, outside Jerusalem on November 2.

All the while, Zionism had few friends within the Jewish leadership. The wealthy thought it impractical; Liberals opposed it because they favored assimilation. The Orthodox were against it because they believed only God Himself could end the exile and bring the Jews home; the Reform were equally opposed because they wanted Judaism to be exclusively a religious denomination wherever Jews happened to live.

---

9   This is the same bellicose kaiser who led Germany into the First World War and who abdicated in November 1918.

10   Under Sultan Mehmed V real power during the First World War rested with the revolutionary Young Turks triumvirate comprised of Enver Pasha, Talaat Pasha, and Djemal Pasha.

Nonetheless, Herzl persevered in his meetings with world leaders and in organizing the Jewish masses. In 1903, for example, on a visit to Vilna, Poland, he was celebrated as "Herzl the King."

This is how he described his trip to Vilna in his diary: "In the numerous addresses, I was enormously over praised, but the unhappiness of these sorely oppressed people was genuine. Afterwards, all kinds of deputations, laden with gifts, called on me at the hotel, in front of which crowds kept regathering as fast as the police dispersed them."[11]

Herzl met the Ottoman Sultan Abdul Hamid II on May 17, 1901. In his diary, Herzl quoted the sultan as saying: "I am and always have been a friend of the Jews."[12]

Back in Constantinople in February 1902, Herzl learned that the financially strapped Ottoman administration was willing to consider creating a safe haven for the Jews in what is today Iraq – on condition that Herzl mobilize Jewish bankers to lend the Ottomans money. Palestine was expressly excluded from the offer.

All the while, the situation of the Jews of eastern Europe was becoming increasingly untenable. Waves of murderous pogroms, or regime-instigated anti-Jewish rioting, erupted in the vast Russian Empire, including, notoriously, at Kishinev. Between 1902 and 1906, the mayhem resulted in over 2,000 Jewish dead and many, many, more terrorized.

Plainly, if a haven could not be achieved immediately in Ottoman-controlled Palestine, a solution of sorts needed to be found elsewhere. There was talk of Argentina, where Baron Maurice de Hirsch (1831–1896), the German Jewish financier, had been funding Jewish agricultural settlements in rural areas as a refuge for Jews, and not for a Jewish state.

In October 1902, sympathetic British officials, among them Colonial Secretary Joseph Chamberlain (1836–1914), put forth El Arish in the Sinai Peninsula as a possible haven for persecuted Jews. Despite the area's proximity to Palestine, the idea was unappealing to the Zionists and proved impractical.

That same year, Herzl published *Altneuland* (*Old New Land*), a novel in

---

11   Herzl and Patai, *Diaries of Theodor Herzl*, vol. 4, 1543.

12   Ibid., 1113. Abdul Hamid II (1842–1918) became sultan in 1876. He mismanaged his rule and lost one possession after another, for example Egypt to the British in 1882. The 1894 massacre of Armenians by Kurdish irregulars and Turks happened under his regime. He was ultimately deposed in 1909 by the Young Turks.

which he depicted a future Jewish state: tolerant, always ready to help less well-off countries, scientifically advanced, cooperative – and a place where Arabs and Jews would enjoy good relations.

In 1903, the British government offered to establish a sanctuary for persecuted Jews in Uganda, East Africa (now part of Kenya).[13] Herzl was inclined to say yes as an interim measure, on the grounds that the first imperative was rescue. But the delegates of the Sixth Zionist Congress, led by Chaim Weizmann – who would become a key player in the Balfour Declaration story – rejected the idea out of hand. Only Zion would do.

Herzl's last diary entry was for May 16, 1904. He was exhausted. It is unsettling to consider that had Herzl not died age forty-four outside Vienna on July 3, 1904, from heart disease and pneumonia, he would have been only in his late fifties when the Balfour Declaration was issued.

Tragedy followed tragedy. His wife Julia Naschauer Herzl (1860–1904) survived Theodor by only three years. Herzl's eldest daughter Pauline lived until 1930; his son Hans committed suicide at age forty soon after Pauline's funeral.[14] Trude, Herzl's youngest daughter, perished in the Theresienstadt concentration camp in 1943. His only grandchild Stephen committed suicide in 1946.

Herzl wrote that in general realists are those in the rut of routine who are incapable of transcending a narrow circle of antiquated notions. His preferred motto was: "If you will it, it is no dream."[15]

His dream a reality, after the War of Independence, one of the new State of Israel's first actions was to move Herzl's remains to Jerusalem and reinter the country's founding father in the Mount Herzl national cemetery.

---

13   Taking endemic Jew hatred to a higher level, between 1881 and 1884 a series of murderous pogroms – or government-sanctioned anti-Jewish riots – took place in the Russian Empire; these resumed in 1903–1906. Also, in 1903, the Russian Tsarist secret police disseminated the fabricated *Protocols of the Elders of Zion* which has ever since been used by Jew-haters to prove the existence of an international Jewish conspiracy. See, for example, David I. Kertzer, "The Modern Use of Ancient Lies," *New York Times*, May 9, 2002, http://www.nytimes.com/2002/05/09/opinion/the-modern-use-of-ancient-lies.html.

14   He had flirted with conversion to Christianity and was known to suffer from depression.

15   Herzl wrote in German, so this famous expression from his *Altneuland* has been variously translated, especially in English. The Knesset of Israel biography of Herzl goes with: "If you will it, it is no fairy-tale." The Hebrew is most often translated as אם תרצו, אין זו אגדה. http://www.knesset.gov.il/vip/herzl/eng/Herz_Bioframe_eng.html.

Chapter 3

BY THE RIVERS OF BABYLON: ZIONISM

Theodor Herzl's political Zionism was a nineteenth century modern phenomenon, but Zionism itself is the central ethos of Jewish civilization. It is the quest for a Jewish return to Israel and is based on a historical and continuous connection of the Jewish people to the Land of Israel. This connection dates back from time immemorial.

Zion is another name for Jerusalem. It was first used in the Bible in the Second Book of Samuel (4:7): "Nevertheless, David took the stronghold of Zion; the same is the city of David."

In sacred history the root of Jewish identity is the covenant, a fundamental motif of Hebrew and Christian Scripture. There is no covenant without the Land of Israel.

In Jewish tradition, codified in the Bible's Book of Genesis, God promised Abraham that his descendants would inherit the Land of Israel. This covenant or contract was reiterated to the patriarchs Isaac and Jacob as well as to the lawgiver Moses.

Sacred history dated the Israelite conquest of Canaan under Joshua to circa 1250 BCE. The biblical stories about the Ark of the Covenant, David and Goliath, and the messianic teachings of the prophet Isaiah all play out in the Land of Israel. Isaiah's hope that "nation shall not lift up sword against nation, neither shall they learn war any more" (Isaiah 2:4) was already part of Jewish civilization by the eighth century BCE.

After being spiritually guided by Deborah, Gideon, and Samuel, the Israelites hankered after a king. Saul became Israel's first monarch followed by David and Solomon. After he died, the kingdom split.

The Northern Kingdom of Israel (Samaria) was eventually conquered by the Assyrians in 722 BCE. To the south, Judea and its capital, Jerusalem, remained intact. The ancient Babylonians, under Nebuchadnezzar, in due course conquered the southern kingdom of Judea, expelled the Jews from the Land of Israel, and destroyed their temple in 586 BCE. The Hebrew poets composed the diaspora lament recorded in Psalm 137:1, "By the rivers of Babylon, there we sat down, yea, we wept, when we remembered Zion."

To gain some perspective, consider that all this happened well *before* Plato appeared on the scene in ancient Greece around 427–347 BCE.

Cyrus, the ruler of Persia, which had become the Middle East regional superpower, allowed the Babylonian Jewish exiles to make their way back to Jerusalem and rebuild their House of God, which became known as the Second Temple.

Invaders came and went.

The Persians were supplanted on the world stage by the Greeks. Next came the Romans.

The Jews battled the Romans during the years 66–70. In 70 CE, taking advantage of internal Jewish divisions, the Roman Empire destroyed the Second Temple. These events took place about thirty years after the Roman crucifixion of Jesus (whose Jewish linage is traced back to Abraham in Matthew 1:17).

Scattered Jewish resistance to Rome continued. The fall of Masada occurred in 73 CE. The Bar Kochba rebellion of 132–135 ended in defeat at Betar.

At the end of the day the Jews were dispersed around the globe. Only a remnant Jewish community was to remain in the land.

Even in exile, Jews' longing for their homeland persisted, however. Finding themselves in the diaspora again, Jews would turn to face Jerusalem three times a day and pray to God: "May our eyes behold Thy return in mercy to Zion."

The apocryphal story goes that Napoleon Bonaparte was once riding past a Paris synagogue in the early nineteenth century and was perturbed to hear wailing coming from within. A servant dispatched to investigate reported that the Jews were mourning their temple, on the fast of Tisha B'Av (the ninth of Av).

"Temple? Where, when?" demanded the emperor.

"The one in Jerusalem destroyed about 1,800 years ago," replied the servant.

Contemplating the remarkable historical memory, he observed, "Any people that can mourn a temple and exile for so long will surely one day return home."[1]

A small number of Jews continued to live in the land. Jews worldwide maintained their religious and cultural connections to the land, through rituals such as the Passover Seder and breaking a glass at a wedding, keeping their connection to the land at the forefront of their national consciousness.

In the event, after the Romans and their Byzantine Christian successors, a string of conquerors followed.

A mere six years after the death in Arabia of Islam's founding Prophet Muhammad, his followers conquered Jerusalem in 638. They prayed in Jerusalem facing Mecca – the holiest city in Islam. Islam's second-holiest city is Medina.

The Umayyad Arab dynasty (661–750 CE) ruled Palestine from Damascus and built the beautiful Dome of the Rock on the Temple Mount. The Abbasid Arab Dynasty (750–1258 and 1261–1517) ruled Palestine from Baghdad.

Islamic tradition holds that both Jews and Christians broke their covenant with God and corrupted his Scripture. Therefore, they believe, only Allah's covenant with Muhammad is true and complete.

Next, in 1099, the first Christian crusaders came.

Then, in 1187, Saladin, who was of Muslim, Sunni, and Kurdish origin, led a counter-crusade and took the city.

After that, came the Khwarizmis, who were Persian Sunnis. And so it went on...

Finally, in 1516, the Muslim Turkish Ottomans claimed the city – indeed all of Palestine – for their empire.

The Arabs of Palestine, meanwhile, saw themselves as descended from the Arabs of Arabia who had conquered the Fertile Crescent (a quarter-moon shape, from the Persian Gulf, through southern Iraq, Syria, Lebanon, Jordan, Israel, and northern Egypt) hundreds of years earlier. By the 1800s, the Arabs naturally thought of themselves as indigenous, having lived in the country for centuries.

Still, the Arabs of Palestine never established an independent polity.

---

1   Samuel Zanvel Pipe, "Napoleon in Jewish Folklore," *Yivo Annual of Jewish Social Science* 1 (1946): 294–304. See, too, Anshel Pfeffer, "It Is Wrong to Fast on Tisha B'Av?" *Haaretz*, July 16, 2010, http://www.haaretz.com/it-is-wrong-to-fast-on-tisha-b-av-1.302241.

There was never an Arab country called Palestine, but only a geographical area known in Arabic as *Filastin*.

Palestinian Arab national identity was a post-WWI development – partly a response to the Zionist movement, partly an element of the overall post-WWI Arab Awakening, but centrally due to the imposition of borders by Britain and France.

Meanwhile, Jews again became the majority in Jerusalem in 1844. By 1855, Sir Moses Montefiore had bought land at Mishkenot Sha'ananim outside the Old City as well as in Safed and Tiberias to enable the resettlement of a small number of Jews in agricultural villages.

When the first Zionist *halutzim* arrived from eastern Europe and from Yemen in Arabia around 1882, they found ultra-Orthodox Jews whose community was known as the Old Yishuv already in Jerusalem. These included Sephardic Ladino-speaking as well as European Hassidic Jews.[2]

The second wave of settlement (aliyah), mostly from the Russian Empire, took place between 1904 and 1914 (before WWI).

A third aliyah came between 1919 and 1923 (after WWI) mostly from Russia, Poland, Romania, and Lithuania. The fourth aliyah took place between 1924 and 1928, mainly from Poland, the USSR, Romania, and Lithuania, but also from Yemen and Iraq. And, finally, the fifth aliyah from Central Europe, including Germany, took place between 1929 and 1939 (the year WWII began).

---

2   Semantics is a key element in all anti-Zionist campaigning. The Hebrew word *Yishuv* means settlement. The early Jewish immigrants to Palestine called themselves *halutzim* or pioneers. After 1967, Israelis who moved over the Green Line preferred the term *mitnahalim* which translates to settlers. The post-modern era has objectified "settlers" by adopting the Palestinian Arab narrative of illegitimacy. So a settler becomes a "land-grabber" and, implicitly, therefore, any measure taken against Israelis who live in the West Bank, no matter how violent, is excusable if not praiseworthy. At the same time, the semantic battle over "Palestinian" has to be ceded to the Arabs. Until after the creation of Israel in 1948, most newspaper mentions of "Palestinians" referred to Jews not Arabs. Hence, the Jerusalem-based English-language Zionist newspaper founded in 1932 was called the *Palestine Post* (today the *Jerusalem Post*).

Chapter 4

ENTER A HERO: ARTHUR JAMES BALFOUR

No statesman is more directly associated with British support for a Jewish national home in Palestine than Arthur James Balfour.

A Conservative grandee who came of age during the Victorian era, Balfour served as prime minister from 1902 to 1905 and, more significantly from the Zionist perspective, as foreign secretary in a wartime coalition government during the First World War. Together with Prime Minister David Lloyd George, Balfour bestowed upon the Jewish people an historic opening to take their destiny back into their own hands.

Arthur James Balfour was born in Scotland on July 25, 1848, to a landowning family. His father James Maitland Balfour, who died when Arthur was not yet ten, was a country squire; his mother Lady Blanche Balfour was the daughter of the second Marquess of Salisbury. Balfour entered Eton at age fourteen and Trinity College, Cambridge in 1866, where he read mostly philosophy.

An early reputation for idleness and frivolity proved deceptive. He gained the respect of those around him, and not just because family connections to Lord Salisbury on his mother's side stood him in good stead.

Balfour was elected a Conservative member of Parliament in 1874 for the constituency of Manchester East, the year Benjamin Disraeli – a Jew whose father had found it expedient to embrace Anglicanism – became prime minister.

Balfour pursued two vocations, philosophy and politics, often concurrently. As a metaphysician, his main concern was to find arguments for religious belief. His writings on religious philosophy include *A Defense of Philosophical Doubt* (1879), *Foundations of Belief* (1896), and the Gifford

Lectures at the University of Glasgow, which were published as *Theism and Humanism* (1915) and *Theism and Thought* (1923).

In *Foundations of Belief* he argued that nothing is certain and that everything rests on belief; science cannot dictate to religion and, indeed, presupposes theism as the basis for its own assertions of rationality.[1]

He became his uncle Lord Salisbury's parliamentary private secretary and accompanied him to the 1878 Congress of Berlin, where the older man as foreign secretary engaged Prussian statesman Otto von Bismarck in a balance of power game. When Salisbury became prime minister in 1895 (until 1902), he appointed Balfour to the cabinet, first as secretary for Scotland (1886) and then as Irish secretary (1887–1892). To the surprise of some, Balfour proved his mettle as a steely politician.

In July 1902, aged forty-seven, Balfour succeeded his uncle as prime minister and remained ensconced at 10 Downing Street until November 1905. He was credited with the Education Act of 1902, which reorganized the administration of schooling at the local level, and the Irish Land Act of 1903, intended to make it possible for peasants to own land.

Balfour supported the 1905 Aliens Act aimed at limiting eastern European immigration. This support stemmed from his conviction that Jews from the Russian Empire could not acculturate and become Britons, but would remain "a people apart." According to his biographer, R. J. Q. Adams, Balfour believed that the Jews shared not just a religion but also a cultural identity which made it difficult for many to "become British."[2]

At the same time, Balfour made clear his opposition to the persecution of Jews. He had his frustrations about Jews, but these were tinged with admiration. "I think that their rigid separation…from their fellow countrymen is a misfortune for us," he said.[3]

He happened to be prime minister in 1903, as Colonial Secretary Joseph Chamberlain weighed up whether to provide refuge to persecuted Russian

---

1   Balfour's early interest in philosophy brought him into contact with Jewish civilization, according to his niece Blanche Dugdale. His interest in Judaism was also rooted in the "Old Testament training" that he received from his mother, which would influence his outlook. "The position of the Jews is unique. For them race, religion, and country are inter-related, as they are inter-related in the case of no other race, no other religion, and no other country on earth," Balfour said. See Gertrude Himmelfarb, *The People of the Book: Philosemitism in England, From Cromwell to Churchill* (New York: Encounter Books, 2011), 133.

2   R. J. Q. Adams, *Balfour: The Last Grandee* (London: John Murray, 2008), 332.

3   Ronald Sanders, *The High Walls of Jerusalem: A History of the Balfour Declaration and the Birth of the British Mandate for Palestine* (New York: Holt, Rinehart and Winston, 1984), 119.

Jews in Britain's East Africa territories (today's Kenya) under the so-called Uganda Plan. Balfour was baffled when, after brutal internecine clashes, the Zionists rebuffed Britain's Africa offer, the desperate imperative to find a haven for oppressed Jews notwithstanding.

Though the territory was then firmly in Turkish hands, they would hold out for a return to Zion – meaning a Jewish national home in Palestine.

Balfour lost power when his Conservative Party (the Tories) split over whether to move away from the party's traditional free trade doctrine. The Tories found themselves defeated in the general election of 1906 by the Liberals, led by Henry Campbell-Bannerman. Balfour himself lost his Manchester constituency.

In short order, a safe seat in the City of London was found for him. He remained leader of the Conservatives in the House of Commons, determined to stymie Liberal social and economic reforms, even employing the House of Lords. When his tactics ultimately failed, he resigned the party leadership in 1911.

After World War I erupted in August 1914, Balfour was brought back into the government as first lord of the Admiralty (1915–16) under the new Liberal prime minister, Herbert Asquith.

Though he respected Asquith as fair-minded and temperate, Balfour did not think he had the grit to be a wartime prime minister. When a new coalition government headed by Liberal David Lloyd George was formed, Balfour became foreign secretary, serving from 1916 to 1919.

In keeping with the era and his class, Balfour was not above the occasional anti-Jewish aside, yet he said of the Jews: "I like them for their history." In France, the 1894 show trial and conviction for treason of Captain Alfred Dreyfus, an assimilated Jewish officer, had drawn Balfour's sympathetic attention.

And on January 9, 1906, just before he lost the premiership to Campbell-Bannerman's Liberals, Balfour fatefully met the Belarus-born chemist and Zionist luminary Chaim Weizmann in Manchester.[4] He found himself im-

---

4   This was their first substantive meeting. Chaim Weizmann, *Trial and Error* (New York: Harper, 1949), 109. See, too, Jehuda Reinharz, *Chaim Weizmann: The Making of a Zionist Leader*, vol. 1 (New York: Oxford University Press, 1985), 227. According to Leonard Stein, "Weizmann met Balfour for the first time in January 1905, when he had been in England less than a year." During a visit to his Manchester constituency on January 27, Weizmann went to hear Balfour and was introduced to him by Dr. Charles Dreyfus. On January 29, 1905, Weizmann reported to Menachem Ussishkin, "We couldn't talk much, but he invited me to see him in London." Cited in Stein, *Balfour Declaration*, 147.

pressed by the force of Weizmann's personality and by the cause he espoused.

On December 12, 1914, with the world war under way, through the good offices of Samuel Alexander, a professor of philosophy, Weizmann secured an appointment to see Balfour. Both men anticipated Turkey's defeat and the dismembering of the Ottoman Empire. Balfour continued to be moved by Weizmann's fervor and the nobility of his cause. Shortly after this talk they saw each other at a luncheon.[5]

The two met again in March 1915, and yet again in March 1916 – and they probably met for a second time that year, according to Leonard Stein, who wrote the seminal history of the Balfour Declaration.[6] In March 1917, Weizmann would recall, their Palestine discussions turned to practical implementation issues.

Then, on June 19, 1917, Balfour met with Weizmann and Lord Rothschild, who had perhaps surprisingly emerged as the preeminent British-born Zionist leader. He asked them to come up with a statement defining Zionist aspirations that he could present to the War Cabinet.[7]

Most of the opposition to such a statement came from within the British Jewish community itself – including from Edwin Montagu, a Jewish cabinet member – out of concern that fulfilling Zionist aspirations in Palestine would undermine hard-won Jewish civil rights in Britain and elsewhere.

Beyond the Jewish community, Lord Curzon, a leading member of the War Cabinet, argued against the Jewish homeland idea on the grounds that Arabs far outnumbered Jews in Palestine. Balfour, however, assumed that the Arabs would take the long view and see the value of a Jewish homeland to the region. He further supposed that the Jews would find a way to win the Arabs over for a Jewish majority in Palestine, and that the Arabs, for their part, would be content with dominion over Arabia and Iraq.

So what, he asked, if the Jews were allowed "a small notch…in what are now Arab territories"? They were, after all, a "people who for all these hundreds of years have been separated" from Palestine.[8]

As Balfour saw it, Zionism was the solution to the Jewish problem:

---

5   Weizmann, *Zionist Leader*, 154. Stein points to a second meeting at Balfour's London home two days after the first meeting. Stein, *Balfour Declaration*, 153.

6   Ibid., 155.

7   Isaiah Friedman, *Encyclopaedia Judaica*, 2nd ed. ed., s.v. "Balfour Declaration."

8   "Case of Jews Absolutely Exceptional and Must Be Treated by Unusual Methods, Said Balfour," *Jewish Telegraphic Agency*, March 20, 1930, accessed June 20, 2017, http://www.jta.org/1930/03/20/archive/case-of-jews-absolutely-exceptional-and-must-be-treated-by-unusual-methods-said-balfour-discussing.

"If a place were provided for them in the land of their historic origins, the Jews would be given the choice of assimilation in their adopted countries or Jewish citizenship in their ancient homeland."[9] Thus, he told the War Cabinet in October 1917, "any danger of a double allegiance or non-national outlook would be eliminated."

After much back and forth on the precise wording of the declaration to be put before the ministers and with solid backing from Lloyd George, Balfour won the cabinet's approval. And on November 2, 1917, on behalf of His Majesty's Government, Balfour wrote the now familiar letter addressed to Lord Rothschild that committed Britain to supporting the creation of a Jewish national home in Palestine.

By the time the war ended on Armistice Day, November 11, 1918, Britain had captured Palestine in its entirety from the Turkish Ottoman Empire.

Following the post-war Versailles Peace Conference, which began in January 1919, Balfour stepped down as foreign secretary though he continued to hold a place in the cabinet. He also continued to represent Britain in the international arena when his presence was demanded.

For that reason, he attended the April 1920 San Remo international conference, which determined the boundaries of the territories – Palestine included – that the Allies had captured from Turkey and the other Axis powers. The San Remo delegates resolved to incorporate the Balfour Declaration into the international mandate granted to Britain for Palestine. The various mandates were under the overall authority of the new League of Nations, whose founding was itself an outcome of Versailles. In February 1920, Balfour personally chaired the first meeting of the League, serving as his country's chief representative.

In 1920, taking cognizance of the self-determination principle and the Arab majority in Palestine, Balfour said: "The deep, underlying principle of self-determination really points to a Zionist policy – however little in its strict technical interpretation it may seem to favor it. I am convinced that none but the pedants or people who are prejudiced by religious or racial bigotry, none but those who are blinded by one of these causes would deny for one instant that the case of the Jews is absolutely exceptional, and must be treated by exceptional means."[10]

On October 13, 1920, Balfour told Lord Curzon, his successor as foreign

---

9   Adams, *Last Grandee*, 332.
10   "Case of Jews," *Jewish Telegraphic Agency*.

secretary: "Whether Zionism be good or bad – and, as you know, I think it good – we are now committed to it, and failure to make it a success will be a failure for us."[11]

The right person, in the right place at the right time makes all the difference. Once Balfour was succeeded by Curzon at the Foreign Office and Lloyd George was replaced by the Conservative Bonar Law at Number 10 Downing Street, Britain's official support for Zionism became wobbly.

Still, Balfour went on to represent Britain at the 1921–1922 Washington Disarmament Conference, which, like the League of Nations, was an initiative taken by the international community intended to end war once and for all.

Balfour was raised to the peerage as the Earl of Balfour in 1922, and took a seat in the House of Lords.

On April 1, 1925, Lord Balfour was enthusiastically welcomed by the Palestinian Jewish community when he visited the country to attend the official opening ceremony of the Hebrew University of Jerusalem on Mount Scopus. Creating the university had been a key Zionist goal and its cornerstones had been laid in 1918. Balfour delivered the opening address and sat through too many mostly Hebrew speeches alongside British High Commissioner Herbert Samuel, Weizmann, Palestine's chief rabbi Avraham Yitzhak Hacohen Kook, and the great Hebrew poet Haim Nahman Bialik.

To this day, a large painting commemorating the event adorns the university's administration building.

After touring Palestine, he was driven north to French-controlled Syria, where he was met by anti-Zionist Arab protesters outside his hotel.

Yet, Balfour did not waver in his belief that it was right to embrace Zionism. His attraction to Zionism was anchored, writes his biographer Adams, "in his belief that it provided solutions to a number of problems: It would solve the problem of Jewish assimilation in the West, strike at the worldwide curse of anti-Semitism, and revitalize Palestine. Furthermore, it would reunite the Jews in the land of their origins, which he believed in a spiritual as well as a historic sense was in fact theirs."[12]

Blanche Dugdale, Balfour's niece and a Zionist in her own right, attributed her uncle's Zionism to his reading of the Bible. And Leonard Stein sug-

---

11   David Gilmour, "The Unregarded Prophet: Lord Curzon and the Palestine Question," *Journal of Palestine Studies* 25, no. 3 (1996): 60–68.

12   Adams, *Last Grandee*, 334.

gested that Balfour was motivated by a need to redress the persecution of the Jews, quoting him as saying, "The treatment of the race has been a disgrace to Christendom."[13]

Balfour had many interests besides philosophy and politics. Back in 1893, for instance, he became president of the Society for Psychical Research, which studied the paranormal. Indeed, on his deathbed he reportedly said, "I am longing to get to the other side to see what it's like."[14]

He never married and had no children. "Whether I have time for Love or not, I certainly have no time for Matrimony," he once wrote.[15]

He valued his solitude even as he relished the elaborate table talk so adored by the Victorians. He ate and drank with restraint – "not least of all," according to his biographer, "because he was repelled by the idea of taking on the rotund shape so common among gentlemen of this time."[16]

Balfour resigned his last high profile position, that of lord president of the council, in 1929, when he was eighty-one, to be replaced by the leader of the House of Lords, Charles Cripps. He had mostly withdrawn from public commitments in the final two years of his life. As the end drew closer, he was visited by an array of officials from across the political spectrum, from David Lloyd George and Winston Churchill to Stanley Baldwin and Neville Chamberlain.

According to Adams, "Chaim Weizmann was the last visitor outside the family to see the dying statesman – it was a silent farewell, with Balfour too weak and the great Zionist too overcome to speak."[17]

Arthur James Balfour died on March 19, 1930, at his brother Gerald's estate near Woking.

"For me, this is the greatest loss of my life," Weizmann told a British Zionist gathering. "Lord Balfour left us at a time when we needed him most. The period of our most beautiful dreams and fondest hopes passes with him. He was working for our cause to his very last."[18]

Weizmann then paraphrased the traditional Jewish response upon

---

13   Stein, *Balfour Declaration*, 149. See, too, Parliamentary Debates, 4th Series, vol. 145, col. 795.

14   J. Gordon Melton, ed., *Encyclopedia of Occultism and Parapsychology* (Farmington Hills, MI: Gale, 2001), s.v. "Arthur James Balfour, 1st Earl of Balfour."

15   Adams, *Last Grandee*, 32.

16   Ibid., 24.

17   Ibid., 378.

18   "Dr. Weizmann Breaks Down as He Eulogizes Balfour," *Jewish Telegraphic Agency*, March 20, 1930, accessed June 20, 2017, http://www.jta.org/1930/03/20/archive/dr-weizmann-breaks-down-as-he-eulogizes-balfour.

hearing of a death: "Let God console us together with all mourners in Zion."

In Palestine, the Jewish community went into mourning. Shops closed, schools held special assemblies, and prayer services were held in synagogues.

Besides Blanche Dugdale, who worked with the Jewish Agency in London and closely collaborated with Weizmann, Balfour's family continued to support the cause. For example, in 1939, his nephew Robert Arthur Lytton, the third Earl of Balfour, offered his family estate at Whittingham as a training school for Jewish refugee children from Germany.

It is fitting, too, that the official residence of Israel's prime minister is located on Balfour Street in Jerusalem. There are many other Balfour Streets in Israel.

The Hebrew Bible (Ezra 1:1–4) records that it was by the decree of Cyrus II the Great, king of Persia, that the Jews were allowed to return to Jerusalem and rebuild their temple, which the Babylonians had destroyed in 586 BCE.

Providentially for Chaim Weizmann and the political Zionists, Arthur James Balfour ardently embraced a new Jewish return. It was his efforts and those of other British friends of Zionism that set the stage – some thirty years after the Balfour Declaration – for the United Nations to vote for the establishment of a Jewish state.

Chapter 5

CHAIM WEIZMANN: INDISPENSABLE MAN

My earliest impressions of Chaim Weizmann (1874–1952) were colored by Ben Hecht's contempt for the man whom he believed had been callously lackadaisical when presented in 1944 with a ghastly opportunity to save Hungarian Jewry from the Nazis.[1] Let me hasten to add that Hecht was not a historian – he was a playwright who collaborated on *Gone with the Wind* and wrote *The Front Page* – and most Holocaust historians disagree with his take. But he left an impression. Moreover, there was my perception that Weizmann took too soft a line against British backtracking on the Balfour Declaration.

Hecht was an admirer of Vladimir Ze'ev Jabotinsky (1880–1940) who led the political camp opposed to Weizmann's policy of Zionist gradualism. Sadly, Jabotinsky died at age 59 in New York at the start of World War II. Interestingly, during WWI and the Balfour Declaration era, Weizmann and Jabotinsky were good friends and allies. The more I explored the Balfour Declaration era and its aftermath the more nuanced became my assessment of Weizmann's predicament and achievements. Bottom line: there can be no debating that without Weizmann's relentless political lobbying, statesmanship, and personal magnetism there would not have been a Balfour Declaration.

---

1   Journalist and Hollywood screenwriter Ben Hecht (1894–1964) was a US Jewish campaigner, active in efforts to rescue European Jewry during the Holocaust. His book, *Perfidy* (1961), which I read soon after college, is a brilliant polemic against the Zionist establishment, Weizmann, David Ben-Gurion, and the Labor (Mapai) Zionist camp. Hecht argued that, in an affair involving Joel Brand and Rudolf Kastner, Mapai chieftains collaborated with British Mandate authorities to torpedo a scheme that might have led to a trade of Allied trucks to the Nazis in exchange for Hungarian Jews. I go into detail about this controversy here: https://elliotjager.blogspot.ie/2007_08_01_archive.html?m=0

Weizmann had no illusions about anti-Semitism. "One of its fundamental causes is that the Jews exist.... We carry the germs of anti-Semitism in our knapsack on our backs," he told the Anglo-American Committee on March 8, 1946.[2]

During World War I, Weizmann became convinced that Britain was the key to Zionist aspirations. And this was the overarching vision that guided his actions.

Chaim Weizmann was born on November 27, 1874 in western Russia, in a shtetl called Motol outside Pinsk, in what is Belarus today. He was the third of fifteen children (three of whom died in infancy), born to parents Oizer and Rachel. The family, whose economic circumstances fluctuated, was religiously observant and Weizmann received a traditional Jewish education in cheder before going on to high school. By age eleven, he had begun to think of himself as a Zionist.

Weizmann maintained that contemporary Zionism preceded Theodor Herzl, the founder of modern political Zionism, and that the persecution of the Jews in Europe was not its true catalyst.

Zionism's true roots, he believed, were ancient, embedded in "the yearning of the Jewish people for its homeland, for a national center and a national life."[3]

In 1892, Weizmann left the confines of the Russian Empire, where a quota or numerus clausus limited how many Jews could obtain a place in the higher education system, to attend college in Germany.

"I was in my second year in Berlin," he wrote later, when he was living in England, "when in 1896 Theodor Herzl published his tract, now a classic of Zionism, *Der Judenstaat* [The Jewish State]."

By then, Weizmann was already active in Zionist affairs and had come under the influence of Ahad Ha'Am (1856–1927). So, while the Zionist idea was hardly new to him, Herzl's personality, drive, and charisma were a draw. Weizmann was struck by the fact that Herzl, an acculturated journalist from a Viennese milieu, so different from his own earthy Russian Jewish one, cared so much about the Jewish future.

---

2   Joseph Baron, *A Treasury of Jewish Quotations* (New York: Crown, 1956).

3   "'Weizmann Year' Launched by WZO Executive-American Section Dr. Goldmann, Sapir, Mrs. Jacobson, Assess," *Jewish Telegraphic Agency*, November 29, 1974, accessed June 20, 2017, http://www.jta.org/1974/11/29/archive/weizmann-year-launched-by-wzo-executive-american-section-dr-goldmann-sapir-mrs-jacobson-assess.

"The very fact that this Westerner came to us unencumbered by our own preconceptions had its appeal," he wrote.[4]

Weizmann missed the First Zionist Congress of 1897, but attended the second congress in 1898. Meanwhile, he earned a doctorate in chemistry from the University of Fribourg in Switzerland.

As an ideological movement Zionism had its factions. Herzl wanted to focus on diplomacy – on building a legal, diplomatic, and political basis for the Jewish return to Palestine. Weizmann was part of Ahad Ha'Am's "cultural Zionist" camp, which wanted to concentrate energies on making Palestine the spiritual, cultural, and educational capital of Jewish civilization. Thus, in Ha'Am's view, the focus needed to be on institution-building – for example, by creating a Hebrew university in Jerusalem.

The ruthless, periodically murderous, persecution of Russian Jews led in 1903 to the floating of a well-intentioned British government proposal to provide eastern European Jews with a safe haven in Africa – in today's Kenya, then British Uganda.

With Palestine firmly under Turkish Ottoman control, it was a stopgap measure. Herzl was willing to present the proposal as an interim solution to the Zionist Congress. Weizmann was vehement in his opposition, and in doing so established a reputation as a young man willing to stand up even to Herzl.

In the event, Herzl died at the age of forty-four on July 3, 1904, leaving the movement devastated.

In the same year, Weizmann left Geneva, where he had been living, to settle in Britain and make a new start. "My flight to England, in 1904, was a deliberate and desperate step.... I was in danger of being eaten up by Zionism, with no benefit either to my scientific career or to Zionism."[5]

Weizmann had a reputation as a ladies' man. The twenty-seven-year-old had first crossed paths with seventeen-year-old Vera Khatzman in the late autumn of 1900 at the Jewish Club in Geneva. Breaking away from her domineering parents in Rostov, Russia, she was in Geneva studying medicine.

Vera attended a chemistry tutorial for Russian students that Chaim – at the time engaged to another woman, Sophia Getzova – was giving at the club. Perhaps it was a case of opposites attract. His Jewish background was deeply

---

4   Chaim Weizmann, *Trial and Error: The Autobiography of Chaim Weizmann* (New York: Harper, 1949), 43.

5   Ibid., 93.

rooted; she had very little attachment to her Jewish culture. Nonetheless, the two were drawn to one another. Vera became part of Chaim's Zionist circle and they eventually became a couple.

When Weizmann took up a post at Manchester University in 1905, Vera remained in Geneva to complete her medical studies.

She also became his political comrade. On January 24, 1905, Weizmann wrote to Vera: "Tonight I am going to a meeting at which Balfour, the prime minister, will speak. Perhaps I shall succeed in having a word with him – though I doubt it."[6]

Later, he reported to her on the Manchester gathering. A mutual friend, (the chemist and Zionist) Charles Dreyfus, had indeed made what would turn out to be a historic Balfour-Weizmann introduction: "I went yesterday to Balfour's meeting and talked to him about Zionism: not for long, only five minutes, but he promised me that when I was in London he would give me a chance to talk to him at greater length and in more detail."[7]

On the personal front, Vera graduated from medical school and the couple married in a modest ceremony outside Danzig, Germany, in 1906. Then they headed together to Manchester.[8]

Their son Benjamin was born in 1907. Vera, who already spoke four languages, now had to learn English. In due course, she was appointed a Manchester public health physician and worked with the city's poorer population.

Weizmann had been elected to the decision-making General Zionist Council and, by and by, become an Anglophile. Indeed, early on in his Zionist career he became convinced that Britain was the key to Zionist aspirations.

The real turning point presented itself on January 9, 1906, when Weizmann had a second encounter in Manchester with Balfour, who was on an election campaign swing. They got to talking about why Zionists had rejected a safe haven in British Uganda for persecuted Jews and Weizmann offered this perspective: "Supposing I was to offer you Paris instead of London, would you take it?"

---

6   This was their first encounter but not a substantive meeting. Vera Weizmann, *The Impossible Takes Longer: The Memoirs of Vera Weizmann* (London: Hamish Hamilton, 1967), 25. In *Trial and Error*, chapter 8, Chaim Weizmann describes the evening: "I was brought in to Balfour in a room in the old-fashioned [Manchester] Queen's Hotel, on Piccadilly, which served as his headquarters."

7   In a note dated January 28, 1905. Vera Weizmann, *Memoirs*, 25.

8   She was less than enamored with the city. "Some of my most difficult and most depressing years were spent in Manchester. They were dark days indeed, both spiritually and physically," she wrote in ibid., 30.

Balfour replied, "But, Dr. Weizmann, we have London."

"That is true," Weizmann said. "But we had Jerusalem when London was a marsh."

"Are there many Jews who think like you?" Balfour asked.

"I believe I speak for millions of Jews whom you will never see and who cannot speak for themselves..." Weizmann replied.

"It is curious. The Jews I meet are quite different," Balfour said.

Weizmann answered: "Mr. Balfour, you meet the wrong kind of Jews."[9]

That was when Balfour became intrigued by the Zionist idea. Weizmann joined up with a group of the best and brightest London and Mancunian Zionists, among them Leonard Stein, who would go on to write the definitive book about the Balfour Declaration, and lawyers Harry Sacher[10] and Herbert Bentwich. He was further and immeasurably aided by Lord Simon Marks, Leon Simon and Israel and Rebecca Sieff.

Together they opened many doors and facilitated numerous contacts with British officialdom and opinion formulators, while also serving as a brain trust.

All the while, Weizmann was evolving his own distinctive approach to Zionism. In 1907, Weizmann told the Eighth Zionist Congress at The Hague that there needed to be a synthesis between practical resettlement efforts in Palestine, the kind he and his mentor Ahad Ha'Am advocated, and the diplomatic overtures to world powers for which Herzl had been known. "Governments will listen to you only when they see that you are capable of being in *possession* of Palestine [through persistent practical work]," he said.[11]

From the eighth congress, Weizmann made his way to Palestine for the first time. He was not impressed with what he saw. "A dolorous country it was on the whole, one of the most neglected corners of the miserably neglected Turkish Empire," he would later record.[12]

---

9   Reinharz, *The Making of a Zionist Leader*, 271.

10   Born in London, Sacher (1881–1971) was a prominent solicitor, author, and Zionist campaigner. He served on the *Manchester Guardian*'s editorial board 1905–1909 and 1915–1919. Sacher was part of the Manchester Zionist Circle that Weizmann headed. He made aliyah in 1919 and practiced law. He also testified before the Shaw Commission: "We do not wish to rule over others, but we do not wish others to rule over us." Sacher returned to England in 1931 to help manage Marks and Spencer, the department store. He also wrote widely on Zionism. See, for instance, Harry Sacher, *Zionist Portraits and Other Essays* (London: Anthony Blond, 1959).

11   Barnet Litvinoff, *The Letters and Papers of Chaim Weizmann* (New Brunswick, NJ: Transaction Books, 1977), vol. 1, August 1898–July 1931, paper 9, 69 (aet. 32).

12   Weizmann, *Trial and Error*, 125.

It was thanks to Vera that Weizmann met Charles Prestwich Scott, the inimitable sixty-seven-year-old editor of the *Manchester Guardian*. Toward the end of November 1914,[13] Vera recalled: "Chaim and I were invited to another afternoon [tea] ritual, this time in the home of Mr. and Mrs. Eckhard. She was the chairman of the clinic for mothers in which I served as medical officer.... Chaim and I went to this tea without an inkling that it would mark a momentous turning point in Chaim's political career and, indeed, in the fortunes of the Zionist movement."[14]

Scott's support for the Zionist cause was instrumental in bringing about the Balfour Declaration, because of the editor's close relationship with British wartime prime minister David Lloyd George. As Vera recalled in her memoir, Scott invited Weizmann to a breakfast in London with Lloyd George, then chancellor of the exchequer, in December 1914. It was there he first heard that Herbert Samuel, then president of the local government board and a member of the cabinet, was positively predisposed to Zionism – unlike some in the Jewish establishment. Early on in World War I Samuel had presented Prime Minister Herbert Asquith (1852–1928) with a memorandum arguing that Britain should establish a Jewish state in Palestine once the Ottomans were ousted.[15]

For her part, in 1916, Vera began to keep a diary recording events in what amounted to be her own political salon. Besides being integral to her husband's efforts to promote the Zionist enterprise, she was a co-founder of the Women's International Zionist Organization (WIZO).

On the Arab question, this was Weizmann's assessment in 1919: "The Arabs are not strangers, they have lived in the country for centuries.... We say: 'There is room both for you and for us; you will benefit by our coming in, and we shall benefit by friendly relations between you and us.'"[16]

In 1920, Chaim Weizmann wrote: "In all our work of colonization and industrial development in Palestine, a guiding principle must be to win and seek the goodwill of the Arabs.... We must be on the best terms with the Arabs of Palestine, because that is the condition of a healthy society of our own and good relations with the Arab world outside Palestine."[17]

---

13   Jonathan Schneer, *The Balfour Declaration: The Origins of the Arab-Israeli Conflict* (London: Bloomsbury, 2010), 131.
14   Vera Weizmann, *Memoirs,* 52.
15   Ibid.
16   Litvinoff, *Letters and Papers,* paper 55, 261.
17   Ibid., paper 58, 293.

Writing in 1923, he was adamant that the Jews were not coming to Palestine as conquerors or to dominate anybody, but as builders. They would build a common homeland in which Arabs would be integral. At the same time, he did not flinch from making explicit the inalienable right of return of the Jewish people.

But it was the First World War that framed Weizmann's career and the Balfour Declaration. The war erupted in August 1914, when Weizmann was aged forty and established in his academic career. His formal status in the Zionist movement had lapsed, but this did not stop him from seizing the initiative when the opportunity presented itself.

As head of the British Admiralty Laboratories from 1917 to 1919, he was engaged in scientific work for the war effort. He discovered a method to produce the synthetic acetone used to create cordite, a military propellant. In this role, he hobnobbed with First Lord of the Admiralty Winston Churchill and with Lloyd George.

When Liberal Party prime minister Herbert Henry Asquith resigned in 1916, his fellow Liberal, David Lloyd George, who had served as chancellor of the exchequer and then, briefly, as minister of munitions, took over.

Balfour was appointed foreign secretary.

By now, Weizmann was firmly established as Zionism's preeminent lobbyist and statesman in England, even though, organizationally, Nahum Sokolow (1859–1936), who had been assigned by the movement to its London bureau, was his senior.

Fortunately, the two collaborated closely in pressing for Britain to embrace the Zionist cause. Paradoxically, the main opposition to their efforts came from the British Jewish opponents of Zionism who, basically, comprised the entire Jewish leadership, which was centered in the Conjoint Committee and the Board of Deputies of British Jews.

Of course, there was also a pro-Zionist camp, which included Chief Rabbi Dr. Joseph Hertz (1872–1946), the head of the Sephardic community haham Rabbi Dr. Moses Gaster (1856–1939), and, crucially, the philanthropist Lord Rothschild (1868–1937).

On February 17, 1917, the Zionists met anew in London to plan strategy, which amounted to advocating that Britain take possession of Palestine after the war and for the British government to commit to facilitating a Jewish homeland.

After intense behind-the-scenes lobbying for and against, on November 2, 1917, Prime Minister David Lloyd George's War Cabinet agreed on a policy which was relayed by Foreign Minister Balfour to Lord Rothschild for transmittal to the Zionist movement:

"His Majesty's Government view with favour the establishment in Palestine of a national home for the Jewish people, and will use their best endeavours to facilitate the achievement of this object."

"While the Cabinet was in session, approving the final text, I was outside," Weizmann relates in his autobiography *Trial and Error*. "[British diplomat Sir Mark] Sykes brought the document out to me, with the exclamation: 'Dr. Weizmann, it's a boy!' Well – I did not like the boy at first. He was not the one I had expected."[18]

But, like Lionel Walter Rothschild, the British Jewish leader and philanthropist, Weizmann knew that delaying the declaration in order to obtain more perfect wording would have played into the hands of the Jewish opponents of Zionism, and, in the end, there would have been no declaration at all.

"A new chapter had opened for us," Weizmann wrote, "full of new difficulties, but not without its great moments."[19]

Leonard Stein (1887–1973), an English lawyer and Weizmann's political secretary whose book *The Balfour Declaration* remains an authoritative work on the subject, posits:

"What, then, were the Zionists promised? The language of the declaration was studiously vague, and neither on the British nor on the Zionist side was there any disposition, at the time, to probe deeply into its meaning – still less was there any agreed interpretation."[20]

---

18   Weizmann, *Trial and Error*, 208.
19   Ibid.
20   Stein, *Balfour Declaration*, 552. A word about demographics at this historic juncture: When the Balfour Declaration was issued; the Jewish people were dispersed across many lands. In 1914, most of the world's Jews were subjects of the Russian Tsar. They lived in a western region of Tsarist Russia known as the Pale of Settlement. Areas outside the Pale were barred to Jews unless they obtained special permission. From the 1880s, approximately two million Jews fled west as a result of pogroms in Russia, religious persecution, and worsening economic conditions. A quarter of a million Jewish immigrants arrived in the United States in 1913 and 1914 alone. The Lower East Side of Manhattan became home to half a million Jews. Meanwhile, over a million Jews lived in western and central Europe where they enjoyed varying degrees of tolerance. Berlin, Vienna, and Budapest were among the largest Jewish communities. But even here a new form of Jew-hatred was growing – racial anti-Semitism. There were also a million Jews living in the Arab world, from Morocco to Iraq. There were thousands of Jews in non-Arab Muslim countries including Iran, Turkey, and Afghanistan. These ancient Middle Eastern communities were traditionally subjected to special taxes and restrictions. The Jewish population in Palestine, then a province in the Ottoman Turkish

Weizmann, now the undisputed leader of the Zionist cause outside Palestine, chaired the Zionist Commission for Palestine.[21] During his 1918 tour of Palestine as commission chair, he met with Emir Feisal, the son of Hussein bin Ali, Sharif of Mecca, in June 1918 (WWI ended November 11). But, by now, it was obvious Turkey was on the brink of defeat.

Feisal was prepared to make an alliance with the Zionists so long as the British delivered on their promise to turn Syria and Iraq over to the Arabs.

Feisal became king of Syria in 1920, but when the French objected, he was installed as king of Iraq in 1921. He died in 1933. Hussein's son Abdullah would become emir of Transjordan in 1921 when that country was carved out of Palestine. He died at the hands of a Palestinian Islamist assassin on Jerusalem's Temple Mount in 1951. As for Hussein of Mecca, he was ousted by the Saud family from Arabia in 1924 and died in Amman in 1931.

Weizmann writes this about Feisal: "This first meeting [on June 4, 1918] in the desert laid the foundation of a lifelong friendship. I met the emir several times afterwards in Europe and our negotiations crystallized into an agreement, drawn up by Colonel Lawrence ["Lawrence of Arabia"] and signed by the emir and myself."[22]

Weizmann led the Zionist delegation at the Paris Peace Conference in Versailles, which commenced in January 1919, although it concluded only in January 1920. On January 3, 1919, before they were called before the conference the two leaders signed an agreement – conditioned on the Arabs gaining independence in Syria – that guaranteed free immigration and settlement for the Jews in Palestine. "All necessary measures shall be taken to encourage and stimulate immigration of Jews into Palestine on a large scale, and as quickly as possible to settle Jewish immigrants upon the land through closer settlement and intensive cultivation of the soil. In taking such measures the Arab peasant and tenant farmers shall be protected in their rights, and shall be assisted in forwarding their economic development."[23]

Empire, numbered approximately seventy-five thousand. Jews formed the majority in Jerusalem.

21   Set up in 1918 with British approval, its task was to liaise between British officials and the local Jewish community. See Raphael Patai, ed., *Encyclopedia of Zionism and Israel*, vol. 2 (New York: Herzl Press, 1971), 1271.

22   Weizmann, *Trial and Error*, 235. The world war was at a critical stage in June 1918, Weizmann writes, adding: "Our conversation lasted over two hours, and before I left he suggested that we be photographed together.... The Emir promised to communicate the gist of our talks to his father, the Sharif [of Mecca] Hussein, who was, he said, the ultimate judge of all his actions, and carried the responsibility for Arab policy." The two men met again in 1918 in London.

23   Ibid., 247.

Notably, on March 3, 1919, Feisal wrote to Felix Frankfurter (1882–1965) – then a Harvard law professor and from 1939 a justice of the US Supreme Court – who was a member of the American Zionist delegation to the Paris talks:

"We feel that the Arabs and Jews are cousins in race, suffering similar oppressions at the hands of powers stronger than themselves and by a happy coincidence have been able to take the first step towards the attainment of their national ideals together." The letter continued: "We Arabs, especially the educated among us, look with the deepest sympathy on the Zionist movement."[24]

The 1917 Balfour Declaration was officially adopted by the international community, first at the April 1920 San Remo Conference, which incorporated the declaration, and then by the League of Nations when it granted Britain the Palestine Mandate on July 24, 1922.

Many years later, Weizmann lamented in his memoirs how regrettable it was that Emir Feisal had not been able to "unite the Arab world" and that he had been forced out of Syria. No less lamentable, from Weizmann's point of view was the rise of Ibn Saud in Arabia and the "practical annihilation of the Hashemite family."[25]

Weizmann's singular focus continued to be on nation-building.

Speaking in Jerusalem on January 30, 1921, he said: "A state cannot be created by decree, but by the forces of a people and in the course of generations; even if all the governments of the world gave us a country it would only be a gift of words. But if the Jewish people will go and build Palestine, the Jewish state will become a reality – a fact."[26]

Not long after the First World War, both Lloyd George and Balfour left government. One thing that distressed Weizmann deeply was that practically from the outset British officials implementing the mandate on the ground, and those making policy in London did not adhere to the spirit of the Balfour Declaration.

---

24 Weizmann reproduced the letter in full in *Trial and Error*, 246.
25 Ibid., 235. The ascendency of the Saudis has had lasting impact. Whereas the Hashemites embraced traditional Sunnism the Saud clan were, and are, proselytizers of Wahhabism. See "What is Wahhabism? The Reactionary Branch of Islam from Saudi Arabia Said to be 'the Main Source of Global Terrorism,'" *The Telegraph*, March 29, 2016, http://www.telegraph.co.uk/news/2016/03/29/what-is-wahhabism-the-reactionary-branch-of-islam-said-to-be-the/.
26 Litvinoff, *Letters and Papers*, paper 60, 301.

Still, during the 1920s and 1930s, Weizmann busied himself with building the infrastructure that would be needed for statehood. This included the opening of the Hebrew University of Jerusalem on April 1, 1925, with the guest of honor, Lord Balfour, declaring:

"This occasion marks a great epoch in the history of the people who have made this little land of Palestine the seed ground of great religions... and who will look back to this day which we are celebrating as one of the great milestones in their future career."[27]

Five years later, on March 9, 1930, "Chaim Weizmann was the last visitor outside the family to see the dying statesman – it was a silent farewell, with Balfour too weak and the great Zionist too overcome to speak," writes historian R. J. Q. Adams in his biography *Balfour: The Last Grandee*.[28]

Alongside the process of nation-building, there were plenty of intramural struggles – ideological and personal – within the world Zionist movement and its many factions. Weizmann quarreled with Louis Brandeis (1856–1941) over what Zionism means and whether it was incumbent upon a Zionist to move to Palestine.

Brandeis did not think aliyah was a Zionist prerequisite: "Let no American imagine that Zionism is inconsistent with patriotism. Multiple loyalties are objectionable only if they are inconsistent. A man is a better citizen of the United States for being also a loyal citizen of his state, and of his city; or for being loyal to his college.... Every American Jew who aids in advancing the Jewish settlement in Palestine, though he feels that neither he nor his descendants will ever live there, will likewise be a better man and a better American for doing so. There is no inconsistency between loyalty to America and loyalty to Jewry."[29]

They argued over how Zionism should be organized and financially supervised. By 1921, an unhappy Brandeis – who was a US Supreme Court justice from 1916 to 1939 – quit the organized movement though remained supportive of Zionism.

Weizmann in addition had his disputes with Jabotinsky, the charismatic head of the Revisionist Party within Zionism and an old comrade of his, over how firmly to press the British to honor their Balfour Declaration commit-

---

27 *The Hebrew University Jerusalem: Inauguration, April 1 1925* (Jerusalem: for the Hebrew University Jerusalem by 'Azriel' Printing Works, 1925), 29.

28 Adams, *Last Grandee*, 378.

29 Louis Dembitz Brandeis, *Brandeis on Zionism: A Collection of Addresses and Statements* (Westport, CT: Hyperion Press, 1976), 28.

ments. They also quarreled over how the Jewish Agency (Palestinian Jewry's quasi-governmental body) was to be structured.

Undoubtedly, it was British backtracking on the Balfour Declaration that gave Weizmann the most grief.

The Zionists became taken up with how to respond to British officials on the ground in Palestine who they perceived as diluting the spirit of the Balfour Declaration.

In the face of increasing Arab violence against the Jews of Palestine, especially in the years 1920, 1921, and 1929, stung by Britain's refusal to implement the mandate wholeheartedly and worn down by rows within the Zionist camp, Weizmann – identified as being too close to the British – was not elected head of the 1931 Seventeenth World Zionist Congress.[30]

By 1935, however, the indispensable Weizmann was again piloting the movement.

In 1936, with a full-blown revolt by the Palestinian Arabs against the British under way, Weizmann spoke plainly and from the heart as he testified before a British Royal Commission of Inquiry headed by Lord Peel:

> We are a stiff-necked people and a people of long memory. We never forget. Whether it is our misfortune or whether it is our good fortune, we have never forgotten Palestine, and this steadfastness, which has preserved the Jew through the ages and through a career which is almost one long chain of inhuman suffering, is primarily due to some physiological or pathological attachment to Palestine.
>
> We have never forgotten it; we have never given it up. We have survived our Babylonian and Roman conquerors. The Roman Empire, which digested half of the civilized world, did not digest small Judea.
>
> And whenever they [Jews] got a chance, the slightest chance, there they returned, there they created their literature, their villages, towns, and communities. And if the commission took the trouble to study the post-Roman period of the Jews, and the life of the Jews in Palestine, they would find that there was not a single century in

---

30 Opposition came from the Jabotinsky and Mizrachi camps as well as some American Zionists. "Congress Elects Nahum Sokolow President of World Zionist Organization," *Jewish Telegraphic Agency*, July 15, 1931, http://www.jta.org/1931/07/15/archive/congress-elects-nahum-sokolow-president-of-world-zionist-organization-coalition-executive-without-r.

the nineteen centuries which have passed since the destruction of Palestine as a Jewish political entity, there was not a single century in which the Jews did not attempt to come back.[31]

But as the promise of the Balfour Declaration continued to unravel other options arose.

In 1937, the Peel Commission determined that Arab opposition had made the mandate unworkable and recommended the partition of western Palestine, the area between the Jordan River and the Mediterranean Sea.

The country had already been partitioned once. On September 16, 1922, the British divided Mandatory Palestine into two administrative areas with eastern Palestine, 77 percent of the country, earmarked for the Arabs to create Transjordan under the leadership of Emir Abdullah.

The background for this: In 1921, France, which had the mandate for Syria, expelled the Hashemite Feisal from his Syrian throne. Britain, which had the mandate for Iraq, offered Feisal the throne of Iraq. But the Iraqi throne had been pledged to Feisal's brother Abdullah. The men were the sons of Hussein, Sharif and Emir of Mecca.

Abdullah then organized a rag-tag force to march on Damascus. He set up camp in Transjordan, on the eastern side of the River Jordan.

Colonial Secretary Winston Churchill headed for Cairo to handle the crisis and brokered an arrangement whereby eastern Palestine would be transformed into Transjordan, with Abdullah made sovereign; Feisal would become king in Iraq.

This was technically possible because the League of Nations had not yet ratified the Palestine Mandate which comprised both Palestine and Transjordan. The draft was now altered giving Britain the right to "withhold" the Jewish homeland provisions of the mandate "in the territories lying between the Jordan and the eastern boundary of Palestine with the consent of the League of Nations. London then asked for and was given the right to exclude Transjordan from the Jewish homeland provisions of mandate."[32]

---

31 Litvinoff, *Letters and Papers*, paper 22, 107. His remarks in full appear in *The Jewish People and Palestine; Statement Made Before the Palestine Royal Commission in Jerusalem, on November 25, 1936, by Dr. Chaim Weizmann* (London: Zionist Organisation, 1937).

32 The original draft was dated December 1, 1920. The final Palestine Mandate including Article 25 was ratified July 1, 1922.

British strategist and diplomat T. E. Lawrence wrote that creating Transjordan "honorably fulfils the whole of the promises we made to the Arabs in so far as the so-called British spheres are concerned."[33]

And still the Zionists continued to build their country. In the 1930s, Weizmann raised funds to create the Daniel Sieff Institute in Rehovot, today the Weizmann Institute of Science.

In 1937, Weizmann reluctantly advocated accepting Peel's plan for the partition of western Palestine and what would have amounted to a truncated Jewish homeland. The Palestinian Arab leadership, however, rejected the creation of a Jewish state within any boundaries.

By then, in January 1933, Adolf Hitler (1889–1945) had come to power and was an established menace.

The führer initially wanted to force the Jews of Germany out of the country, but immigration quotas and outright barriers limited where European Jews could go. Under intense Palestinian Arab pressure, the British closed the doors of Palestine ever more tightly.

On August 23, 1939, Hitler's Nazi Germany and Stalin's Communist Russia signed a non-aggression pact. Land would be traded, thereby putting even more Jews under Nazi jurisdiction.

Germany's September 1939 invasion of Poland ignited World War II, and millions of Polish Jews fell under Hitler's control.

On the day the Nazi-Communist alliance was announced, the Twenty-First Zionist Congress was meeting in Geneva in neutral Switzerland. A photograph of the Zionist Congress dais, snapped just after the news of the Hitler-Stalin pact broke, shows Weizmann and his colleague David Ben-Gurion.

In *The Siege: The Saga of Israel and Zionism* (1986), Conor Cruise O'Brien picks up the photograph's story:

"The copy before me shows twelve heads fully – four, including Weizmann, have a hand over their face or their head. Ben-Gurion, beside Weizmann, has his head bowed over his hands, which are crossed on his chest. They do not look like people who have just heard a piece of political news. They look like people who have heard a death sentence pronounced on members of their family."[34]

---

33   "Letter from T. E. Lawrence to William Yale," curated by Jeremy Wilson, T. E. Lawrence Studies, http://www.telstudies.org/index.shtml.

34   Conor Cruise O'Brien, *The Siege: The Saga of Israel and Zionism* (London: Paladin Grafton, 1988), 242.

Weizmann spent most of World War II (1939–1945) outside Palestine. Despite his good relationship with Churchill, including occasional wartime meetings, the British government kept Weizmann and the Zionists at arm's length. Offers of scientific and military cooperation were mostly rebuffed.

As Hitler's war against the Jews built up steam, the British authorities kept Palestine closed to Jewish asylum seekers. In February 1942, Weizmann in London personally protested Britain's policy after 750 Jewish refugees from Romania aboard the *Struma* drowned at sea off Turkey, having been denied entry to Palestine.

Weizmann traveled to the United States in 1940 to call, along with Jabotinsky, for the creation of a Jewish army to fight the Nazis and to raise funds, via the United Jewish Appeal, for the Zionist enterprise – specifically immigrant absorption, land purchases, and the Hebrew University.

The United States did not enter the war until December 7, 1941.

In March 1943, Weizmann addressed a protest rally of 20,000 at New York's Madison Square Garden to denounce the ongoing Nazi atrocities against Europe's Jews. Another 75,000 demonstrators were turned away, the JTA news service reported.[35]

All along, Nazi Germany, in its Arabic-language broadcasts, called Weizmann an "international criminal Jew" and "head of international Jewish gangs," the JTA reported.

Weizmann's pleas to the Jews and Arabs in Palestine to put aside their differences and unite against the Nazis were met with derision. "The Arabs will not be deceived by such Jewish English tricks and the Arabs will not allow a mean Jew to speak on their behalf," German broadcasters taunted.[36]

Indeed, in 1941, the leader of the Palestinian Arabs, Haj Amin al-Husseini, fled to Germany, where he parlayed with Hitler and other Nazi leaders. In addition to conducting Arabic-language propaganda broadcasts, he also helped to recruit Bosnian Muslim volunteers for the Nazi-SS forces.

For his Zionist critics, Weizmann had been permanently tarnished by

---

35 "Huge Demonstration in New York Appeals to All Governments to Save Jews in Europe," *Jewish Telegraphic Agency*, March 2, 1943, accessed June 20, 2017, http://www.jta.org/1943/03/02/archive/huge-demonstration-in-new-york-appeals-to-all-governments-to-save-jews-in-europe. See, too, "75,000 Sought Entrance to New York Meeting Protesting Nazi Massacres of Jews," *Jewish Telegraphic Agency*, March 3, 1943, accessed June 20, 2017, http://www.jta.org/1943/03/03/archive/75000-sought-entrance-to-new-york-meeting-protesting-nazi-massacres-of-jews.

36 "Nazi Radio Excoriates Weizmann on Arrival in New York," *Jewish Telegraphic Agency*, March 25, 1941, accessed June 20, 2017, http://www.jta.org/1941/03/25/archive/nazi-radio-excoriates-weizmann-on-arrival-in-new-york.

his close identification with Britain. Perhaps unfairly, he was seen as too tolerant of the British backsliding on Balfour.

Like David Ben-Gurion, Weizmann denounced as immoral and counterproductive Jewish militant violence against British forces in Palestine by the Lehi or Stern Gang while the war was being waged. Jabotinsky's Irgun did not, in the main, target British forces during the war. Under Ben-Gurion's leadership the Haganah, the biggest Zionist underground force, allied with the British during the war.

By the time the Second World War officially ended on September 2, 1945, Weizmann was over seventy years old. Britain's wartime prime minister Winston Churchill lost the 1945 election to Clement Attlee's Labour Party.[37] And British policy toward Zionism remained solidly antagonistic. Holocaust survivors were blocked from entering Palestine; tens of thousands were housed in displaced persons camps in Germany.

Weizmann lobbied the Labour government to return to the spirit of the Balfour Declaration, to no avail. At the same time, he continued to denounce armed opposition to Britain in Palestine by the Irgun and Stern Gang.

"No one understands better than I the state of mind out of which the recent events have come. Nevertheless, I deplore and disapprove of them, and urge that for the sake of our cause they should not recur. We have loyal friends on both sides of the ocean who firmly believe in the justice of our cause, and share our faith in the power of reason and justice. The overwhelming moral force of our cause must ultimately triumph."[38]

In June 1946, with no letup in Jewish terror against British targets, Weizmann criticized Attlee and Foreign Secretary Ernest Bevin, whose policies he said promoted instability in Palestine. This did not mean, he emphasized, that he approved of Jewish violence. He decried the July 1946 bombing of the British military headquarters at the King David Hotel by the Irgun as an "unspeakable outrage."[39]

On the streets of Palestine Weizmann was received with appreciation.

37   "1945 Elections," BBC News, accessed July 2, 2017, http://www.bbc.co.uk/news/special/politics97/background/pastelec/ge45.shtml.

38   "Weizmann En Route to Washington; Counsels Jews of Palestine Against Further Violence," *Jewish Telegraphic Agency*, November 5, 1945, accessed June 20, 2017, http://archive.jta.org/1945/11/05/archive/weizmann-en-route-to-washington-counsels-jews-of-palestine-against-further-violence.

39   "Weizmann Issues Statement Deploring Jerusalem Bombing as 'Unspeakable Outrage,'" *Jewish Telegraphic Agency*, July 24, 1946, accessed June 20, 2017, http://www.jta.org/1946/07/24/archive/weizmann-issues-statement-deploring-jerusalem-bombing-as-unspeakable-outrage.

And yet, fairly or not, by 1946, his popularity had become ever more tainted by the harsh British policies toward Zionism. The Twenty-Second Zionist Congress in Basel removed him as its leader; he was not deemed the suitable figure to lead the struggle against British policy. The torch was formally passed to David Ben-Gurion.[40]

Though he now held no official position in the Zionist hierarchy, Weizmann continued to meet with world leaders, including US president Harry S Truman, and he served as the chief Zionist spokesman before the United Nations.

Despite his failing eyesight and frail health, Weizmann made the Zionist case for the partition of western Palestine into two states – one Arab and one Jewish – before the international community. His efforts were crowned with success when the UN General Assembly voted on November 29, 1947, for partition.

"The time will come," he said in January 1948, "when Arabs and Jews will meet on common economic and cultural grounds."[41]

The Palestinian Arabs and the greater Arab world rejected the General Assembly partition decision and mobilized to strangle the newborn Jewish state in its infancy. Meanwhile, Britain's pullout from Palestine was set for Friday, May 14, 1948.

That same day, Zionist leaders in Tel Aviv, led by Ben-Gurion, declared Israel's independence. Weizmann was still in New York on Zionist business. The United States granted Israel de facto recognition that very day. The Soviet Union was the first country to recognize Israel de jure on May 17, 1948.

On May 16, 1948, with the country under military attack on all fronts, the provisional government elected Chaim Weizmann to the largely ceremonial position of state president. He sent word: "I dedicate myself to the service of the land and people in whose cause I have been privileged to labor these many years."[42]

Weizmann's first order of business was to see Truman in a meeting fa-

40 "New Zionist Executive Elected: Ben-Gurion, Chairman, Silver Heads Washington Section," *Jewish Telegraphic Agency*, December 30, 1946, http://www.jta.org/1946/12/30/archive/new-zionist-executive-elected-ben-gurion-chairman-silver-heads-washington-section.

41 "Dr. Weizmann Predicts Differences Between Jews and Arabs Will Be Resolved," *Jewish Telegraphic Agency*, January 26, 1948, accessed June 20, 2017, http://www.jta.org/1948/01/26/archive/dr-weizamnn-predicts-differences-between-jews-and-arabs-will-be-resolved.

42 "Chaim Weizmann First President of Israel, Sends Acceptance Message to Government," *Jewish Telegraphic Agency*, May 18, 1948, accessed June 20, 2017, http://www.jta.org/1948/05/18/archive/chaim-weizmann-first-president-of-israel-sends-acceptance-message-to-government.

cilitated by Edward Jacobson, Truman's former business partner and friend, that took place on May 25. Weizmann appealed, unsuccessfully, for an end to the American arms embargo.

Chaim and Vera Weizmann were honored with new Israeli passports – numbers one and two – issued by the Jewish state's Foreign Ministry. That summer, Weizmann gave up his British passport.

His health continued to deteriorate; glaucoma had temporarily robbed him of his vision and he flew to Switzerland for special surgery.

On February 18, 1949, he was officially sworn in as Israel's first president.

The *New York Times*, which did not support the Zionist idea, nonetheless editorialized: "Few men of our time have dreamed a dream so long and lived to see it fulfilled," as Weizmann had.[43]

In May 1949, Israel's first president was back in New York to address 250,000 supporters of the Jewish state at an outdoor meeting to mark the country's first anniversary.

In August 1949, Weizmann was once again in Switzerland for medical treatment when Herzl's remains were brought from Vienna to be reinterred on Mount Herzl. His message was read by Knesset Speaker Joseph Sprinzak: "Fortunate is the generation which has been privileged to implement the dream of its leader."[44]

August 1949 was also around the time when most of the Arab states that had invaded Israel signed on to a UN-sponsored armistice agreement.

On November 2, another dream was realized: The Daniel Sieff Institute, which Weizmann founded, was renamed the Weizmann Institute of Science, with Weizmann declaring: "We live in a pioneering land. We are pioneers in settling desolate areas, in agriculture and in industry. Here in Rehovot we are involved in a pioneering act of a special kind: pioneering in science."[45]

Weizmann's health continued to deteriorate and he was limited – both physically and politically – in what he could do as president. Still, there were government coalition crises to resolve and diplomatic credentials to receive.

---

43   "A Dream Come True," *New York Times*, February 18, 1949, accessed June 20, 2017, http://query.nytimes.com/gst/abstract.html?res=9E05E5DD103FE43ABC4052DFB4668382659EDE&legacy=true.

44   "Herzl's Remains Brought to Israel; Coffin Placed in Public Square; Reburial Today," *Jewish Telegraphic Agency*, August 17, 1949, accessed June 20, 2017, http://www.jta.org/1949/08/17/archive/herzls-remains-brought-to-israel-coffin-placed-in-public-square-reburial-today.

45   The Weizmann Institute, www.chaimweizmann.org.il/en/timeline#1948.

He commuted the death sentences of Arabs charged with killing Jews. He received leaders of the country's Arab community on the third anniversary of Israel's creation. And on July 20, 1951, he was briefed on the assassination that day of King Abdullah of Jordan by a Palestinian Arab at the Dome of the Rock on the Temple Mount.[46]

On November 20, 1951, Weizmann was reelected president. Unable to travel to Jerusalem due to ill health, he was sworn in at home in Rehovot. In December 1951, Knesset Speaker Sprinzak was named acting president. Weizmann's condition had improved enough by June 1952 for him to receive Helen Keller, who was visiting Israel.[47]

But the end was near. Chaim Weizmann died at home in Rehovot on November 9, 1952, just short of his seventy-eighth birthday. "The announcer on the Voice of Israel, who informed the people of the state of their loss, burst into tears in the midst of the announcement. When he was able, he concluded the official statement in a heavily choked voice," the JTA reported.[48]

The Zionist leader was buried in the garden of his estate in Rehovot, and Israel went into mourning with public activities cancelled that Sunday night. On Monday, schools were closed, many businesses did not open and the Israeli cabinet met in special session. Prime Minister Ben-Gurion described Weizmann as carrying two crowns on his head – a crown of statesmanship and a crown of learning.

At the end of the traditional seven-day mourning period, the Knesset met to eulogize Weizmann and hear Ben-Gurion declare that Weizmann had provided the Zionist cause with both vision and a practical appreciation of what needed to be done on the ground in Palestine.

---

46 "Abdullah, Jordan King, Slain by an Arab in Old Jerusalem," *New York Times*, July 21, 1951, http://www.nytimes.com/1951/07/21/archives/abdullah-jordan-king-slain-by-an-arab-in-old-jerusalem-abdullah-is.html. The 1949 armistice agreement had left Jordan in control of eastern Jerusalem including the Old City as well as the West Bank. The king often went to Friday prayers at the Dome of the Rock. The assassin was a member of an Islamist group, Jihad Mukadess, aligned with Amin al-Husseini, the exiled Mufti of Jerusalem. The Islamists opposed Jordan's annexation of Jerusalem.

47 "Helen Keller Leaves Israel After Two-Week Visit," *Jewish Telegraphic Agency*, June 4, 1952, http://www.jta.org/1952/06/04/archive/helen-keller-leaves-israel-after-two-week-visit. Keller, a writer and political activist, was both deaf and blind.

48 "Israel Mourns Death of President Weizmann; Funeral Tomorrow," *Jewish Telegraphic Agency*, November 10, 1952, accessed June 20, 2017, http://www.jta.org/1952/11/10/archive/israel-mourns-death-of-president-weizmann-funeral-tomorrow.

Weizmann was survived by his wife Vera, who lived on until September 24, 1966, and his son Benjamin. His other son, Michael, had been killed in action in 1942, while serving in the British Royal Air Force. "Difficult things take a long time, the impossible takes a little longer," Weizmann wrote.[49] He managed to accomplish "the impossible" in his own lifetime and witness the rebirth of Israel.

---

49   Vera Weizmann, *Memoirs*, iii.

Chapter 6

DUTY FIRST:
LIONEL WALTER ROTHSCHILD

The document that came to be known as the Balfour Declaration was addressed to Lionel Walter Rothschild (1868–1937) and delivered by hand to his London home at 148 Piccadilly.

Born into the legendry Rothschild banking family, Walter took on, perhaps reluctantly, the business and civic responsibilities necessitated by his position. He served as a Conservative member of the House of Commons and on the boards of Jewish communal institutions. His attachment to Zionism was heartfelt and of incalculable value to the movement; yet, his greatest passion was reflected in his lifelong commitment to the natural sciences.

He came into this world in London on February 8, 1868, the eldest son of Nathaniel Mayer de Rothschild (1840–1915), who was the first Lord Rothschild and the first Jewish peer in England. His mother was Emma Louisa (1844–1935), daughter of Mayer Carl von Rothschild of Frankfurt.

Walter was educated at home, then at Bonn University, and later at Magdalene College, Cambridge (1887–1889), where he came under the influence of the renowned ornithologist Alfred Newton. Pressed by and under the tutelage of Nathaniel Mayer de Rothschild, Walter left academia to learn the business – banking – that had made the Rothschild name renowned. Between 1889 and 1908, he worked at N. M. Rothschild and Sons in London. In tandem, he served as a member of Parliament with the Liberal Unionists (1899–1910), a faction that had broken away from the Liberal Party in opposition to Irish Home Rule. The Liberal Unionist and Conservatives eventually merged.

By 1910, Walter had retired from Parliament and banking to devote himself to the natural sciences. He wrote scores of well-received articles on biology, zoology, ornithology, and entomology. An avid collector, he opened a public museum at Tring in Hertfordshire that housed his specimen collection, just as he had said he would when he was only seven years old.[1]

Besides being a trustee of the British Museum, Rothschild was the de facto head of Britain's Jewish community serving as a governor of the Board of Deputies, the United Synagogue, the Anglo Jewish Association, and the Jews' Free School.

When Nathaniel Mayer de Rothschild died in 1915, Walter succeeded his father to the peerage. Nathaniel Mayer's father Baron Lionel Nathan de Rothschild (1808–1879) was the first observant Jew to serve as a member of Parliament. Lionel Nathan was first elected in 1847, but was not allowed to take his seat because he refused to take the oath on a Christian Bible. In 1858, the House rules were amended allowing him to take office.

Britain's first Lord Rothschild, Nathaniel Mayer, had served on the 1902 Royal Commission on Alien Immigration. He met Theodor Herzl when the father of political Zionism went to London to testify before the commission.

Nathaniel Mayer was concerned that Herzl's testimony should not prejudice the Jews' position in England or his own efforts to champion the immigration of eastern European Jewry. Herzl indeed took care not to do this and the two men got on well, though their collegiality did not convert the elder Rothschild to Zionism.

As Zionist leader Chaim Weizmann remarks in his memoirs: "The House of Rothschild, perhaps the most famous family in Jewish exilic history, was divided on the issue of Zionism."[2]

But Nathaniel Mayer did eventually have a change of heart about Zionism not long before his death in March 1915, according to historian Jehuda Reinharz.[3] His sons, Walter and Charles, were both Zionists.

Indeed, Walter even managed to relate his work in the natural sciences to his commitment to Zionism, as the scientist and historian Stephen Jay Gould notes: "When Chaim Weizmann, the Zionist leader, left for Palestine to see if he could facilitate the implementation of Balfour's Declaration, Rothschild gave him another mission" – to find out what had happened

---

1   "Lionel Walter (Walter) Rothschild (1868–1937)," The Rothschild Archive, accessed June 21, 2017, https://family.rothschildarchive.org/people/102-lionel-walter-walter-rothschild-1868–1937.
2   Weizmann, *Trial and Error*, 160.
3   Reinharz, *The Making of a Zionist Leader*, 126.

to two ostriches he had gifted to a Jaffa-based naturalist. Needless to say, Weizmann carried out the mission.[4]

"Exactly when and how" Walter Rothschild was "moved to take an active interest in Zionism is uncertain," writes Leonard Stein, chief historian of the Balfour Declaration.[5] It probably happened around November 1916, although Rothschild's public allegiance to the cause came, powerfully, on May 28, 1917, in a letter to the *Times*.

Rothschild, furthermore, worked diligently with Weizmann to counter the influence of the opponents of Zionism both in and outside the British cabinet. On February 7, 1917, he told his coterie of Zionist insiders, in the presence of Sir Mark Sykes, the Middle East strategist and government emissary, that he was for a Jewish state under the sponsorship of the British crown.

In response to those Jewish opponents of Zionism who worried that the rights of British Jewry would be jeopardized if Zionism were embraced abroad, Rothschild argued that a Jewish homeland in Palestine under British protection was meant for those who "could not" or "did not" desire to be citizens in the country where they lived.

"I can truly say that national Zionism has done nothing, and would never do anything, inconsistent with the status of the true British citizen of which I am proud to be one, just as proud as I am of being a Jew," Rothschild declared.[6]

On June 19, 1917, Foreign Minister Arthur James Balfour met with Rothschild and Weizmann. He asked them to draft a communiqué regarding Palestine for the cabinet to consider, and that would be acceptable from the Zionist viewpoint.

A draft with the imprimatur (by a 56–51 margin in favor) of the previously anti-Zionist Board of Deputies, which by this point was under Rothschild's leadership, was submitted on July 18. "At last I am able to send you the formula you asked me for," Rothschild wrote. "If His Majesty's Government will send me a message on the lines of this formula, if they and you approve of it, I will hand it in to the Zionists' Federation and also announce it at a meeting called for that purpose."[7]

---

4   Stephen Jay Gould, "Dear Lord Rothschild," *Science* 227 (1985), 159.
5   Stein, *Balfour Declaration*, 183.
6   Schneer, *The Balfour Declaration*, 313.
7   Stein, *Balfour Declaration*, 470.

One of the two Jewish ministers in Prime Minister David Lloyd George's cabinet – the Liberal Party's Edwin Montagu, secretary of state for India – made the anti-Zionist case when the cabinet discussed the draft in September 1917. As it happened, both the prime minister and Foreign Minister Balfour were away from London during the deliberations.

In the event the tide was with the Zionists and under the helm of Lloyd George and Balfour, the cabinet's ultimate approval came on October 31, 1917. The tidings were delivered by messenger from Balfour to Rothschild, in his capacity as president of the English Zionist Federation, and arrived at 148 Piccadilly dated November 2. In the legendary letter, which began "Dear Lord Rothschild," the British government declared its support for the establishment in Palestine of "a national home for the Jewish people."

It would take about a week for the newspapers to report the story to the wider world.

On the evening of the declaration, the news was cabled to Baron Edmond de Rothschild in Paris. Before heading to his own flat, Chaim Weizmann went to Ahad Ha'Am's home in Maida Vale. According to Shmuel Tolkowsky, an aide to both Weizmann and Nahum Sokolow, Weizmann was overjoyed and "embraced me for a long time," saying *mazel tov* over and over again.[8] Numerous other leading Zionists, including Ze'ev Jabotinsky, Tolkowsky, and Eliezer Margolin (who had commanded a Jewish battalion of the British Army formed to fight the Turks in Palestine) had dinner at Weizmann's place.

Before they sat down to eat, the group, which by now included Vera Weizmann, danced in a circle, Hassidic-style, in Weizmann's study.[9]

On December 2, 1917, Rothschild chaired a meeting of thanksgiving at the Royal Opera House in central London. Besides Zionist dignitaries led by Chaim Weizmann, Herbert Samuel, Chief Rabbi Dr. Joseph Hertz, and Nahum Sokolow, the British government officials present included Under-Secretary of State for Foreign Affairs Robert Cecil and Sir Mark Sykes.

After the world war, Rothschild continued to play an important supporting role in the Zionist movement. One key task was to reach out for Arab support. On December 21, 1918, Rothschild tendered a dinner for Emir Feisal of Arabia, who would, in January 1919, reach an agreement with

---

8   Schneer, *The Balfour Declaration*, 346.
9   Reinharz, *The Making of a Zionist Leader*, 205. The scene is first described by Vera Weizmann in *Memoirs*, 78.

Weizmann on Arab-Zionist cooperation. Rothschild also sat on the advisory committee of the Hebrew University of Jerusalem, the institution whose establishment was seen as a crucial milestone in Zionist nation-building.

For all his involvement in communal and civic affairs, Walter Rothschild was basically a nonpolitical man who was profoundly, and more contentedly, invested in the natural sciences.

He had grown up at Tring Park in Hertfordshire, just north of London, and from an early age dreamt of building a zoological museum to show off his collection of insects, butterflies, and other creatures. But his childhood was perhaps less idyllic than one might imagine; out riding near his home one day, he was dragged off his horse and roughed up by apparently anti-Semitic louts. The incident stayed with him.

As a youngster, Rothschild was delicate, introverted, and had a speech impediment. As an adult, he was an imposing man of six foot three, eventually weighing three hundred pounds. He never married, though as a young man he was purported to have had dalliances with chorus girls and in later life kept mistresses – one of whom bore him a daughter, and another who is said to have blackmailed him.

After a long illness, Lionel Walter Rothschild died on August 27, 1937, at the age of sixty-nine.

At that Royal Opera House mass meeting a month after the Balfour Declaration, Rothschild struck a tone of gratitude and conciliation. The declaration, he said, was the most momentous occasion in the history of Judaism in 1,800 years. For the first time since the Roman dispersion of the Jewish people from Palestine in 70 CE, they had received international recognition of their aspirations for a national home. Now they had to take care to respect the rights and privileges of their non-Jewish neighbors in Palestine and reconcile with those in the Jewish community who did not, in the first instance, embrace the Zionist cause.

He called on those gathered in the hall to adopt a resolution that "conveys to His Majesty's Government an expression of heartfelt gratitude" and to pledge their own continuing support for the Zionist cause.[10]

While Rothschild's name is linked in perpetuity to British support for

---

10   Nahum Sokolow, *History of Zionism, 1600–1918* (New York: Ktav, 1969), 101. Speeches of thanksgiving were also delivered by, among others, Lord Robert Cecil, the Under-Secretary of State for Foreign Affairs, MP Herbert Samuel, Chief Rabbi Joseph Hertz, Sir Mark Sykes, Haham Dr. Moses Gaster, and Sheikh Ismail-Abdul al-Akki, an Arab spokesman.

a Jewish national home in Palestine, his contributions to scientific inquiry, his support for taxonomy in biology, his establishment of scientific journals, and his natural history museum at Tring Park could hardly be less central to the achievements for which he would have wanted to be remembered.

Despite the vicissitudes that have accompanied the Jewish people on their journey these past one hundred years, one constant has been the Rothschild family's civic-mindedness – manifested through extraordinary contributions that have enhanced Jewish life in Europe and have made a lasting imprint on the Israeli landscape, and boosted human capital by fostering a democratic polity committed to equal opportunity for all Israel's inhabitants. At home, the tapestry of Rothschild generosity is evident in the arts, British heritage, education, and the environment.

Continuity has been a cornerstone of the Rothschild ethos. Nathaniel Charles Jacob Rothschild holds the peerage today as the centenary of the Balfour Declaration is commemorated. He was just sixteen months old when his great-uncle died.

One hundred years ago, providence placed Lionel Walter Rothschild in partnership with a small group of other men and women including David Lloyd George, James Arthur Balfour, Chaim Weizmann, and Vera Weizmann. Together they made it possible for the Zionist enterprise to achieve its chief goal of creating a Jewish homeland in Palestine. Like all human endeavors the outcome of their efforts has been imperfect. Yet, this can in no way detract from the magnitude of their accomplishment.

Chapter 7

A CONFLUENCE OF FACTORS

No one really knows where the expression came from, but "two Jews, three opinions," seems to encapsulate the fractious nature of Jewish history from time immemorial. We began as the Tribes of Israel circa 1280 BCE and we remain a twenty-first century tribal people.[1] Why did Britain issue the Balfour Declaration? Everyone has an opinion: Weizmann's acetone, Christian Zionism, British national interest, and the cabinet's quest for international Jewish support during wartime usually top the list.

It seems to me that the cabinet's decision to go with the pro-Zionist camp was actually the result of a confluence of factors.

On June 13, 1917, Foreign Secretary Arthur Balfour met with Lord Rothschild (Walter), leader of the British Jewish community, and Zionist statesman Chaim Weizmann and suggested they submit a draft document encapsulating their hopes for Palestine that he could submit for cabinet discussion.

The formula which the Zionists preferred was submitted by Rothschild to Balfour on July 18, 1917.

But the to-and-fro over the letter's wording continued as we shall see further on. The phraseology needed to be crafted so as to promote a national home for the Jews in Palestine while protecting the political status of Jewish people who would never move there and, at the same time, ensure that Arab civil and religious rights would not be prejudiced in the Jewish homeland.

---

1 I think of the tribes of Israel today as encompassing Ashkenazi, Sephardi, Edot HaMizrah, Ethiopian, Orthodox, modern Orthodox, national Orthodox, ultra-Orthodox, ultra-Orthodox Zionist, ultra-Orthodox anti-Zionist, ultra-Orthodox non-Zionist, insular Haredi, Chassidic (there are dozens of dynasties from Belz to Vizhnitz), Mitnagdim-Litvish-Yeshivish, Conservative (ranging from neo-Orthodox to neo-Reform), Masorti, conservodox, post-denominational, Reform, Liberal, Progressive, Reconstructionist, unaffiliated, secular, Zionist, post-Zionist, Israeli atheist, and humanist.

Paradoxically, perhaps, the most vocal opponents of issuing the declaration were some British Jews, among them David Alexander, president of the Board of Deputies of British Jews, and Lucien Wolf, a journalist who held what amounted to the foreign affairs portfolio at the Board of Deputies. Claude Montefiore (1858–1938), a great-nephew of Sir Moses and a proponent of Liberal Judaism, was another fierce adversary of Zionism.

Leon Simon, a leading Zionist campaigner, civil servant, and intellectual, rebutted the anti-Zionist claims in his pamphlet "The Case of the Anti-Zionists: A Reply."

The declaration's opponents, concerned that Jewish nationalism would raise doubts about their own loyalty to the Crown, argued that the Jews were solely a religious community.

One of the two Jewish ministers in Lloyd George's cabinet, the Liberal Party's Edwin Montagu, secretary of state for India, made the anti-Zionist case. His cousin and fellow cabinet member Herbert Samuel (1870–1963), also a Liberal, not only supported Zionism, but within months of the outbreak of the world war, presented the cabinet with a memorandum on the benefits of a British protectorate for Palestine to support Jewish immigration.

On October 6, 1917, the War Cabinet decided to send out the latest draft text to eight Jews – four anti-Zionists and four Zionists – for comment. The cover letter acknowledged that "in view of the divergence of opinion expressed on the subject by the Jews themselves," the government "would like to receive in writing the views of representative Jewish leaders, both Zionists and non-Zionists."[2]

Letters of support were submitted by Chief Rabbi Dr. Joseph Hertz (1872–1946), Rothschild, Sokolow, and Weizmann.

The anti-Zionist case was made, also in separate letters, by Leonard Cohen of the Jewish Board of Guardians, MP Philip Magnus, president of the Anglo-Jewish Association Claude Montefiore, and the newly elected president of the Board of Deputies Stuart Samuel.

Often lost in the haze of history is the fact that the anti-Zionists didn't oppose Jewish immigration to Palestine. The anti-Zionist Jews of the early twentieth century fully accepted Palestine's special significance to the Jewish people.

---

2   Stein, *Balfour Declaration*, 525.

Lucien Wolf was an opponent of political Zionism and director of the Conjoint Foreign Committee which largely concerned itself with battling anti-Semitism. Its Palestine position was articulated in March 3, 1916:

"In the event of Palestine coming within the spheres of influence of Great Britain or France at the close of the war, the governments of those powers will not fail to take account of the historic interest that country possesses for the Jewish community. The Jewish population will be secured in the enjoyment of civil and religious liberty, equal political rights with the rest of the population, reasonable facilities for immigration and colonisation, and such municipal privileges in the towns and colonies inhabited by them as may be shown necessary."[3]

Edwin Montagu, recently appointed secretary of state for India, was the most persistent opponent of political Zionism inside the David Lloyd George government. He asserted that "there is not a Jewish nation" and that if Palestine were declared the national home of the Jews, "every country will immediately desire to get rid of its Jewish citizens." He also worried how any Zionist declaration would affect his ability to preside over the Indian subcontinent.[4] Nonetheless, this is what he wrote on August 23, 1917:

"I would say to Lord Rothschild that the Government will be prepared to do everything in their power to obtain for Jews in Palestine complete liberty of settlement and life on an equality with the inhabitants of that country who profess other religious beliefs. I would ask that the Government should go no further."[5]

And while his aim was to head off political Zionism, on September 14, 1917, Montagu came back – in a letter addressed to Lord Robert Cecil, the assistant foreign secretary – with yet another alteration for the Government to consider:

"His Majesty's Government accepts the principle that every opportunity should be afforded for the establishment in Palestine for those Jews who cannot or will not remain in the lands in which they live at present, will use its best endeavours to facilitate the achievement of this object, and will be

3   Isaiah Friedman, *The Question of Palestine: British-Jewish-Arab Relations, 1914–1918*, vol. 1 (New Brunswick: Transaction, 1992), 52.
4   "How would he negotiate with the people of India on behalf of His Majesty's Government if the world had just been told that His Majesty's Government regarded his national home as being in Turkish territory?" Cited in Stein, *Balfour Declaration*, 515.
5   Great Britain, Public Record Office, Cab. 24/24, August 23, 1917. Lord Edwin Samuel Montagu (1879–1924), an Anglo-Jewish statesman, was British Minister of Munitions in 1916 and Secretary of State for India, 1917–1922. See, too, Reinharz, *The Making of a Zionist Leader,* 181.

ready to consider any suggestions on the subject which any Jewish or Zionist organisations may desire to lay before it."[6]

Like their opponents, the anti-Zionists were products of their milieu. They worried – among other things – that hard won Jewish rights in western Europe would be withdrawn if Jews had their own national home. That said, there were no Jewish voices which argued against immigration to Palestine or denied its special place in Jewish civilization.

To reiterate, the cabinet's decision to go with the pro-Zionist camp was the result of a confluence of factors, the foremost being British national interest.

There was also compassion for persecuted Jewry. Back in 1840, prompted by the Christian Zionism of the young Lord Shaftesbury, then secretary of state for foreign affairs Lord Palmerston instructed the British ambassador to the Ottoman Empire to encourage the sultan to allow Jews to resettle in Palestine. Shaftesbury's hope was that they would in due course embrace Christianity.

In 1903, Joseph Chamberlain, secretary of state for the colonies, floated the idea of finding the Jews a homeland somewhere in East Africa or in the Sinai Peninsula at El Arish.

Balfour himself, very much in keeping with his age and class, was ambivalent about Jews, but believed that the Christian world owed a moral debt to Jewish civilization over centuries of persecution and contempt.

Adding to the atmosphere, George Eliot's 1876 novel *Daniel Deronda* raised the idea of restoring Palestine to the Jews. Back in 1833, Benjamin Disraeli, prime minister of Britain from 1874 until 1880, had written *The Wondrous Tale of Alroy*, a novel set partly in Jerusalem about a young Jewish man trying to survive in a non-Jewish world. Disraeli's father had converted to Christianity when Benjamin was twelve years old.[7] The future prime minister visited Palestine in 1831.

---

6   Naomi Levine, *Politics, Religion, and Love: The Story of H.H. Asquith, Venetia Stanley and Edwin Montagu, Based on the Life and Letters of Edwin Samuel Montague* (New York: New York University Press, 1991), 439. Montagu was not a member of the War Cabinet and in his capacity as Secretary of State for India was already on his way there when the Balfour Declaration was issued.

7   I have a tendency to idealize Disraeli. I really shouldn't. Out of pique over being nominated a warden at London's Bevis Marks synagogue, Disraeli's father Isaac quit the community in 1813 and in 1817 baptized his children as Christians. Benjamin would soon have been eligible for bar mitzvah. See, André Maurois, *Disraeli: A Picture of the Victorian Age* (New York: D. Appleton and Co., 1928), 13. Moreover, as British premier, Disraeli was no particular friend of Jewish people. See Todd Endelman, *Disraeli's Jewishness* (London: Mitchell, 2002), 6–7.

At the end of the day, Balfour envisaged, those Jews who could not or would not fully assimilate in their countries would move to their national home. This was more or less Herzl's vision too.

A second factor was the British leadership's rather inflated view of Jewish influence. It imagined Jews, irrespective of whether they were Russian, American or German, as a unified collective that could be used to further British interests. Zionist leaders in London had done nothing to disabuse the British of this belief.

Up until the world war, Zionist leaders had simply hedged their bets. The movement sought to sway any leader – from the Turkish sultan to the German kaiser, and from the British prime minister to the Catholic pope – who would lend an ear to supporting the restoration of the Jews to Palestine.

So it was that Britain hoped the Jews could help with the war effort. London needed Russia to stay in the Great War and the United States to accelerate its military involvement in the fighting. But Russia's Kerensky, despite his Jewish-sounding name, was actually Russian Orthodox. The revolutionary Leon Trotsky was Jewish though certainly no Zionist. US president Woodrow Wilson had nominated Louis Brandeis (who was indeed a Zionist) to the US Supreme Court in 1916. Another Zionist, Felix Frankfurter, a law professor and later also a member of the US Supreme Court, worked in the War Department and elsewhere in the Wilson administration.

Ultimately, Wilson signaled that he would welcome a Jewish homeland declaration by Britain.[8]

Asked later about the Balfour Declaration, Lloyd George would make the case that the Zionist movement was "exceptionally strong in Russia and America," so winning its backing was good politics.

There was of course a dark side to this overrating of Jewish influence, and taken to the extreme it led to anti-Semitic conspiracy theories. Some went so far as to convince themselves that a Jewish "hidden hand" wanted the world war to continue and was profiteering off it.

In fact, about 1.5 million Jews fought in World War I for their respective countries and, wretchedly, battled their co-religionists across the trenches. Some 100,000 German Jews fought in the war and 12,000 gave their lives for the fatherland. About 500,000 Russian Jews were conscripted – not that they wanted to fight for the anti-Jewish Tsar. Roughly 250,000 American Jewish

---

8   Wilson's influential aide "Colonel" Edward House was no friend of Zionism but Brandeis was able to overcome this hostility. Stein, *Balfour Declaration*, 505.

soldiers also went to war. Some 60,000 Jews from throughout the British Empire enlisted and 3,500 were killed; and about 35,000 Jews served in the French army. There were Jewish field marshals and Jewish generals commanding the Austro-Hungarian forces.

Finally, the cabinet's decision to go with the pro-Zionist camp was in no small measure due to the indefatigable Zionist campaigners led by Chaim Weizmann who would become the first president of the State of Israel.

Chapter 8

CHRISTIAN LOVE FOR ISRAEL

BY ELWOOD MCQUAID

The role that philo-Semitic Christians played in setting the stage for the Balfour Declaration is laid out in the pages that follow written by Rev. Elwood McQuaid. I have known and esteemed Elwood for nearly twenty years and we have become as close as friends can be who are separated by six thousand miles.

First some background: Most Christian Zionists are Protestants belonging to an Evangelical or "fundamentalist" church. Their roots are traceable to early nineteenth-century American and British Evangelical movements. In theological terms, Christian Zionists believe that the return of the Jewish people to the Land of Israel is a precursor to the second coming of Jesus whom they believe is the Messiah. He would then establish God's kingdom on Earth. One of Christianity's great theological dilemmas is the Jews' rejection of Jesus as the Messiah – a matter that comes up also in the following chapter about the Catholic Church and Zionism. One way in which Christian theologians deal with this rejection is in the belief that it does not represent the Jews' final word.

I realize that many Jewish people are discomfited by end-of-time, apocalyptic prophecies, and undoubtedly by Christian proselytizing of the Jewish people. To be fair, spreading the gospel is a pillar of Christianity. Rather than expect a Christian to change their creed, I would invite Jewish people to become more literate about their own civilization. I am convinced that in the twenty-first century we "lose" far more millennial Jews to "none of the above" than to Christianity – to indifference and Jewish illiteracy rather than conversion.

What matters in connection with the Balfour Declaration is that

Christian Zionism was an element in the War Cabinet's decision. More generally, Christian Zionists take seriously passages in the Hebrew Bible such as Genesis 12:3: "And I will bless them that bless thee, and curse him that curseth thee: and in thee shall all families of the earth be blessed."

One hundred years after the declaration, Christian Zionists are selfless supporters of Israel. Let me give you an example. I have a Christian friend, a man in his late seventies who, when visiting Israel, has held quiet prayer vigils through long, cold, and damp nights at the Western Wall. Like McQuaid, he has stood with Israelis when the missiles and rockets were falling and when the buses and cafes were being blown up.

I know that Christian Evangelicals are by and large not rich folks, yet many a hard-earned dollar is tithed to support soup kitchens for elderly and destitute Jews in Israel. A Christian lady I know opts to live in Israel even though it means she is separated from her son and grandchildren. She does so not to proselytize, but to lead her life in the Holy Land and walk in the footsteps of Jesus. Contrast these Evangelicals with mainline liberal church leaders in the United Kingdom and the United States who have mostly abandoned Israel. Some have even taken to symbolically equating Palestinian Arabs with Jesus on the cross.

Gratitude is a Jewish value. So I am delighted and grateful to Rev. McQuaid for this contribution. It is based on a chapter from his *The Zion Connection* (The Friends of Israel, 2003).

* * *

The return of evangelical commitment to giving Israel her proper place in future events ran roughly parallel to the rising desire of Jewish people to return to the land of their fathers. The phenomenon takes on immense significance when we look at what was developing simultaneously within the Zionist movement and in the evangelical community. Such stirrings were not recognized as a formal alliance by either group at the time. In hindsight, however, they seem to have been pushed in the same direction by a higher hand.

For Jews, the terrible pogroms that took place in Tsarist Russia in 1881 were forcing the issue of where Jews could find a safe haven. Of course, the enduring dream of scattered Jewry had always been "the Hope" – a return to

Zion. For nearly two thousand years, "next year in Jerusalem" had been the final word around Jewish Passover tables the world over.

That hope is memorialized today each time Israelis rise to sing their national anthem, *Hatikva*.

> *So long as still within our breasts*
>
> *The Jewish heart beats true,*
>
> *So long as still towards the east*
>
> *To Zion looks the Jew,*
>
> *So long our hopes are not yet lost –*
>
> *Two thousand years we cherished them –*
>
> *To live in freedom in the land*
>
> *Of Zion and Jerusalem*[1]

Events crescendoed to a climax of sorts with the 1894 trial of Alfred Dreyfus in Paris. Dreyfus, the only Jewish member of the general staff of the French army, was accused of treason. After two trials and wearying years in prison, the officer was exonerated of all charges against him. However, the anti-Semitic fervor fanned by the trial left European Jewry in shock.

Among the stunned observers was a Jewish journalist, Theodor Herzl, who had for some time had doubts about the quality of European hospitality toward the Jew. Those doubts were confirmed by the Dreyfus Affair, and Herzl became convinced that it was time for European Jews to prepare to make a move. Herzl, revered as the father of modern Zionism and founder of the Jewish state, began to promote the dream of a return of Jews to their ancient homeland in Palestine. The tone of his urgings was summarized in a simple phrase: "If you will it," said Herzl, "it is no dream."[2]

On August 31, 1897, in Basel, Switzerland, Herzl convened the First Zionist Congress. When it ended, Herzl wrote in his diary, "At Basel I found-

---

1   For a range of translations see, "Hatikvah," Wikipedia, August 5, 2017, accessed August 10, 2017, https://en.wikipedia.org/wiki/Hatikvah.

2   As noted earlier, Herzl wrote in German so this famous expression from his *Altneuland* has been variously translated especially in English. The Knesset of Israel biography goes with: "If you will it, it is no fairy-tale." The Hebrew is often translated as אם תרצו, אין זו אגדה. http://www.knesset.gov.il/vip/herzl/eng/Herz_Bioframe_eng.html

ed the Jewish state."[3] Although the realization of Herzl's dream was still some years away, a page had been turned in Jewish history, and a new reality entered the world of the Jew.

In the Christian world, on both sides of the Atlantic, a similar tide was rising among those biblically committed to a Jewish return.

An American milestone was reached with the 1878 publication of William E. Blackstone's book *Jesus Is Coming*. The book instantly became a phenomenal success, and sales were soon being counted in the hundreds of thousands. The work, which is read as a classic today, has sold well over a million copies and has been translated into forty-seven languages.

Jewish author Michael Pragai, in his book *Faith and Fulfillment*, sized up Blackstone with the following words:

> The author was a Chicago businessman, William E. Blackstone, a stout Christian Evangelist missionary and an ardent supporter of a Jewish revival in Zion. Blackstone was an outstanding Biblical scholar, and his "Zionist" views sprang from his Millenary theology. In his book, which came out in many translations, including Hebrew, he saw the Jewish Restoration of Zion as the fulfillment of the Biblical prophecies heralding the approach of the Second Advent of Christ.
>
> Like other Christian theologians, he raised the question of how Israel's survival over generations is to be interpreted. And Blackstone answered:
>
> "And the wonderful preservation, as a distinct people, through all the persecutions, vicissitudes, and wanderings of the past eighteen centuries down to this present moment, is a standing miracle, attesting to the truth of God's word, and assuring His purposes in their future history.
>
> "Said Frederick the Great to his chaplain: 'Doctor, if your religion is a true one, it ought to be capable of a very brief and simple truth. Will you give me an evidence of its truth in one word?' The good man answered – 'Israel.'
>
> "Other nations come and go, but Israel remains. She passes not away.

---

3   Herzl and Patai, *Diaries of Theodor Herzl*, vol. 2, 581.

"God says of her: 'For a small moment have I forsaken thee, but with great mercies will I gather thee. In a little wrath I hid my face from thee for a moment, but with everlasting kindness will I have mercy on thee, saith the Lord, thy Redeemer' (Isaiah 54:7, 8). [4]

Blackstone's belief, "Happy is the people that shall intercede on Israel's behalf, for God hath said: 'I will bless them that bless thee,'" was something he practiced literally. President Woodrow Wilson was favorably influenced through Blackstone's intercession to support the Balfour Declaration, which called for a homeland for Jews in Palestine.

As with other premillennial thinkers, Blackstone believed firmly that the Jewish people had never relinquished their rights to the land given by God to Abraham. [5] He said:

> The Jews have never abandoned this land of their own will, and they have not signed any treaty of capitulation, but they have succumbed in a desperate battle before the crushing power of Rome.... They were sold as slaves.... The violence by which Israel was kept out of her land, without means of appeal, is in principle equivalent to a continual conflict.... No entreaty can change this situation until Israel will have the opportunity to present its demands before the one and only competent Authority, an international Conference.

From another Jewish source, *The Encyclopedia of Zionism and Israel*, we find an assessment of other evangelicals who were supportive of a Jewish return. [6]

> It should be noted that the idea of a Jewish return to Palestine had long found strong support among prominent Christians in Western Europe, particularly in England. Eminent men and women lent themselves to what came to be known as the Restoration Movement, which favored the ingathering of Jews to their Homeland on the ground of Christian doctrine.... It is difficult to say to what extent such pro-Zionist sentiments among Christian leaders influenced

---

4   Michael J. Pragai, *Faith and Fulfillment: Christians and the Return to the Promised Land* (London: Vallentine, Mitchell, 1985), 57.

5   Premillennialism is the Christian belief that Jesus will physically return to the earth (the Second Coming) before the Millennium, a literal thousand-year golden age of peace. "Premillennialism," Wikipedia, July 18, 2017, accessed August 11, 2017, https://en.wikipedia.org/wiki/Premillennialism.

6   Patai, *Encyclopedia of Zionism*, 1264.

the Jews, but in all likelihood they helped pave the way for British acceptance of Zionism later on.

As early as the 1840s, some influential Christians were telling their peers that they should be encouraging the concept of a Jewish return. There were many who held this conviction and who to a greater or lesser degree played active roles in the movement. Among the better known was the great social reformer Lord Shaftsbury. Pragai notes:

> He fought for the idea of the Return just as much as for his many other social or philanthropic undertakings. But in the case of the Jews there were many additional dimensions: attachment to the Bible and the opportunity of helping biblical prophecy to its fulfillment. Lord Shaftsbury, like many other stout Protestants, held the belief of the Second Advent. And since, according to prophecy, the Return of the Jews is indispensable to this great event, [he] never doubted that the Jews were to return to their own land. This was his daily prayer, his daily hope. "Oh, pray for the peace of Jerusalem" were the words engraved on the ring he always wore on his right hand.[7]

Laurence Oliphant was also among those in the British Restoration Movement who favored a Jewish return to Palestine. Oliphant, an officer in the British Foreign Service, served in Parliament in the late 1860s. Deeply moved by the anti-Semitic outbursts he witnessed in Romania, he proceeded to survey lands east of the Jordan – ancient Gilead – as a place to resettle Jews from Europe. Oliphant took his plan to the sultan in Constantinople and to the Turkish cabinet, both of whom approved of designating 1.5 million acres for Jewish settlement. The plan was scuttled, however, by Sultan Abdul Hamid II, who suspected British political intrigue.

Oliphant's Christian passion, which he urged from a "Biblical point of view," never wavered. Following the massive pogroms against Jewish communities in Russia in 1881, he gathered a group of influential Christians in London to promote the idea of building Jewish villages in Gilead. Furthermore, Oliphant advised Jewish organizations, who sought to save Jews in Russia by aiding their immigration to the United States, to encourage them instead to go to Palestine.

---

7   Pragai, *Faith and Fulfillment*, 45.

So strong and obvious to the Jewish people was Oliphant's desire to aid in a Jewish return that Israel has honored his memory by naming a street in Jerusalem after him.

Theodor Herzl had his dream, but he clearly needed influential people who shared it. Yes, there were other Jews, visionaries, who saw the future as he did. But, strange as it may seem now that we are on the other side of the Holocaust, he had stern opposition from unlikely sources. Among Herzl's own friends were those who confided that he had gone quite mad. Some went so far as to counsel him to see a psychiatrist. Frontal opposition came from prominent rabbinical forces in Germany, who officially advised Jews to shun Zionism.

There were others, however, who thought Herzl was right on the mark and a person who, like Esther of old, was called into the arena "for such a time as this" (Esther 4:14). Among them was the venerable British clergyman William H. Hechler. When Herzl and Hechler first met, on March 10, 1896, they seemed like an odd pairing. Herzl was the picture of a dignified Jewish journalist. Hechler, on the other hand, was an unconventional Christian who was, in Herzl's words, "curious and complicated...given to pedantry, undue humility, and much pious rolling of the eyes."

Hechler, however, was a man with an enormous circle of contacts that ran through the ranks of Protestant officials and into the courts of European royalty. Yes, Herzl needed contacts badly, and in Hechler he had found the right man.

When all was said and done, Herzl would declare of the man who became a trusted and valued friend, "He counsels me superbly, and with unmistakably genuine good will. He is at once shrewd and mystical, cunning and naive. So far, with respect to myself, he has backed me up in quite a wonderful way.... I would wish the Jews to show him a full measure of gratitude."[8]

The British clergyman's enthusiasm for what he saw in Herzl and for the Zionists he was coming in contact with was hard for him to conceal.

> We are now seeing the stirrings of the bones in Ezekiel's valley: O! May we soon see the glorious outpourings of the spiritual life predicted in Ezekiel 36. The religious element is, according to God's word, to become the inspiring force, and, I think, I can see that it is the religious faith in Zionism, which is now influencing the whole

---

8   Claude Duvernoy, *The Prince and the Prophet* (Jerusalem: Christian Action for Israel, 1979), 43.

nation of the Jews...what food for reflection to every thoughtful student of the Bible and history.

The Jews are beginning to look forward to and believe in the glorious future of their nation, when, instead of being a curse, they are once more to become a blessing to all.[9]

The quality of their relationship is reflected in a letter that Hechler wrote to Herzl from Vienna when the latter was perplexed over being rebuffed by some important members of European royalty.

I am very worried on your account. I am afraid that in your impulsiveness you will only succeed in hitting your head against the wall. Let me ask you not to rush too much. The great ones of the world have to be tamed. If all this [the Jewish return to Palestine] seems impossible to thousands of the children of Abraham, and not so desirable, how much more impossible will it seem to those [Gentiles] who know nothing about the matter? Please be very discreet concerning the subject of which you write and the manner in which you do it. For the good of your cause, I pray that you will let me see what you write before sending it, being one who can judge impartially from the side.[10]

But for all their camaraderie, there was still the lurking suspicion that Jewish people, in the best of relationships with caring Christians, find hard to shake. After Hechler issued an invitation to Herzl to attend an Anglican service at which he was preaching and the British ambassador would be reading Scripture, Herzl made a revealing observation. Hechler wrote to his friend:

It is nearly midnight, and my thoughts are flying toward Jerusalem and the Holy Land.... What can be done to awaken those sleeping lazy Christians? On Sunday morning I will preach about the return of the Jews to Palestine.... Do come, Dr. Herzl. Come Sunday morning at 11 o'clock. The sermon is given at ten minutes to twelve, but one should be there at eleven in order to hear His Excellency officiate. This is good advice.... May God guide and bless us![11]

---

9   Ibid.
10   Ibid., 48.
11   Ibid., 50.

In his journal on the same day, after commenting on the exceptional devotion of Hechler, Herzl added, "But I think he wants to convert me."[12]

Certainly Hechler would have liked to restore the messianic aspiration to his friend Herzl. But on that particular occasion he wished only for Herzl's presence to make a favorable impression on the ambassador, Sir Monson, and thus promote the cause so dear to them both.

Herzl's passing was a traumatic event for Hechler. He spoke for many Jews when, after Herzl's funeral in Vienna, he said, "But this evening they [Jews] will be clear of the streets of this anti-Semitic city, taking their trains back to their reserved neighborhoods…. Only now they ask with tears of despair: Who will lead us now to the promised, inaccessible land?"[13]

For many years after his friend's death, Hechler continued to champion among sluggish Christians the return of the Jews to Zion. And he was not alone; there were others who stood ready to make the dream a reality.

Another of Herzl's Christian counselors, Philipp Newlinski, was also an ardent supporter of the biblical concept of a Jewish return. While Hechler's contacts had been for the most part in England and the royal courts of Europe, Newlinski took Herzl in another direction. As a journalist appointed to the Austro-Hungarian embassy in Constantinople, he knew the situation in Turkey and the Near East well. It was a time when the Muslim Ottoman Turks were ruling Palestine from Constantinople.

On Herzl's behalf, Newlinski contacted the Turkish sultan, the crown prince of Bulgaria, the German chancellor, and the Vatican. While not successful in every attempt, he relentlessly promoted the return of Jews to Palestine, with the net effect of making the movement well-known in many royal courts.

In December 1917, General Edmund Allenby led the British Expeditionary Force in a World War I campaign that routed Turkish forces from Palestine and captured the city of Jerusalem. Allenby and the allied Western forces would occupy the largest area in the Middle East ever conquered by "Christian" nations.

One of the most moving demonstrations of Christian reverence for the city so loved by Jews was displayed by the conquering commander of the British Expeditionary Force. General Allenby rode at the head of a long procession toward the Old City on his way to officially accept the surrender of

---

12   Herzl and Patai, *Diaries of Theodor Herzl*, vol. 2, 475.
13   Duvernoy, *Prince and the Prophet*, 95.

Jerusalem from the Turks. Upon arriving at the Jaffa Gate, the general suddenly reined in his horse and dismounted. When asked why he was doing such a thing, he replied: "Because it is not fitting that I should ride mounted across the stones where my Lord carried His cross."[14]

Even before Allenby's famous entry into Jerusalem, however, the British government had declared itself in favor of a homeland for Jews in Palestine.

On November 2, 1917, the British took a major step toward the rebirth of the modern State of Israel. It came in a letter from the British foreign secretary, Lord Arthur James Balfour, to the renowned Jewish leader Lord Rothschild. The text of the declaration read:

> Dear Lord Rothschild,
>
> I have much pleasure in conveying to you, on behalf of His Majesty's Government, the following declaration of sympathy with Jewish Zionist aspirations which has been submitted to, and approved by, the Cabinet.
>
> "His Majesty's Government view with favour the establishment in Palestine of a national home for the Jewish people, and will use their best endeavours to facilitate the achievement of this object, it being clearly understood that nothing shall be done which may prejudice the civil and religious rights of existing non-Jewish communities in Palestine, or the rights and political status enjoyed by Jews in any other country".
>
> I should be grateful if you would bring this declaration to the knowledge of the Zionist Federation.
>
> Yours sincerely,
>
> Arthur James Balfour

As was true with the development of early Zionism, the road to the Balfour Declaration was paved with relationships between Jews and those special

---

14   The story may be apocryphal yet it is laden with Christian symbolism. Charles Leaming, *Key to Fulfillment of Bible Prophecy* (Oklahoma: Tate Publishing and Enterprises, 2007), 15, has Allenby saying, "I am thinking of Another who walked" as he entered Jerusalem. There is no question that he dismounted as a sign of humility. See "Allenby Enters Jerusalem Again Delighting 87-year-old Witness," *Jewish Telegraphic Agency*, December 10, 1992, http://www.jta.org/1992/12/10/archive/allenby-enters-jerusalem-again-delighting-87-year-old-witness.

types of Christians who believed that they should help make a way home for the Jewish people.

As World War I was progressing, men like Lieutenant Colonel John Henry Patterson were putting feet to their biblical convictions. Patterson was a devout Christian who was brought up under a strict biblical discipline, which included intense Bible study. Bible geography, prophecies about Israel, and a thorough familiarity with the great stories of the Book stood him in good stead when he was appointed to command the Zion Mule Corps. He also became a strong advocate for the formation of a Jewish Legion to fight with the British against the Turks. When Patterson, the Christian, was appointed to lead the newly formed Jewish fighting force, he became the commander of the first Jewish fighting brigade to campaign in the Holy Land since the Bar Kochba rebellion against the Romans in 135 CE. Patterson related his feelings as a Christian about the Balfour Declaration.

> Christians, too, have always believed in the fulfillment of prophecy, and the Restoration of the Jewish people is of no little interest to them, so it can be imagined with what feelings of joy and gratitude the masses of the Jewish people looked upon the promise of England, holding out as it did the prospect of the realization of their dearest hope. Nothing like it has been known since the days of King Cyrus. It is not too much to say that this epoch-making declaration uplifted the soul of Israel the world over.[15]

Sir Wyndham Deedes was known for "the humble simplicity of his faith [which] was at one with the humble simplicity of his nature. He spent much time in contemplation, especially in the early hours of the morning, and a Bible was always at his bedside."[16]

During World War I, Deedes was stationed in Cairo, serving in the British Intelligence Service. It was there that he met Dr. Chaim Weizmann, a Jewish champion of Zionism who would later become Israel's first president. It was Deedes who informed a rather surprised Weizmann of the taint of anti-Semitism infecting the British military – a fact that was to become a decided problem for Jews during the pre-state days of the British Mandate.

At their first meeting in the tent of General Allenby, Deedes pulled out a typed copy of the so-called *Protocols of the Elders of Zion.*

---

15   Pragai, *Faith and Fulfillment*, 82.
16   Ibid.

Weizmann asked him what "this rubbish" was.

Deedes told the baffled Jew, "You will find it in the haversack of a great many British officers here – and they believe it!"

The British intelligence officer went on to explain that copies of the *Protocols* had been brought over by the British military mission that had been serving on the staff of Grand Duke Nicholas in the Russian Caucasus.[17]

Exposing Weizmann to the *Protocols* would greatly enhance his perspective in future dealings with certain elements in the British military.

Like the others who were Christian lovers of the land and its people, Wyndham Deedes's fervor was nurtured by deep biblical roots. Professor Norman Bentwich, an associate in the early Palestine administration, wrote of him:

> He was a deeply religious Christian and conscious of the inhumanity which the professed Christian states of Europe had shown to the Jews for centuries. He was convinced that the Christian society should make retribution for that age-long injustice, and assist the Jews to establish their National Home in the Bible Land.[18]

Two key players in the British government at the time of the Balfour Declaration were Prime Minister David Lloyd George and British Foreign Secretary Lord Arthur James Balfour.

Balfour, who would lend his name to the famous declaration, was steeped in the Old Testament from his childhood. Historian Michael Pragai said of him:

> He was one of those devout Christians who was able to view the Jews with insight and simple, down-to-earth understanding. For Balfour, the Jews were not the instruments of a Christian Millennium or, as others had suggested, tools of development projects in the neglected Ottoman Near East. They were, rather, exiles who needed help to get back to their homeland. Why there? "The answer is," he wrote, "that the position of the Jew is unique. For them race, religion, and country are inter-related as they are inter-related in the case of no other religion and no other country on earth.[19]

---

17 Ibid., 99. See, too, Leon Poliakov, *Encyclopaedia Judaica*, 2nd ed., s.v. "Elders of Zion, Protocols of the Learned," 297.

18 Pragai, 100.

19 Ibid., 84.

For a man the likes of Arthur Balfour, the declaration bearing his name was simply the honorable and biblical thing to do.

David Lloyd George, England's prime minister from 1916 to 1922, was no less a Biblicist; regarding the Balfour Declaration, he was emphatic: "It was undoubtedly inspired by natural sympathy, admiration, and also by the fact that, as you must remember, we had been trained even more in Hebrew history than in the history of our own country. I was brought up in a school where I was taught far more about the history of the Jews than about the history of my own people. I could tell you all the kings of Israel. But I doubt whether I could have named half a dozen of the kings of England and not more of the kings of Wales...[but] we were thoroughly versed in the history of the Hebrews."[20]

Lloyd George felt a deep debt of gratitude to Chaim Weizmann, a biochemist who had invented a chemical process which the British urgently needed during the war. This no doubt weighed heavily upon his and the War Department's decision regarding the Balfour Declaration. But, in the minds of many, this was a subsidiary consideration to what their biblical backgrounds were prompting them to do.

In fact, it was Lloyd George who insisted that the original borders of the proposed Jewish homeland approximate those laid out in the Abrahamic covenant.

Speaking of these men and their storied declaration, Lieutenant Colonel Patterson wrote:

> Britain's share towards the fulfillment of prophecy must...not be forgotten and the names of Mr. Lloyd George and Sir Arthur Balfour, two men raised up to deal justly with Israel, will, I feel sure, live for all time in the hearts and affections of the Jewish people. It is owing to the stimulus given by the Balfour Declaration to the soul of Jewry throughout the world that we are now looking upon the wonderful spectacle unfolding before our eyes, of the people returning to the Land promised to Abraham and his seed forever.[21]

Among the host of dedicated Christian women who shared a biblical zeal for a Jewish national home was Blanche Dugdale. She was the niece of Lord Balfour and an outspoken advocate of Jewish rights in the Middle East.

---

20   Himmelfarb, *The People of the Book*, 137.
21   Pragai, *Faith and Fulfillment*, 88.

Lady Dugdale knew and loved the Word of God. Consequently, she had a great heart for the Jewish people and Israel. She was a particular favorite of Dr. Weizmann, who spoke of her as "an ardent, lifelong friend of Zionism." For many years, she promoted Zionism among British statesmen. In addition, she functioned as an adviser to the Zionist leadership during the years of the British Mandate.[22]

Blanche Dugdale had the perception to see what was ahead for the Jews in Hitler's Europe. During World War II she worked tirelessly, constantly speaking in public meetings, attempting to secure help for children who had been victimized by the Nazis.

This good woman believed that there was no alternative for the Jewish people, who had been ravished in the trauma that was World War II, than to create a national safe haven in Israel. Her conviction was based on her unwavering belief that this was true because Israel was a land grant made by God to the Jewish people in perpetuity.

She died on May 15, 1948 – the day that the State of Israel became a reality.

Perhaps the best known of all the true friends of Israel associated with the return to the Promised Land was a British army captain named Orde Wingate.

Wingate was not a person who moved in the higher echelons of government. He was rather an officer who, like Patterson, served in the field, working shoulder to shoulder with the Jewish defenders of life and land.

Wingate arrived in Palestine in 1936 while, under British Mandatory rule, Jewish returnees were attempting to maintain their still-fragile presence in their settlements. Unfortunately, they were not receiving overwhelming support from the British, who by this time had taken a turn toward the Arabs. Indeed, with all the foreboding developments in Europe, the British were moving toward a policy that would severely restrict Jewish immigration. The policy was deployed in 1939, through a series of White Papers, which announced an absolute limit of seventy-five thousand on Jewish immigration into Palestine.

It was during this time that Arabs were harassing Jewish settlers by, among other things, attacking buses, burning Jewish homes and fields, and carrying out sniping attacks on Jews traveling on the roads or working in the

---

22   Weizmann, *Trial and Error*, 154.

fields. With the arrival of Orde Wingate, the Jews received a gift that would materially contribute to their ability to defend themselves. Of even greater importance was his aid in preparing them for the coming military struggle, when the very survival of the state was in question.

He entered Palestine with little knowledge of what was transpiring on the ground. He was well-versed in the arguments taking place among the British as to whether the Jews should have their own state or be kept a controlled minority living among the Arabs. These arguments, however, carried no weight with Wingate. He knew where his sympathies rested; he had learned them as a boy on the knee of his mother in far-off England.

His sister, Rachel, remembered that it was "mother who taught Orde about religion.... She gave him regular and systematic Bible training. She suckled him on the strong milk of the Old Testament and weaned him on the Psalms and Proverbs."[23] Through her patient spiritual nurturing, Wingate became a lover of the Bible – so much so that it eventually shaped the whole course of his life.

Being in Israel, the place he already knew so much about, was an exhilarating experience for Wingate. Among his great delights was touring the land. He is well remembered for singing, in Hebrew, the 126th Psalm as he strode through the fields: "When the Lord turned again the captivity of Zion, we were like them that dream. Then was our mouth filled with laughter, and our tongue with singing; then said they among the nations, the Lord hath done great things for them. The Lord hath done great things for us, whereof we are glad."

When a prominent Jew from Haifa asked the captain about Zionism, Wingate replied, "I have met few Jews in my life, but my sympathies are with Zionism."

The man then asked him if he had read anything about Zionism. Wingate was ready with his answer: "There is only one important book on the subject, the Bible, and I have read it thoroughly."[24]

It was Wingate who trained the Jewish settlers in the military art of disciplined self-defense. He developed the Special Night Squads, which soon struck fear into the Arab attack units that had been making night raids on Jewish kibbutzim. Arab guerrilla units crossing from Syria and Jordan soon found that they were being met by well-trained, professionally led opponents

---

23   Pragai, *Faith and Fulfillment*, 112.
24   Ibid.

who were up to the task of thwarting their attempts to attack inadequately armed civilians.

To all those who trained and fought at his side – men like the famed Moshe Dayan – he became not only respected, but revered as a leader. To his young Jewish comrades he became the *Yedid*, the friend. And that friendship has endured. To this day, you can meet, as I have, many Jews who were trained by Orde Wingate. To the man, they speak of fond memories and unbridled appreciation for the young English soldier who was willing to give so much of himself for them and their land.

Of his part in their preparation, Wingate said:

> This is the cause of your survival. I count it as my privilege to help you fight your battle. To that purpose I want to devote my life. I believe that the very existence of mankind is justified when it is based on the moral foundation of the Bible. Whoever dares lift a hand against you and your enterprise here should be fought against. Whether it is jealousy, ignorance or perverted doctrine such as have made your neighbors rise against you, or politics which make some of my countrymen support them, I shall fight with you against any of these influences. But remember that this is your battle. My part, which I say I feel to be a privilege, is only to help you.[25]

At a farewell party given in his honor, Orde Wingate let the Scriptures express his feelings: "If I forget thee O Jerusalem, let my right hand forget her cunning. If I do not remember thee, let my tongue cleave to the roof of my mouth; if I prefer not Jerusalem above my chief joy" (Psalm 137:5, 6).

A Jewish village, Yemin Orde, has been named in Wingate's honor.[26] It could be viewed as tangible evidence of Jewish appreciation for him and the multitudes of evangelical Christians who have shared the single-hearted love for the land and the people of the Book exhibited by Orde Wingate.

I feel it is incumbent to make an important point here. What these lives have said to us is that what we are witnessing today is nothing new. Since long before the rebirth of the modern State of Israel there has been an un-shakable alliance between some Bible-believing Christians and some Bible-

---

25   Ibid., 113
26   Yemin Orde Youth Village is situated atop Mount Carmel in northern Israel. It provides a haven for at-risk youth. Also named after him is the Wingate Institute for Physical Education and Sports located south of Netanya.

believing Jews. They have been inseparably linked in the cause of the return of the Jews to their homeland and the resurrection of the nation.

This is an alliance forged by the emergence of the returns – a return by evangelical Christians to a literal, historical interpretation of the prophetic Scriptures regarding Israel, and the return of an insatiable desire among Jews to again claim their ancient homeland. In these respects, the returns have converged. They have converged and cooperated in one of the greatest national enterprises ever seen on the face of the planet.

What we are witnessing today in America, I believe, is that old alliance taking on a new dimension. It is, if you will, a maturing of relationships. Perhaps it is being pressed upon us, as in the Holocaust experience, by a certain environment-borne desperation. Nonetheless, it is there. And it is a phenomenon that must be nurtured rather than discouraged.

Chapter 9

THE CHURCH SAYS NO

Had Britain remained a Catholic country the Balfour Declaration would almost certainly not have been issued.[1]

From its inception as a modern political movement, Zionism sought support in the international arena from kings, prime ministers, presidents – and popes. The quest for backing from the Catholic Church began with Theodor Herzl.

For centuries, Jews had been viewed by Christian civilization as a despised people. As Jules Isaac argues in *The Teaching of Contempt* (1964), the Church saw the dispersion of the Jews as providential punishment for the crucifixion.

From the First Zionist Congress in 1897 onward, the Church has found it necessary to evolve its policy with regard to the role of the Jewish people in history.

Before he thought up the concept of political Zionism, Herzl had an interest in the Catholic Church of another sort. His focus was anti-Semitism and what the Church might contribute to solving the problem. His initial answer was far removed from his later thinking. Herzl's early surreal solution to the Jewish problem involved mass conversion to Christianity.

Biographer Amos Elon picks up the story:

> Herzl's...scheme was an extravaganza with a cast of millions. Herzl would go to the pope and say to him, "Help us against anti-Semitism. In return, I shall initiate a great mass movement for the free and honourable conversion of all Jews to Christianity." It would be a diplomatic peace treaty, concluded behind closed doors. But its sequel would be public.

---

1   The Church of England (part of the Anglican Communion) broke away from the Roman Catholic Church in the 1500s.

The mass conversion of the Jews would take place in different European cities in a series of pageants and ceremonies. Even in this plan, Herzl saw himself as a Jewish leader. Interestingly, he would lead the Jews but would not convert with them.[2]

Herzl soon came to believe that neither conversion to Catholicism nor political emancipation were practical responses to solving the Jewish question. Because, as Elon points out, Herzl believed that the Jewish problem was a national one and not due to anything the Jews did or failed to do. Once that realization hit, the Zionist idea grew within him and would not leave him – and became the obsession of his life.

Not long after the First Zionist Congress in Basel, *La Civiltà Cattolica*, a periodical issued by the Jesuits in Rome, had this to say:

> 1,827 years have passed since the prediction of Jesus of Nazareth was fulfilled, namely, that Jerusalem would be destroyed.... [A]ccording to the sacred Scriptures, the Jewish people must always be dispersed and vagabonds (wandering) among the other nations, so that they may render witness to Christ not only by the Scriptures... but by their very existence.

> As for a rebuilt Jerusalem which might become the centre of a reconstituted State of Israel, we must add that this is contrary to the predictions of Christ Himself who foretold that, "And they shall fall by the edge of the sword, and shall be led away captive into all nations: and Jerusalem shall be trodden down of the Gentiles, until the times of the Gentiles be fulfilled." (Luke 21:24) That is…until the end of the world.[3]

Esther Feldblum, in her doctoral thesis on Catholic reaction to Zionism, wrote that, "Embedded in Christian thinking is the notion that Jews can have no support as long as they deny Christ and that this may have been a

---

2   Amos Elon, *Herzl* (London: Weidenfeld and Nicolson, 1975), 115.

3   Esther Yolles Feldblum, *The American Catholic Press and the Jewish State, 1917–1959* (New York: Ktav, 1977), 15. My interest in Catholic attitudes toward Zionism was piqued when I was an undergraduate at Brooklyn College. My history professor Rabbi David Berger pointed me to Feldblum's doctoral dissertation. I was captivated by the topic and cited her thesis in the seminar paper I did for Berger. Later, I learned that Feldblum, the daughter of a Hasidic rebbe, had begun teaching at Brooklyn College. Most tragically, however, she was killed in a 1974 automobile accident at the age of forty-one. Her dissertation was published as a book posthumously.

key stumbling block for Catholics in coming to grips with the political realities of Zionism."[4]

Feldblum saw the *Civiltà Cattolica* article as a clear warning that Zionism "was on a collision course with the Catholic Church."

In his ongoing quest for international support, Herzl sought a meeting with the pope. He anticipated some difficulties with the pope over the Holy Places and had written in the *Jewish State* that Christian shrines "would be safeguarded by assigning to them extraterritorial status such as is well known in the law of nations. We should form a guard of honor about these sanctuaries."[5]

But his main interest with the Church was the hope that the Vatican would support the Zionist movement.

Herzl's contact person at the Vatican was the Austrian papal portraitist Count Berthold Dominik Lippay, whom Herzl had met in Venice. Lippay was instrumental in arranging an audience for Herzl first with Vatican Secretary of State Cardinal Merry del Val on January 22, 1904, and then with Pope Pius X (1835–1914) on January 25.

Herzl, still very much the journalist and dramatist, describes in his diary the pageantry of the Vatican while he waited for his audience with Cardinal Merry del Val. He takes note of the Swiss Guards, chamberlains, prelates, and the colors "that harmonized magnificently."[6] This is what he recorded on January 22:

> Lippay informed me that he had already told both of them a good deal about me, and had relegated other matters to the background. It had made an especially fine impression that I had expressed myself "so favourably" about Jesus Christ. (That was at the beer hall in Venice, when I explained to him my artistic and philosophic attitude toward the touching figure of Jesus, whom, after all, I consider a Jew.)
>
> He said I should tell Merry del Val that mine was the Catholic point of view.
>
> "That, sir, I shall not!" I replied categorically. "The very idea!

---

4 Feldblum, *American Catholic Press*, 15.

5 Theodor Herzl, *Jewish State: An Attempt at a Modern Solution of the Jewish Question* (Tel Aviv: Newman, 1956), 66.

6 Herzl and Patai, *Diaries of Theodor Herzl*, vol. 4, 1591.

After all, I am not going to the Vatican as a proselyte, but as a political spokesman for my own people."

He picks up the story in an entry dated January 23:

When the waiting came to an end I was taken into the next room, the council chamber of the Sacred College. A green table, surrounded by red and gold armchairs. In the background, once again, the tortured God upon the Cross.

...My turn came at last.

Lippay ushered me in, kissed Cardinal Merry del Val's hand, and introduced me. Then he took his leave, kissed the Cardinal's hand a second and a third time, and left.

Merry del Val bade me to be seated, and soon the conversation, which I conducted in French, was in full swing.

Herzl goes on to describe Merry del Val as thirty-eight years old, tall, slim, aristocratic looking.

Fine, large, brown, serious, inquiring yet not unreligious eyes in a still young but already grave face; the hair at his temples showed the first streaks of grey.

I told him what I wanted: the good will of the Holy See for our cause.

He said: "I do not quite see how we can take any initiative in this matter. As long as the Jews deny the divinity of Christ, we certainly cannot make a declaration in their favour. Not that we have any ill will toward them. On the contrary, the Church has always protected them. To us they are the indispensable witnesses to the phenomenon of God's term on earth. But they deny the divine nature of Christ. How can we...agree to their being given possession of the Holy Land again?

Herzl answered, "We are asking only for the profane earth; the Holy Places are to be extraterritorialized.... It would be consonant with the greatest policy of the Church...if the Holy See declared itself in our favour – or, let us say, as not against us...

Merry del Val held firm. "But in order for us to come out for the Jewish people in the way you desire, they would first have to be converted."

Herzl took a different tack. He did not expect the Vatican to take an initiative on behalf of Zionism; rather, what he wanted was "the spiritual approval of the Roman Church" – nothing more. The cardinal promised that his requests would be considered and agreed to ask the pope to grant Herzl an audience.

The meeting with Cardinal del Val had, to Lippay's "astonishment," lasted some forty-five minutes.

On January 25, Herzl was granted an audience with Pope Pius X. His diary records the events of the day.

Herzl arrived early for the meeting and was conducted through several small rooms to the pope's reception room. The pope held out his hand, but Herzl did not kiss it though he felt uncomfortable not doing so. Herzl had considered the issue of kissing the pope's hand and decided against it the night before the meeting.

From his diary entry dated January 26:

Yesterday I was with the pope. The route was already familiar since I had traversed it with Lippay several times. Past the Swiss lackeys, who looked like clerics, and clerics who looked like lackeys, the papal officers, and chamberlains [administrators]....

He received me standing and held out his hand, which I did not kiss.

Lippay had told me I had to do it, but I didn't.

I believe that I incurred his displeasure by this, for everyone who visits him kneels down and at least kisses his hand. This hand kiss had caused me a lot of worry. I was quite glad when it was finally out of the way.

He seated himself in an armchair, a throne for minor occasions. Then he invited me to sit down right next to him and smiled in friendly anticipation.

I began:

Ringrazio Vostra Santità per il favore di m'aver accordato quest'udienza [I thank Your Holiness for the favor of according me this audience].

È un piacere [It is a pleasure], he said with kindly deprecation.

I apologized for my miserable Italian, but he said:

No, parla molto bene, signor Commendatore [No, Commander, you speak very well].

For I had put on for the first time – on Lippay's advice – my Mejidiye ribbon [a knightly order of the Ottoman Empire]. Consequently, the pope always addressed me as Commendatore.

He is a good, coarse-grained village priest, to whom Christianity has remained a living thing even in the Vatican.

I briefly placed my request before him. He, however, possibly annoyed by my refusal to kiss his hand, answered sternly and resolutely:

"We cannot give approval to this movement. We cannot prevent the Jews from going to Jerusalem – but we could never sanction it. The soil of Jerusalem, if it was not always sacred, has been sanctified by the life of Jesus Christ. As the head of the Church, I cannot tell you anything different. The Jews have not recognized our Lord; therefore, we cannot recognize the Jewish people."

Hence, the conflict between Rome, represented by him, and Jerusalem, represented by me, was once again opened up.

At the outset, to be sure, I tried to be conciliatory. I recited my little piece about extra-territorialization, *res sacrae extra commercium* [holy places removed from business]. It didn't make much of an impression.

Gerusalemme, he said, must not get into the hands of the Jews.

And its present status, Holy Father?

"I know it is not pleasant to see the Turks in possession of our Holy Places. We simply have to put up with that. But to support the Jews in the acquisition of the Holy Places, that we cannot do."

Herzl tried to steer the conversation away from theology.

> I said that our point of departure had been solely the distress of the Jews and that we desired to avoid the religious issues.
>
> The pope wouldn't have it.
>
> "Yes, but we, and I as the head of the Church, cannot do this. There are two possibilities. Either the Jews will cling to their faith and continue to await the Messiah who, for us, has already appeared. In that case, they will be denying the divinity of Jesus and we cannot help them. Or else they will go there without any religion, and then we can be even less favorable to them."

Next, the pope gets to the crux of the matter: the Catholic belief that Christianity has replaced Judaism in God's favor:

> "The Jewish religion was the foundation of our own; but it was superseded by the teachings of Christ, and we cannot concede it any further validity. The Jews, who ought to have been the first to acknowledge Jesus Christ, have not done so to this day."
>
> It was on the tip of my tongue to say, "That's what happens in every family. No one believes in his own relatives." But I said instead: "Terror and persecution may not have been the right means for enlightening the Jews."
>
> But he rejoined, and this time he was magnificent in his simplicity:
>
> "Our Lord came without power. *Era povero* [He was poor]. He came in *pace* [peace]. He persecuted no one. He was persecuted.
>
> "He was forsaken even by his apostles. Only later did he grow in stature. It took three centuries for the Church to evolve. The Jews therefore had time to acknowledge his divinity without any pressure. But they haven't done so to this day."

Herzl tried to appeal to the pope on purely humanitarian grounds.

> But, Holy Father, the Jews are in terrible straits. I don't know if Your Holiness is acquainted with the full extent of this sad situation. We need a land for these persecuted people.

"Does it have to be *Gerusalemme*?"

We are not asking for Jerusalem, but for Palestine – only the secular land.

"We cannot be in favor of it."

Does Your Holiness know the situation of the Jews?

"Yes, from my Mantua [a city in Italy] days. Jews live there. And I have always been on good terms with Jews. Only the other evening two Jews were here to see me. After all, there are other bonds than those of religion: courtesy and philanthropy.

"These we do not deny to the Jews. Indeed, we also pray for them: that their minds be enlightened. This very day the Church is celebrating the feast of an unbeliever who, on the road to Damascus, became miraculously converted to the true faith. And so, if you come to Palestine and settle your people there, we shall have churches and priests ready to baptize all of you."

Count Lippay had had himself announced.

The Pope permitted him to enter. The Count kneeled, kissed his hand, and then joined in the conversation by telling of our "miraculous" meeting in Bauer's Beer Hall in Venice.

The miracle was that he had originally planned to spend the night in Padua. Lippay said Herzl had expressed the wish to be allowed to kiss the Holy Father's foot.

Herzl continues:

At this the pope made *une tête* [a long face], for I hadn't even kissed his hand. Lippay went on to say that I had expressed myself appreciatively on Jesus Christ's noble qualities. The pope listened, now and then took a pinch of snuff, and sneezed into a big red cotton handkerchief. Actually, these peasant touches are what I like best about him and what compels my respect.

In this way, Lippay wanted to account for his introducing me, perhaps to excuse it. But the pope said: "On the contrary, I am glad you brought me the *Signor Commendatore*."

As to the real business, he repeated what he had told me: *Non possumus* [We can't]!

Until he dismissed us, Lippay spent some time kneeling before him and couldn't seem to get his fill of kissing his hand. Then I realized that the pope liked this sort of thing. But on parting, too, all I did was give him a warm hand-squeeze and a low bow.

Duration of the audience: about twenty-five minutes.[7]

Fast forward to May 10, 1917. Now it is Nahum Sokolow who as the Zionist representative has been granted an audience with Pope Benedict XV. His pontificate has been eclipsed by the Great War. His efforts at peacemaking brushed aside by all parties.

It is still six months before the Balfour Declaration will be issued. Sokolow wants the Vatican to support the Zionist idea. Remarkably, the pope's reaction seems positive, "Yes, I do hope that we shall be good neighbours."[8]

On November 2, 1917, the Balfour Declaration is issued. The Church's silence lasted only until December 17, 1917, when the pope "conveyed his concern to Sir John Francis Charles de Salis, the British representative to the Vatican, "that the Jews might gain direct control over Palestine to the detriment of Christian interests," according to Feldblum.

For a while the Church took a wait-and-see approach. For one, it was focused on internal matters; for another, there was reason to suppose at first that the declaration would come to nothing.

Then, on March 10, 1919, in a consistorial allocution – a solemn speech from the throne delivered to the cardinals alone – the pope expressed his growing concern over the Jewish role in Palestine. "It would be a great grief to the Holy See if in Palestine the preponderating position were given over to the infidels."[9]

---

7   Ibid.
8   The meeting is described more fully in chapter 13, which sketches Sokolow's life and crucial role in the Balfour Declaration.
9   Sergio Minerbi, *The Vatican and Zionism: Conflict in the Holy Land: 1895–1925* (New York: Oxford University, 1990), 29. The pope's remarks in the original Italian are now publicly available at Allocuzione Antequam ordinem ai cardinali durante il Concistoro Segreto nel Palazzo Vaticano (10 Marzo, 1919), accessed June 21, 2017, https://w2.vatican.va/content/benedict-xv/it/speeches/documents/hf_ben-xv_spe_19190310_antequam-ordinem.html.

Evidently, as political Zionism moved closer toward its ultimate aim, the position of the Church grew increasingly more hostile.

Carl-Ludwig Diego von Bergen, the German Weimar Republic's ambassador to the Holy See, reported to his government on February 7, 1922: "The friendly attitude of the Vatican has meanwhile changed visibly.... [T]he Latin patriarch in Jerusalem...uses every opportunity to express himself against the Jewish colonies and sides openly with the Arabs.... It is known that he also represents the interests of the Christian Arabs politically. It is quite possible that his influence will greatly contribute to a Vatican stand hostile to Jewish settlement."[10]

And, indeed, it does appear that in the years immediately prior to and after 1920 the pope had come under the influence of advisors who were, shall we say, not favorably disposed toward the Zionist settlement enterprise in Palestine.

Thus, in another papal allocution on June 13, 1921, Pope Benedict XV declared that the new civil arrangement [meaning the British Mandate] weakened Christianity and strengthened Judaism, Feldblum wrote. The Pontiff said: "We...warmly exhort all Christians including non-Catholic governments to insist with the League of Nations on the examination of the British Mandate in Palestine."[11]

Inexorably, the Church was becoming increasingly identified as being opposed to the Jewish return to Palestine. On May 24, 1922, von Bergen reported that Vatican Secretary of State Cardinal Pietro Gasparri and Monsignor Luigi Barlassina, the Latin patriarch of Jerusalem, who spoke out vehemently against the Zionist movement, were of the same mind. Barlassina claimed that the Jews were turning Palestine into a den of sin and communism: "Zionism had already caused grave damage to the country.... There were public houses [of prostitution] and in Jerusalem alone lived 500 whores. Furthermore, some of the new settlements [kibbutzim] lived according to communist principles of the most extreme kind," which he didn't care to dwell on.[12]

Chaim Weizmann visited Cardinal Gasparri in Rome during May of 1922 to try to repair some of the damage done by Barlassina. Apparently

---

10 Pinchas Lapide, *Three Popes and the Jews* (New York: Hawthorn Books, 1967), 269.

11 "Pope Criticizes Jews for Acts in Palestine; Urges Appeal to League to Define Mandate," *New York Times,* June 14, 1921.

12 Lapide, *Three Popes*, 270.

reassured, the cardinal indicated that Zionist resettlement did not cause him anxiety. This was after Weizmann had made it clear that the British were responsible for the legal administration of Palestine – not the Zionists.

But the best the Zionists could hope for was Vatican ambivalence rather than outright opposition.

On May 1, 1948, only two weeks before the British Mandate expired, Pope Pius XII – whose pontificate was overshadowed by WWII and the Holocaust – issued his encyclical Auspicia Quaedam urging public prayers to the Virgin Mary. "We desire that supplications be poured forth to the Most Holy Virgin for this request: that the situation in Palestine may at long last be settled justly and thereby concord and peace be also happily established."[13]

When Israel declared independence on May 14, 1948, and even as Arab armies poured in to destroy the fledgling Jewish commonwealth, the Vatican's newspaper *L'Osservatore Romano* had this to say: "Modern Zionism is not the true heir of Biblical Israel, but a secular state...therefore the Holy Land and its scared sites belong to Christianity, the true Israel..."[14]

In its reporting about the 1948 War of Independence, *La Civiltà Cattolica* made clear that its sympathies were with the Arabs. Israeli troops were referred to as "the Jews" whose expanding "occupation" of Palestine was "deplored."[15]

And on June 19, 1948, Jesuits charged that the Jews had poisoned the wells in Gaza.[16]

The Vatican throughout the period leading up to the end of the mandate had been calling for the internationalization of Jerusalem and the Holy Places. As an outcome of the 1949 armistice lines, the key holy places, including Jerusalem's Church of the Holy Sepulchre, actually fell under Jordanian control until the city was reunited in 1967 under Israeli sovereignty.

Since those early days, the Catholic Church has made huge strides both on the ecumenical and political level. The Vatican implicitly granted Israel de facto recognition directly after the 1948 War of Independence. Under the

---

13   Ibid., 282.
14   Ibid.
15   Feldblum, *American Catholic Press*, 39.
16   Lapide, *Three Popes*, 283.

pontificate of Pope John XXIII (1958–1963), the Church turned away from teaching contempt of the Jews.

The Vatican finally established diplomatic relations with Israel in 1993 after the Palestine Liberation Organization and Israel signed the Oslo Accords.[17]

---

17 The Church has extensive interests in the Middle East and it would be impolitic to seem overly friendly toward the Zionist enterprise. Pope John Paul II first met with Palestine Liberation Organization chief Yasser Arafat on September 15, 1982, soon after his expulsion from Lebanon during the first Lebanon War. See Henry Kamm, "Arafat Sees Pope and Italy's Leader," *New York Times*, September 15, 1982, http://www.nytimes.com/1982/09/16/world/arafat-sees-pope-and-italy-s-leader.html. Vatican officials had long been meeting with Forouk Kaddumi, the PLO's then-foreign minister. The Holy See and the PLO established official relations on October 26, 1994 and the relationship has been incrementally upgraded since. In February 2013, the Catholic Church recognized the "Palestinian state." On June 26, 2015, the Vatican entered into its first treaty with the "State of Palestine." Pope Francis met with Mahmoud Abbas most recently in January 2017 at the Vatican. All the while, the Mideast has become increasingly inhospitable to Christians. The Christian population in the Middle East has dropped dramatically since the pre-WWI period (the Balfour era) from about 14% to approximately 4%. The Christian population in the non-Arab countries of Turkey and Iran is gone. See Eliza Griswold, "Is This the End of Christianity in the Middle East?" *New York Times*, July 22, 2015, https://www.nytimes.com/2015/07/26/magazine/is-this-the-end-of-christianity-in-the-middle-east.html?_r=0. Only Egypt and Lebanon have sizable Christian communities. In Egypt, Coptic Christians are regular targets of Islamist violence. In Lebanon, the remaining Christians have learned to accommodate Shi'ite Hezbollah, the country's dominant powerbroker. About 1–2.5% (mainly Greek Orthodox) Christians reside in the West Bank and even fewer in Gaza; the number of Palestinian Catholics is miniscule, according to "The World Factbook: West Bank," Central Intelligence Agency, June 15, 2017, accessed June 21, 2017, https://www.cia.gov/library/publications/the-world-factbook/geos/we.html. It's noteworthy that Sirhan Sirhan (assassin of Robert F. Kennedy), George Habash (founder of the Popular Front for the Liberation of Palestine), and Nayef Hawatmeh (founder of the Marxist Democratic Front for the Liberation of Palestine) are all Palestinian Christian Arabs. For more on the Church's attitude toward Israel, see "Israel-Vatican Diplomatic Relations," Israel Ministry of Foreign Affairs, accessed August 1, 2017, http://mfa.gov.il/MFA/ForeignPolicy/Bilateral/Pages/Israel-Vatican_Diplomatic_Relations.aspx.

Chapter 10

FINDING THE RIGHT WORDS

Many of history's great documents and speeches not to mention works of literature, art, and music were repeatedly modified and refashioned before they were finalized.

Alfred Lord Tennyson's poem "The Charge of the Light Brigade" went through multiple revisions until it was published on December 9, 1854. The American Declaration of Independence underwent repeated amendments after Thomas Jefferson's first draft until it was issued on July 4, 1776. So did the preamble to the 1787 US Constitution. During the American Civil War, President Abraham Lincoln began drafting the Emancipation Proclamation on July 22, 1862. The finalized version was not ready until January 1, 1863.

Even Winston Churchill tinkered with the first draft of his WWII-era 'Finest Hour' speech, which was broadcast on June 18, 1940, after France fell to the Germans.

So it was that on June 19, 1917, British government officials led by Foreign Secretary Arthur James Balfour asked Zionist leaders Chaim Weizmann and Lord Rothschild (Lionel Walter) to produce a draft formulation, for British support of a Jewish homeland in Palestine, which the cabinet could consider.

The Zionists along with British officials (many of whom were sympathetic) had already been working on the contours of such a statement. Among those involved were Mark Sykes, Ronald Graham, Nahum Sokolow, Joseph Cowen, Israel Sieff, Simon Marks, Ahad Ha'Am, Leon Simon, and Harry Sacher.

There were basically four prior drafts of the statement before the final Balfour Declaration was issued.[1]

---

1   In *The Balfour Declaration*, Leonard Stein sketches out the successive drafts on page 664. The so-called Lord Rothschild draft was actually drafted with British input.

Lord Rothschild Draft – July 18, 1917

> His Majesty's Government accepts the principle that Palestine should be reconstituted as the national home of the Jewish people. His Majesty's Government will use its best endeavours to secure the achievement of this object and will discuss the necessary methods and means with the Zionist Organisation.

The so-called Lord Rothschild version was based on a rather long and detailed working draft by the Zionists.

In his capacity as the titular head of the British Jewish community, Rothschild sent it to Balfour with a cover note mentioning that, if acceptable, he would "hand it on to the Zionist Federation and also announce it at a meeting called for that purpose."[2]

Historian Jonathan Schneer, author of *The Balfour Declaration: The Origins of the Arab-Israeli Conflict*, is struck by the very first sentence – the use of the term "reconstituted," which he notes, "implies an unbroken link between Jews and Palestine despite the nearly two-thousand-year separation."[3]

Indeed, that is precisely the Zionist position.

The reference to the Zionist Organisation as the official representative of Jewish interests had several purposes. Much later, when Britain was granted the mandate for Palestine by the League of Nations in 1922, Article 4 formalized a role for a "Zionist organisation."

That organization evolved into the quasi-governmental Jewish Agency. In 1917, though, it was meant to play up the (hugely embroidered) impression of worldwide Jewish influence. Britain's interest was for Russia to remain in World War I and for the United States, which had entered only in April 1917, to assume a major role in the fighting. It was no secret that neither American nor Russian Jews were enthusiastic about the war continuing. London's hope was that giving the Zionists a direct stake in the war's outcome would persuade Jews in Russia and America to urge their governments to support the war.

---

2   Stein, *Balfour Declaration*, 470. The next day, in a "My dear Walter" note, Balfour replied that he would take the matter up with the cabinet. See Ronald Sanders, *The High Walls of Jerusalem: A History of the Balfour Declaration and the Birth of the British Mandate for Palestine* (New York: Holt, Rinehart and Winston, 1984), 560.
3   Schneer, *The Balfour Declaration*, 335.

The idea of a commitment addressed to the Zionist Organization was also intended to deflate rumors that Germany might yet issue its own statement of support for a Jewish homeland in Palestine.

And Balfour himself had used terminology that asked for "any suggestions which the Zionist Organisation may desire to lay before" the cabinet, according to the Anglo-Jewish historian Leonard Stein in *The Balfour Declaration* (1961).

This first draft is also modest in its wording. It refrains from using the phrase "Jewish state," which Sacher had argued for, and instead employed the more restrained "national home of the Jewish people." Although statehood was not explicitly mentioned in any of the drafts, the expression "national home for the Jewish people" is consistent in four of the five drafts, including the final Balfour Declaration.

This phrase echoed back to the 1897 First Zionist Congress in Basel.

Some British Zionists were already vaguely thinking of a self-governing Jewish Commonwealth, presumably under British sovereignty. Balfour himself figured the matter of statehood, if it was to happen, would be the outcome of a gradual political development.

Arthur Balfour Draft – August 2, 1917

> His Majesty's Government accept [sic] the principle that Palestine should be reconstituted as the national home of the Jewish people… [and] will use their best endeavours to secure the achievement of this object and will be ready to consider any suggestions on the subject which the Zionist Organization may desire to lay before them.

Foreign Secretary Arthur Balfour replied to the Rothschild draft with his own draft seen here.

He sent it to Lord Rothschild on August 2, 1917, according to Jehuda Reinharz in his biography, *Chaim Weizmann: The Making of a Statesman*.

Balfour had made adjustments – some stylistic, others substantive.

Gone was the first draft's statement that "His Majesty's Government" would "discuss the necessary methods and means with" the Zionist Organization. Balfour preferred: "be ready to consider any suggestions on the subject which…may desire to lay before them."

Milner Draft – August 4, 1917

> His Majesty's Government accepts the principle that every oppor-
> tunity should be afforded for the establishment of a home for the
> Jewish people in Palestine and will use its best endeavours to fa-
> cilitate the achievement of this object and will be ready to consider
> any suggestions on the subject which the Zionist organisations may
> desire to lay before them.

With this third draft, everything seemed to be on track, but as Balfour expert Leonard Stein notes, it would be "more than three months" until the first draft, which was "drastically amended" would be ultimately translated into the Balfour Declaration.[4]

Sir Alfred Milner, a Conservative party minister without portfolio in the War Cabinet "with an eye toward the anti-Zionist Jews in Britain," writes Jehuda Reinharz, deleted "reconstituted."[5]

Palestine would be constituted as a home for the Jewish people but not as a national home – a change that might appeal to anti-Zionist Jews.

Milner introduced the phrase: "every opportunity should be afforded for the establishment of a home for." The minister-without-portfolio inserted "in Palestine" to suggest that not the whole of Palestine should be allocated to the Jews. Milner also preferred "facilitate" in place of the more solid "se-cure." Milner understood that these measures were undertaken to smooth the progress of the declaration, not to torpedo it.

The War Cabinet met on September 3, 1917, but both Prime Minister David Lloyd George and Foreign Secretary Arthur Balfour were away on hol-iday. Chancellor of the Exchequer Andrew Bonar Law presided and Edwin Montagu, an anti-Zionist Jewish member of the broader cabinet, was invited to make his case.

The cabinet's main action was to send the latest draft with a query to the Wilson Administration in Washington asking where it stood regarding Zionist aspirations.

President Woodrow Wilson's powerful aide Edward M. "Colonel" House was unsympathetic to Zionism (and exploring the possibility of a separate peace with Ottoman Turkey). It took the intervention of US Zionist leader

---

4   Stein, *Balfour Declaration*, 471.
5   Reinharz ,*The Making of a Zionist Leader,* 180.

and jurist Louis Brandeis to, at the end of the day, bring forth a positive reply to the War Cabinet's query.

Milner-Amery Draft – October 4, 1917

> His Majesty's Government views with favour the establishment in Palestine of a national home for the Jewish race and will use its best endeavours to facilitate the achievement of this object, it being clearly understood that nothing shall be done which may prejudice the civil and religious rights of existing non-Jewish communities in Palestine or the rights and political status enjoyed in any other country by such Jews who are fully contended with their existing nationality (and citizenship).

At Milner's instruction, Leo Amery, a member of the War Cabinet secretariat, reworked the draft so that the concerns of anti-Zionist Jews, recently aired in the *Times* newspaper, were clearly taken into account.

He further removed reference to a Zionist organization. He added language intended to indicate concern for Arab sensibilities. He reinserted the idea of a "national" home and also introduced the term "race" in relation to the Jews. This use of "race" rather than "people" was not favored by either Zionist or anti-Zionist Jews.

"Views with favour" was a somewhat more passive phraseology. To safeguard against their possible dilution, "the civil and religious rights of existing non-Jewish communities in Palestine" were made explicit for the first time. This formulation, intended to meet both Jewish and pro-Arab objections, survived into the final draft.

It was significant that the reference was to "civil and religious rights" of existing non-Jewish communities in Palestine, in contrast to the reference of the "rights and political status" of Jews in other countries.

The national home was to be established "in Palestine" for Jews who didn't want to live elsewhere. Also, it was thought helpful to facilitate approval to add "and citizenship," notes historian and biographer Jehuda Reinharz.[6] Plainly, the Zionists could not but be disappointed with this draft because it missed out the historic claim to Palestine being "reconstituted as the national home of the Jewish people."

---

6   Ibid., 196.

On October 4, 1917, the War Cabinet was presented with this fourth draft and again took up the Zionist issue with Lloyd George chairing. Lord Curzon offered a realpolitik case against any "sentimental" declaration, which among other things seemed to ignore Palestine's Muslim population. He also pointed out that Zionism was hardly the unanimous position among Britain's Jewish community.

It was at this point, on October 6, 1917, that the War Cabinet decided to send out the latest draft text to eight Jews – four opposed to Zionism and four in favor – for comment.

Balfour Declaration – November 2, 1917

Finally, on October 31, 1917, the War Cabinet agreed to a slightly amended version of the Milner-Amery formula. Sir Ronald Graham at the Foreign Office sent Weizmann the text on November 1.[7] The final, now famous, text – banged out on an old-fashioned typewriter – was delivered by messenger to Lord Rothschild's London home at 148 Piccadilly. It read:

> Foreign Office
> November 2nd, 1917
>
> Dear Lord Rothschild,
>
> I have much pleasure in conveying to you, on behalf of His Majesty's Government, the following declaration of sympathy with Jewish Zionist aspirations which has been submitted to, and approved by, the Cabinet.
>
> "His Majesty's Government view with favour the establishment in Palestine of a national home for the Jewish people, and will use their best endeavours to facilitate the achievement of this object, it being clearly understood that nothing shall be done which may prejudice the civil and religious rights of existing non-Jewish communities in Palestine, or the rights and political status enjoyed by Jews in any other country".
>
> I should be grateful if you would bring this declaration to the knowledge of the Zionist Federation.
>
> Yours sincerely,
>
> Arthur James Balfour

---

7   Stein, *Balfour Declaration*, 547.

And so, Foreign Secretary Arthur Balfour was authorized to send the letter[8] to Rothschild – who had after all initiated the process when he asked Balfour to "send me a message" regarding the government's stance.[9]

While Chaim Weizmann was the driving force behind the declaration, he was not the most senior Zionist official in London – Nahum Sokolow was, but he was not a British citizen.

As explained by historian Leonard Stein, addressing the declaration to Rothschild resolved protocol issues and "had the decisive advantage of associating the declaration with the most potent name in Jewry."[10]

The final version was aimed at ensuring that there would be no deleterious impact on the rights and political status of Jews who lived outside the Jewish homeland nor on the civil and religious rights of existing non-Jewish communities in Palestine.

The reference to Jewish "race" was replaced with "people" – terminology preferred both by Zionist and anti-Zionist Jews.

As Stein points out, "The language of the declaration was studiously vague. It did not give any assurance that the British government would make itself directly responsible for the establishment of the Jewish national home."[11] For, on November 2, 1917, Britain did not fully control the territory.

When Britain eventually did take possession of Palestine, it still needed an international imprimatur to exercise power. And the declaration was not a legal document; it was more a statement of political intent.

There was no mention of Arab political rights in Palestine – or, indeed, of Jewish political rights.

Regarding the Arab population, Weizmann anticipated that by the time

---

8   The original Balfour Declaration was presented to The British Museum in 1924 by Lionel Walter, 2nd Lord Rothschild. It is now at the British Library. For the text see "The Balfour Declaration," Government of Israel, Ministry of Foreign Affairs, http://altawasul.com/MFA/ForeignPolicy/Peace/Guide/Pages/The%20Balfour%20Declaration.aspx.

9   Of course, it was Balfour in the first place who'd asked Rothschild for a draft that he could present to the war cabinet. Rothschild sent him this draft with a cover note on July 18 saying, "At last I am able to send you the formula you asked me for. If His Majesty's Government will send me a message on the lines of this formula, if they and you approve it, I will hand it on to the Zionist Federation and also announce it at a meeting called for that purpose." See Sanders, *High Walls*, 600.

10   Stein, *Balfour Declaration*, 548. Weizmann, who had become a British citizen in 1910, was president of the English Zionist Federation, but Sokolow a non-citizen was the most senior World Zionist Organization official in England.

11   Stein, *Balfour Declaration*, 552.

Palestine became a Jewish Commonwealth, the Arabs would have become a minority – in the Muslim majority Middle East – with their full civil and religious rights guaranteed, writes Stein.[12]

Indeed, according to Stein, in a June 1917 letter to Leon Simon, Harry Sacher expressed a worry: "At the back of my mind, there is firmly fixed the recognition that, even if all our political scheming turns out in the way we desire, the Arabs will remain our most tremendous problem. I don't want us in Palestine to deal with the Arabs as the Poles deal with the Jews, and with the lesser excuse that belongs to a numerical minority. That kind of chauvinism might poison the whole *Yishuv* [settlement enterprise]. It is our business to fight against it."[13]

Balfour Declaration Postscript

Lord Rothschild replied to Foreign Minister Balfour on November 4, 1917, in a handwritten note:

> Dear Mr. Balfour,
>
> I write to thank you most sincerely for your letter and also for the great interest you have shown in the wishes of the large mass of the Jewish people and also for the efforts and trouble you have taken on our behalf. I can assure you that the gratitude of ten millions of people will be yours, for the British government has opened up, by their message, a prospect of safety and comfort to large masses of people who are in need of it.
>
> I dare say you have been informed that already in many parts of Russia renewed persecution has broken out.
>
> With renewed thanks to you and His Majesty's Government,
>
> I remain,
>
> Yours Sincerely,
>
> Rothschild[14]

---

12   Ibid., 623.
13   Ibid., 622.
14   National Library of Israel, "What was the Balfour Declaration?" accessed August 1, 2017, http://www.nli-education-uk.org/what-was-the-balfour-declaration.

Chapter 11

WHEN HISTORY HAPPENS

T he Balfour Declaration was a turning point for Jewish civilization and a game changer for the Middle East. Some realized its import immediately; for others grasping its significance necessarily took longer. In *Modern Times*, Paul Johnson writes that, "History is concerned not merely with moments, and decades, of time but with the long-term consequences of actions which change their significance and value continuously as the years unfold."[1] Even as the "long-term consequences" continue to play out 100 years on – here are some observations from those personally touched by the announcement:

David Ben-Gurion (1886–1973) was in New York City. Born in Plonsk, Poland, he would go on to become one of the most consequential Zionist politicians of his era and Israel's first prime minster. His colleague Yitzhak Ben-Zvi (1884–1963) was born in Poltava, Ukraine. He and his wife, Rachel were among the leading pioneers of the Second Aliyah and settled in Jerusalem. Ben-Zvi went on to become the country's second president.

> On November 2, 1917, the day on which the Balfour Declaration was promulgated, I was in American exile with my friend Yitzhak Ben-Zvi. In 1915, we had been expelled "forever" from the Ottoman Empire, which included the Land of Israel, by order of Turkish dictator Kemel Pasha....
>
> A few days after the publication of the Balfour Declaration, which made an enormous impression on the Jews of America, I published an article on the declaration in *Der Yiddische Kempfer*, the Labor Zionist weekly in the United States. The article, which appeared on November 14, 1917, stated inter alia:

---

1   Paul Johnson, *Modern Times* (New York, NY: Harper Perennial, 2001), 234.

"England has not given us back the Land of Israel. It is at this very moment, when we feel joy at the great victory, that we must make it very clear: England cannot give us back the Land of Israel. This is not because the country is not or not yet, under her control. Even after England exercises sovereignty over the entire Land of Israel, from Beersheba to Dan, it will not become ours simply because that is her desire, not even if all the other countries of the world agree as well. A land can be won by a people only through their own efforts and creativity, their building and settlement.

England has done a great deal: she has recognized our existence as a political entity and our right to the country. The Jewish people must now transform this recognition into a living reality, by investing their strength, spirit, energy, and capital in building a National Home and achieving full national salvation.[2]

Golda Meir (1898–1978), born in Kiev, Ukraine, was a founding mother of the State of Israel and prime minister from 1969 to 1974. She spent much of her childhood in Milwaukee and moved to Mandate Palestine in 1921.

Fortunately, though he still had reservations about Palestine, [my fiancé] Morris was sufficiently drawn to the idea of living there to agree to go with me. His decision was undoubtedly influenced to some extent by the fact that in November 1917, the British government announced that it favored "the establishment in Palestine of a national home for the Jewish people".... The Balfour Declaration.... Against the background of this historic event...we were married on December 24, 1917, at my parents' home.[3]

Abba Eban (1915–2002) was an eloquent spokesman for Israel, UN representative and foreign minister. He was born in Cape Town, South Africa. For anyone over the age of sixty, Eban's tone of voice resonates as the Voice of Israel.

Early in November 1917, my mother had obeyed a nocturnal call

---

2   David Ben-Gurion, *Israel: A Personal History* (New York: Funk and Wagnalls, 1971), 40.

3   Golda Meir, *My Life* (New York: G.P. Putnam's Sons, 1975), 65.

from the Zionist leaders to leave my cradle and go to the office on a foggy night to translate the Balfour Declaration into French and Russian. It was a sensational document because, in promising the Jewish people a national home in Palestine, it took the Jews, for the first time since antiquity, into the world of politics and law. It deserves to be acknowledged to this day as the authentic starting point of the process that led to the State of Israel. The translation of a document sounds a modest chore, but it linked my family to an unforgettable drama.[4]

Abraham Yitzhak Kook (1865–1935), born in Griva, Latvia, was the first Ashkenazic chief rabbi of British Mandatory Palestine. He found himself in London during World War I. A scholar and mystic, he is considered the founder of national religious Zionism which sought to imbue Jewish law into the Zionist ethos. In a series of letters to his son Zvi Yehudah, Kook wrote:

> Truly great things for our future are being done here [in England]…. Our obligation now is to illuminate things, raise and exalt them…. It's very hard these days to write in clear lines about the broad things happening before our eyes. The acts are so wondrous, to the point where the eye dims from looking and the ears from all the hearing and listening.[5]

Max Isidor Bodenheimer (1865–1940), one of the key figures in German Zionism, was the founding president of the Zionist Federation of Germany and one of the founders of the Jewish National Fund. His sardonic view:

> Lloyd George had grandly proclaimed that England had set the Jewish people into the saddle, and that now they must show that they could ride. We did not yet know that it was no more than a wooden horse on a merry-go-round operated by the Colonial Office.[6]

---

4   Abba Eban, *Personal Witness* (New York: G.P. Putnam and Sons, 1992), 15.

5   Yehudah Mirsky, *Rav Kook* (New Haven: Yale, 2014), 149.

6   Max Isidor Bodenheimer, *Prelude to Israel: The Memoirs of M. J. Bodenheimer* (New York: Yoseloff, 1963), 281.

Nahum Goldmann (1895–1982), the founder and president of the World Jewish Congress from 1948 to 1977, was a powerbroker who balanced his Zionism with support for a vibrant and independent diaspora.[7]

> We thought we held a promissory note in our hands, and we were impatient to see it honored. We took the hesitant British policy as a breach of promise and felt it to be anti-Zionist. As a result, soon after the "honeymoon" that followed the Balfour Declaration, most Jews felt a deep dissatisfaction with British policy that varied in intensity according to party and temperament, but in effect dominated everything. Young and radical, I was among the more dissatisfied. I had never overestimated the importance of the Balfour Declaration. Without rationally knowing why, I sensed that the main factor Zionism had to reckon with was not Britain but the Jewish people, and that the second factor was the Arabs. All the same, I was among the bitterest critics of British policy because I was unable or unwilling to understand the British attitude to the Palestine problem.

Louis Dembitz Brandeis (1856–1941), US-born jurist, made these remarks in 1915. He formally led the US Zionist movement from 1914 until 1916 when he joined the US Supreme Court. It is understood that Brandeis approached Woodrow Wilson's White House urging it to reverse its initial opposition to a proposed British statement on Zionism. Wilson's reluctance stemmed partly from the fact that while the United States entered WWI in April 1917, it did not declare war on the Ottoman Empire.

> Let no American imagine that Zionism is inconsistent with patriotism. Multiple loyalties are objectionable only if they are inconsistent.... Every American Jew who aids in advancing the Jewish settlement in Palestine, though he feels that neither he nor his descendants will ever live there, will likewise be a better man and a better American for doing so. There is no inconsistency between loyalty to America and loyalty to Jewry.[8]

---

7   Nahum Goldmann, *The Autobiography of Nahum Goldmann: 60 Years of Jewish Life* (New York: Holt, 1969), 107.

8   Louis Dembitz Brandeis and Felix Frankfurter, *Brandeis on Zionism: A Collection of Addresses and Statements* (Hanover, NH: University Press of New England Brandeis University Press, 2008), 28.

Judah Magnes (1877–1948), US-born Reform rabbi and WWI-era paci-
fist, spoke these words in 1929. He had served as the first chancellor of the
Hebrew University of Jerusalem (1925–1935) and as its president (1935–
1948).

> The Balfour Declaration having been confirmed so often and with
> such solemnity must in my opinion remain and should become
> the basis of an agreement between Jews and Arabs instead of a
> cause of quarrel. In addition, the interpretation given the Balfour
> Declaration, as contained in the Churchill-Samuel White paper of
> 1922, which was accepted by the Zionist Organization, should serve
> as a basis for an active, constructive policy looking toward the ren-
> dering of Palestine not as a Jewish State, not as an Arab State, but as
> a bi-national country. According to this policy, Jewish immigration
> and settlement of land, as well as the use of the Hebrew language,
> would be recognized as of right and not as of sufferance.[9]

Stephen Wise (1874–1949), born in Budapest, Hungary, was a Reform rabbi and leading Zionist – in contrast to most Reform rabbis at the time. Wise
was a founder of both the American Jewish Congress and the World Jewish
Congress. He attended the post-WWI Paris Peace Conference as a representative of the US Jewish community and was later present at the founding of
the UN. Wise was co-author with Jacob de Haas of *The Great Betrayal* (1930)
about Britain's abandonment of the Balfour Declaration. In a 1918 message
on the first anniversary of the declaration he wrote:

> The declaration has transferred Zionism from the field of national
> aspirations to the realm of political fact. Not in centuries has any
> word been spoken of equally vital consequence to the well-being of
> Israel. Two things may be assumed on the basis of the historic utter-
> ance of the British Minister of Foreign Affairs: the one that Britain
> is not acting alone. It is not for us to predicate that England has spo-
> ken and acted in concert with her Allies, but we are justified in be-
> lieving that England, ever working in closest co-operation with her

---

9   "Balfour Declaration Must Be Basis of Agreement Between Jews and Arabs, Says Magnes,"
Jewish Telegraphic Agency, December 1, 1929, http://www.jta.org/1929/12/01/archive/balfour-
declaration-must-be-basis-of-agreement-between-jews-and-arabs-says-magnes.

Allies in the war, will in the day of peace find herself not only supported by France and Italy, but above all by the American government and people, which, under the leadership of President Wilson, must needs insist that the destruction of the Prussian ideal must be followed by the establishment and maintenance of the integrity of the lesser nations. The other fact that is bound inevitably with the declaration of the British Cabinet is that it is to be taken for granted that opposition to Zionism is ended.[10]

Felix Frankfurter (1882–1965), Vienna born, was a justice of the United States Supreme Court and had served in 1919 as a Zionist delegate to the Paris Peace Conference. These remarks recalling the Balfour Declaration were made in 1960.

I need not tell you that the phrase "that Palestine be established as a Jewish National Home" was a phrase of purposeful ambiguity and gave rise to a good deal of subsequent discussion. Did it mean that there should be a home for Jews in Palestine, or was Palestine to be the national home? Events have largely answered the question as events usually answer the lawyer's ambiguity – that is…events pour meaning into the words and give them one vitality rather than another.[11]

Winston Churchill (1874–1965), in an address to the House of Commons May 23, 1939, came out against a limit on Jewish immigration to Palestine imposed by Prime Minister Neville Chamberlain. Churchill took over the premiership in 1940. Historian Martin Gilbert points out that Churchill opposed breaking faith with the Balfour Declaration to buy Arab calm.[12] Yet, for the most part, though he was premier, his officials did indeed manage to keep the doors to Palestine closed.

---

10   *Great Britain, Palestine and the Jews: Jewry's Celebration of its National Charter*, (New York: George H. Doran, 1918), 36.
11   Deborah Mark and Sandee Brawarsky, *Two Jews, Three Opinions* (New York: Penguin, 2000), 559.
12   Martin Gilbert, *Churchill and the Jews: A Lifelong Friendship* (New York: Henry Holt and Co., 2008).

It was…on the basis of [The Balfour Declaration] that…after the war we received from the Allied and Associated Powers the Mandate for Palestine…. Either there will be a Britain which knows how to keep its word on the Balfour Declaration and is not afraid to do so, or believe me, we shall find ourselves relieved of many overseas responsibilities other than those comprised within the Palestine Mandate.[13]

Sylva Gelber (1910–2003), rejected by Barnard College in 1929 because the Jewish quota was full, became the first graduate of the social work program at the Hebrew University of Jerusalem and went on to found the Ottawa-based Sylva Gelber Music Foundation.

Although I had been but a child at the time, I could still remember that day when Toronto Jewry, like that of other Jewish communities of other Canadian cities, celebrated that historic declaration. I recalled how our whole family piled into my father's Page automobile, a touring car sufficiently large to accommodate family. A large Union Jack and an equally large Zionist flag bedecked the back of the open vehicle, as we drove downtown to join an assembling crowd. I may not have understood the significance of the celebration, but I still remembered it as a happy day.[14]

George Antonius (1891–1941) was a Cairo-born Christian Arab of Lebanese descent, leading opponent of Zionism and author of *The Arab Awakening* (1938):

In those parts of the Arab world which were in direct touch with the Allies, the Balfour Declaration created bewilderment and dismay…. It was taken to imply a denial of Arab political freedom in Palestine.[15]

---

13   Aaron Berman, *Nazism, the Jews, and American Zionism, 1933–1988* (Detroit: Wayne State University Press, 1992), 71.
14   S. M. Gelber, *No Balm in Gilead: A Personal Retrospective of Mandate Days in Palestine* (Montreal: McGill-Queens University Press, 2014), 2.
15   George Antonius, *The Arab Awakening* (London: Hamish Hamilton, 1938), 267.

Edward Atiyah (1903–1964), a Lebanese-born Christian Arab, was the Arab League representative in London in 1949. In *An Arab Tells His Story* (1946) he wrote:

> The Balfour Declaration promised the Jews a national home in Palestine, in terms whose bearing on the promise made to the Arabs became the subject of an endless controversy. The Arabs maintained that they were a flagrant violation of that promise; the British protagonists, that Palestine had under the stipulated reservations been excluded from it, or alternatively, that the promise of a "national home" for the Jews, under the safeguards provided in the Declaration, was not incomparable with independence for the Palestine Arabs. The Arabs felt betrayed by Britain…whatever the literal interpretation of the promise made to them might be…[16]

Sheikh Ismail Abdu-al-Akki. Not much is known about Sheikh Ismail except that he was a member of the Arab national movement and had been sentenced to death by Turkish authorities. Sheikh Ismail took part in the Zionist rally of thanksgiving to the British government held on December 2, 1917, at the London Opera House. In his *History of Zionism*, Nahum Sokolow picks up the story:

> He spoke in Arabic, which was translated by Mr. Israel Sieff.… He not only spoke as an Arab, but as a 'Moslem' Arab, having studied five years in theological schools and being granted a degree, and it was the duty of every Moslem to participate in the movement for the liberation of their countrymen. The meeting was to celebrate the great act of the British Government in recognizing the aspirations of the Jewish people, and he appealed to them not to forget in the days of their happiness that the sons of Ishmael suffered also. They had been scattered and confounded as the Jews had been, and now began to rise, fortified with the sense of martyrs. He hoped that Palestine would again flow with milk and honey.[17]

---

16   Edward Atiyah, *An Arab Tells His Story* (London: John Murray, 1946), 199.
17   Sokolow, *History of Zionism*, 109–10. The (London) *Times* story on the meeting appeared on December 3, 1917, on page 2.

Chapter 12

GUARDIAN ANGEL: CHARLES PRESTWICH SCOTT

It may come as a revelation to readers of the British newspaper the *Guardian* that in its original incarnation the *Manchester Guardian* was highly supportive of the Zionist enterprise.[1]

In point of fact, no one did more than Charles Prestwich Scott (1846–1932), the *Manchester Guardian's* editor, to open doors for Chaim Weizmann in his quest for British support of the Zionist enterprise.

It was a stroke of fate that Scott met the Manchester-based Weizmann on September 16, 1914, at a tea party.[2] Weizmann had accompanied his wife Dr. Vera Weizmann, a public health physician, to a gathering held in the south Manchester suburb of Withington at the home of a German-Jewish couple who had taken an interest in Vera's work.

Introduced by his host to the white-bearded, sixty-nine-year-old editor, Weizmann did not at first catch the older man's name. The editor asked if Weizmann was Polish. "No," came the reply. "I am not a Pole. I am a Jew," and Weizmann proceeded to talk about Zionism and foreign affairs. He expressed fervent opposition to Russia even though Saint Petersburg was allied with London in the Great War that had recently erupted in August 1914.[3]

Weizmann later recalled: "I saw before me a tall, distinguished-looking

---

1   While few would dispute that the *Guardian* is one of the most critical publications on Israel, it nonetheless comes under attack from hard-left and stridently pro-Palestinian opponents of Israel's existence. See, for example, Benjamin Counsell, "The Guardian of Zionism: The 'Liberal' Press and its Missing Contexts," *The Electronic Intifada*, February 11, 2017, https://electronicintifada.net/content/guardian-zionism-liberal-press-and-its-missing-contexts/5300, and David Cronin, "How The Guardian Told Me to Steer Clear of Palestine," *The Electronic Intifada*, February 11, 2017, https://electronicintifada.net/blogs/david-cronin/how-guardian-told-me-steer-clear-palestine.
2   Jehuda Reinharz, *Chaim Weizmann: The Making of a Statesman* (Lebanon, NH: Brandeis University Press, 1985), 18.
3   Weizmann, *Trial and Error*, 148–49.

gentleman, advanced in years, but very alert and attentive. He was inquisitive about my origin and work."[4]

Afterwards Weizmann wrote to a Zionist colleague about his "long talk" with the editor, noting that Scott had seemed "quite prepared to help us in any endeavor."

"He carries great weight and may be useful," Weizmann commented.[5]

That assessment turned out to be an understatement. Scott offered to introduce Weizmann to Chancellor of the Exchequer David Lloyd George. To a dubious Weizmann, Scott also offered to establish a connection with Herbert Samuel, the first non-baptized Jewish government minister, who Weizmann incorrectly assumed to be an anti-Zionist.

The two met again soon after at Scott's place. And in November 1914, Scott wrote to Weizmann: "I was immensely interested in what you told me of your hopes and plans. There are so few people who have the courage of an ideal and at the same time the insight and energy which make it possible."[6]

More than a political comrade, Scott became Weizmann's mentor, providing the forty-year-old Zionist campaigner with an entree to the highest echelons of British political circles. He found Weizmann "extraordinarily interesting, a rare combination of idealism and the severely practical, which are the two essentials of statesmanship."[7]

Soon after they met, Weizmann candidly wrote his indispensable counselor, "It is the first time in my life I have 'spoken out' to a non-Jew all the intimate thoughts and desiderata, you scarcely realize what a world of good you did to me in allowing me to talk out freely. In this cold world we 'the fanatics' are solitary onlookers, more especially now. I shall never see the realization of my dream – the 100% Jews – but perhaps my son will see it. You gave me courage and please forgive my brutal frankness. If I would have spoken to a man I value less, I would have been more diplomatic."[8]

In his autobiography Weizmann recorded: "It became a practice with me, whenever I happened to be in London [from Manchester], and Mr. Scott came up on the night train, to meet him at Euston Station for breakfast. His usual greeting to me was: 'Now, Dr. Weizmann, tell me what you want me

---

4   Ibid., 149.
5   Stein, *Balfour Declaration*, 131.
6   Ibid.
7   Ibid., 136.
8   Sanders, *High Walls*, 106.

to do for you,' and breakfast would pass in conversation on Zionist affairs."[9]

Scott soon became thoroughly immersed in the Jewish problem and believed, as did Weizmann, that Britain could help make possible the rebirth of a Jewish homeland.

Thanks to Scott, Weizmann met Lloyd George over a breakfast at which Samuel was also present. And when Lloyd George became minister of munitions during the Great War, Scott alerted him to Weizmann's important contribution as a chemist to the war effort.

Born in Bath on October 26, 1846, Charles Prestwich Scott was one of the eight children of Isabella and Russell Scott. His father was a coal company executive and Charles was raised as a Unitarian (a liberal Christian denomination). In 1869, he graduated from Oxford's Corpus Christi College with a BA in literature.

The extended Scott family owned the *Manchester Guardian* and Scott's father was the paper's owner for a short while. He himself joined the paper in 1871, and became its editor in January 1872.

Remarkably, from 1895 to 1906, Scott served as both a Liberal Party parliamentary backbencher and as *Manchester Guardian* editor, thus wielding a great deal of influence. By 1906, he had retired from Parliament. Eventually, he purchased the *Manchester Guardian* outright.

Scott backed Irish Home Rule and opposed the imperialist camp within his Liberal Party on South Africa.[10] He would later oppose Britain's intervention against the Bolsheviks (1918–1919) and the military's campaign against the Irish in 1920–1921.

On the domestic front, he championed the right of women to vote. Women's suffrage in Britain was achieved in 1918.

Scott was against Britain's entry into World War I and had earlier been tarred by critics as "unpatriotic" for his parliamentary opposition to the South African War (1899–1902).[11] Yet, he was a realist. Once the country was in World War I and the collapse of the Ottoman Empire, which controlled Palestine, was in the offing, he did not want to see Britain outmaneuvered by France in the Middle East. Though aware of a local Arab population

---

9   Weizmann, *Trial and Error*, 150.
10   Imperial can simply connote pre-capitalist empire building. During the seventh and eighth centuries, for example, Muslim Arab imperialism defined the Middle East. These days, imperialism is the term generally used as an invective to mean a country maintaining an empire or colonies in order to control their raw materials, markets, and political affairs.
11   *Oxford Dictionary of National Biography*, s.v. "Scott, Charles Prestwich."

in the country, he saw a Jewish Palestine as being in the British interest, a friendly buffer.

Chaim Weizmann's biographer, Jehuda Reinharz, writes that "Weizmann's relationship to Scott was never explained by either man. It is not clear what the two had in common, how often they met, and whether their conversations ranged beyond Zionism and Weizmann's contribution to the British war effort."[12]

Historian of Zionism Walter Laqueur offers a possible clue. Scott was a "Bible-reading man" who had considered becoming a Unitarian minister.[13] In Weizmann, Scott wrote, he saw a "perfectly clear conception of Jewish nationalism, an intense and burning sense of the Jew as Jew just as strong, perhaps more so, as that of the German as German or the Englishman as Englishman."[14]

Scott acknowledged that Weizmann had opened his mind to the Jewish Question. He admired the Zionist's combination of idealism and practicality. For his part, Weizmann made almost no move regarding British politics without consulting Scott. According to Reinharz, "More than anyone else, C. P. Scott was instrumental in bringing Weizmann in contact with many of the policymakers of the empire." He was, adds Reinharz, Weizmann's "closest and most loyal non-Jewish patron" during the Balfour Declaration era.

For example, as described by historian Jonathan Schneer, at a meeting on April 12, 1917, with Vicomte Robert de Caix, an editor at the Paris-based *Le Journal des Debats*, Scott learned about the Sykes-Picot accord, which had been agreed to by Britain and France a year earlier. He informed Weizmann that the secret deal to divide Syria and Palestine between the two powers with the remainder being internationalized would leave nothing for a Jewish homeland.[15]

Scott was also a member of the British Palestine Committee, which was established toward the end of 1916 to lobby for British sponsorship of the Zionist idea. His efforts came to fruition when, on November 2, 1917, the British government, led by Scott's comrade Prime Minister Lloyd George, issued the Balfour Declaration in support of a national home for the Jewish people in Palestine.

12 Reinharz, *The Making of a Zionist Leader,* 19.
13 Walter Laqueur, *A History of Zionism* (New York: Holt, Rinehart and Winston, 1972), 182.
14 Schneer, *The Balfour Declaration*, 131.
15 Ibid., 221. Sykes himself quickly soured on the deal, became a friend of Zionism, and worked to upend the pact which bore his name.

When C. P. Scott died aged eighty-five on January 1, 1932, Mancunians turned out en masse for his funeral. His university-educated wife, Rachel Cook Scott, had predeceased him in 1905. They had four children.

Scott was editor of the *Manchester Guardian* for fifty-seven years, retiring in 1929 when his son Edward Taylor Scott took over. Still, he continued to serve on the newspaper's board of governors. Until he was about eighty he would cycle daily from his estate to the newspaper's offices.

In eulogizing Scott, the *Times* wrote: "He consulted and was consulted by men of good will in all parties, and if ever his diaries see the light, it will be revealed how helpful was the part he played behind the political scene in the last twenty years of his life."[16]

Nobel Peace Prize winner Robert Cecil (1864–1958) allowed that C. P. Scott had "made righteousness readable."[17]

Scott, who was associated with his newspaper for the better part of sixty years, famously encapsulated his journalistic philosophy:

> A newspaper is of necessity something of a monopoly, and its first duty is to shun the temptations of monopoly. Its primary office is the gathering of news. At the peril of its soul it must see that the supply is not tainted. Neither in what it gives, nor in what it does not give, nor in the mode of presentation must the unclouded face of truth suffer wrong. Comment is free, but facts are sacred.[18]

---

16   "Mr. C.P. Scott – Obituary," *Times*, January 2, 1932.
17   Ibid.
18   Ibid.

Chapter 13

THE PERFECT DIPLOMAT: NAHUM SOKOLOW

As Nahum Sokolow (1859–1936) approached the podium at Manhattan's Carnegie Hall in March 1913 to deliver a speech on behalf of Zionism, he could not have helped but notice that there was not an empty seat in the house.

Though nowadays Sokolow is probably less well known than fellow Zionist statesman Chaim Weizmann, the extent of their partnership should not be underrated. In 1917, Sokolow played a crucial role in the framing of the Zionist proposals – which eventually became the Balfour Declaration – for the consideration of the British War Cabinet.

Actually, he was the highest-ranking Zionist official on the scene in London.

Sokolow was a man of practical bent who embraced both political and cultural Zionism.

The tormented Jews of eastern Europe needed a home – in Palestine. And that home needed to be a global center for Jewish education, learning, literature, and a wellspring of idealism. Sokolow wanted Palestine to be a place where the language of the Bible would be reborn, where Jewish civilization itself would be resurrected and Jewish creativity find expression.

His dream, moreover, was that in the ancient, long-neglected home of their fathers the Jews would develop a vibrant agricultural class.

As France and Britain wrangled over Middle East spheres of influence, Sokolow represented the Zionists in important discussions with British strategist and diplomat Sir Mark Sykes and with French diplomat François Georges-Picot. According to Leonard Stein, who remains the preeminent chronicler of the Balfour Declaration, Sokolow was charged with the "delicate task" of gauging French, Italian, and Vatican support for Zionist aspirations.

In his memoirs, Weizmann, who was not known for bandying compliments about, described Sokolow as a remarkable Zionist, a genius, extraordinarily versatile, cool under pressure, astonishingly prolific and hardworking; his only shortcoming being, according to Weizmann, that he was somewhat disorganized and perhaps too conciliatory.[1]

Sokolow was born in Wyszogrod, Poland, in 1865. When he was a small child the family moved to nearby Plotzk. He hailed from an illustrious rabbinic family and was considered a child prodigy. He studied under several Talmudists, but was also drawn to science and languages and could write in Hebrew, Yiddish, German, Polish, and English; he even wrote an English primer for Yiddish speakers. And he published his first book when he was eighteen.

Despite growing up within the confines of a Polish Jewish ghetto, Sokolow had personal poise and an air of sophistication. These would serve him well as a Zionist diplomat.

In 1876, while he was still a student, Sokolow married Regina Segal and the couple lived with her parents in Makow, Poland. There, he helped pioneer Hebrew-language journalism and broadened its readership. In 1880, the couple moved to Warsaw where Sokolow wrote a popular column for the Hebrew weekly (later daily, thanks to him) *Ha-Zefirah*, which was aimed at a broad readership that spanned Jewish sectarian differences. He had begun contributing to the newspaper in 1876.

In 1885, he became *Ha-Zefirah*'s editor and covered the First Zionist Congress in Basel (1897), coming away an ardent admirer of modern political Zionism's founder, Theodor Herzl.

He soon transformed *Ha-Zefirah* into a Zionist platform and translated Herzl's utopian novel *Altneuland* (Old New Land) into Hebrew. He also worked to promote political Zionism among the Orthodox.

With Zionist work taking up more and more of his time, Sokolow left *Ha-Zefirah* in 1906 to become secretary-general of the World Zionist Organization. (His former newspaper later folded.) He established *Ha'Olam* as the Zionist movement's own Hebrew weekly and in 1913, joined the Zionist executive.

---

1   Weizmann, *Trial and Error*, 77–79.

Sokolow traveled broadly on behalf of the Zionist cause. On trips to the United States he would meet with Zionist supporters such as Solomon Schechter of the Conservative movement, Supreme Court Justice Louis Brandeis, and Henrietta Szold, founder of the Hadassah Women's Zionist Organization. Once when he was in town, the March 23, 1913, *New York Times* took note of his presence by carrying a longish essay of his translated from the Yiddish.

Over the years Sokolow raised hundreds of thousands of dollars for Zionist settlement and reclamation in Palestine. He first visited the country in March 1914, when he met the Parisian-based philanthropist Baron Edmond de Rothschild (1845–1934), Eliezer Ben-Yehuda (1858–1922), the father of Modern Hebrew, and a long roster of other Zionist notables. He also learned about Hashomer, the Zionist self-defense group set up in 1909, which by 1920 would meld into the Haganah.

At the end of 1914, with the Great War under way, Sokolow moved to London together with Yechiel Tschlenow (1863–1918), a physician and fellow Zionist executive member. The World War divided the Zionist organization both philosophically and geographically and Sokolow and Tschlenow were instructed to toe the movement's line of neutrality. That, apparently, was Tschlenow's inclination – though not necessarily Sokolow's.

With Turkey's entry into the war on November 5, 1914, the prospect that Zionist aspirations could be realized grew more real. The Ottoman Turkish Empire had captured Palestine from earlier Sunni Muslim conquerors around 1512. Now there was a good chance that Turkey's Empire would crumble and the Allies would take the Holy Land.

Sokolow teamed up with Weizmann, who headed a cluster of uncommonly talented British Zionist campaigners. These included civil servant and intellectual Leon Simon (1881–1965), solicitor Harry Sacher (1881–1971), future secretary of the London office of the World Zionist Organization Samuel Landman (1884–1967), businessmen Simon Marks (1888–1964), philanthropist Israel Sieff (1889–1972), haham or rabbi of the Spanish and Portuguese congregation Moses Gaster (1856–1939), and merchant Joseph Cowen (1868–1932).

There was also the *Jewish Chronicle* publisher Leopold Jacob Greenberg (1861–1931), journalist and engineer Leopold Kessler (1864–1944), lawyer Herbert Bentwich (1856–1932), historian Paul Goodman (1875–1949), principal of Redman's Road Talmud Torah Rev. Joseph Koppel Goldbloom (1872–1961), and author and advocate of cultural Zionism Israel Zangwill (1864–1926).

On May 10, 1917, with the war's outcome uncertain, Sokolow traveled to the Vatican, thereby becoming the first Jew to meet with Pope Benedict XV (1854–1922), who had been installed shortly after the outbreak of the conflict. The pope patently acknowledged that Sokolow had come as the representative of the Zionist movement. The Italian-born Benedict said he viewed it as providential that the Jews were now claiming back their land and described the Zionist plan laid out by Sokolow as a wonderful idea.

The pope asked what he could do for the Zionists.

Sokolow replied: "We count on the sympathy and moral support of Your Holiness."

The pope then spoke about the importance of safeguarding the holy places. The meeting concluded with the pope again asking, "What else could I do for you?" and Sokolow once more requesting moral support.

The pope responded: "*Si, si io credo che noi saremo buoni vicini*" – "Oh yes, I do hope we shall be good neighbors."[2]

It was British Foreign Secretary Arthur Balfour who recommended that the Zionists sketch out a statement to be brought before the War Cabinet that harmonized their aspirations with a British role in a post-Ottoman Palestine.

As the highest Zionist official empowered by the World Zionist Organization who was in London, Sokolow played an essential role in drafting a version of what would eventually become the Balfour Declaration – and in so doing ignored his original instructions about remaining neutral in the war between Germany and Britain. He, apparently, coined the politically ambiguous though emotionally expressive term "Jewish national home."[3] In fact, Sokolow's diplomacy had already helped set the stage for the Balfour Declaration.

On June 4, 1917, he was the recipient of correspondence from French diplomat Jules Cambon, which expressed France's sympathy toward Zionism. The letter hailed the "renaissance of Jewish nationhood in that land from which the people of Israel were exiled so many centuries ago."[4] In London,

---

2   Laqueur, *History of Zionism*, 192.
3   Sokolow, *History of Zionism*, 119.
4   Stein, *Balfour Declaration*, 416.

Cambon's dispatch, given the French-British rivalry, was seen as having eased the way for the British cabinet approval of the Balfour Declaration.

After the Balfour Declaration – addressed to Lord Walter Rothschild in his capacity as head of the British Jewish community and dated November 2, 1917 – was made public, Sokolow first lobbied intensively to gain it wide international support and subsequently to ensure its implementation by Britain.

Of the declaration itself, Sokolow would write: "It was at once clear that a great moment in the history of the Jewish people had arrived through this Declaration…. Great new horizons of free national constructive work are revealed before our eyes. The fate of the Jewish land depends not only on the powerful protection of governments, but first and foremost on the steadfastness and capacity for sacrifice of the Jewish people itself."[5]

The First World War finally ended on November 11, 1918. And on February 27, 1919, Sokolow appeared before the Paris Peace Conference at Versailles to help make the Zionist case. Later, he would become the Jewish representative to the League of Nations, founded on June 28, 1919.

All the while, Sokolow continued to publish. In 1919 he brought out his *History of Zionism, 1600–1918*, which also spotlighted non-Jewish support for Zionism. Implicitly, he argued that the Balfour Declaration was but one more link in a venerable chain of Christian Zionism. Balfour himself wrote the introduction to the book.

Sokolow seemed to be in a perpetual state of motion. In 1920, he played a crucial role in launching Keren Hayesod, which was tasked with raising monies for Jewish settlement in Palestine. He was a founding member of the Hebrew writers' union in Eretz Yisrael (Land of Israel). As head of the British government-authorized Zionist Commission, which had been created to make recommendations on how Britain could best implement the Balfour Declaration, Sokolow was present for a March 29, 1921, speech by British Colonial Secretary Winston Churchill. The occasion was a palm tree-planting ceremony on Mount Scopus at the Hebrew University of Jerusalem.

On January 13, 1922, Sokolow met with President Warren Harding at the White House in connection with the dreadful state of affairs facing eastern European Jewry.

Though he fell seriously ill in 1924, Sokolow was back in Palestine in spring 1925 and then again traveled continuously: to the United States,

---

5   Sokolow, *History of Zionism*, 84.

South Africa, Italy, Poland and – lastly – Lebanon for meetings with Arab leaders aimed at gaining their understanding for Zionism.

By 1929, Arab violence, including the massacre of nearly seventy Jews in Hebron, and British backtracking on Jewish immigration were creating tensions within the Zionist camp. The dilemma was whether the Zionists should press harder or trust that Britain would ultimately fulfill its Balfour Declaration commitments. While it is unclear whether he differed substantively with Weizmann's unpopular seemingly pro-London line, this was nonetheless the context in which Sokolow replaced Weizmann for a while at the top of the Zionist hierarchy.[6]

This happened at the Seventeenth Zionist Congress in Basel, held during July 1931; Weizmann was thwarted in his presidential reelection bid because of a bitter combined challenge from Vladimir Ze'ev Jabotinsky's Revisionist Party, the Orthodox Mizrachi Party, and some general Zionists. Sokolow, broadly respected by most factions, was elected in his place.

It was not the outcome that either Weizmann or Jabotinsky wanted. In any event, Jabotinsky led a walk-out after losing a motion to have the congress go on record as demanding a reversal of the 1922 Partition of Palestine. As we'll see further on, Churchill had given 76 percent of the original Palestine Mandate land to Emir Abdullah and renamed the area Transjordan (today's Kingdom of Jordan).

Ten years later, the Zionists were more fearful than ever that Britain was abandoning its Balfour Declaration commitments altogether.

But on January 8, 1932, Colonial Secretary Philip Cunliffe-Lister wrote to Sokolow pledging that the British government would fulfill not only the letter, but also the spirit of those solemn Balfour obligations "which it is their privilege to discharge."[7]

Sokolow's tenure as WZO president spanned the Great Depression, which in the United States had begun on September 4, 1929, as well as the rise of the Nazi regime in Germany. Adolf Hitler became chancellor on January 30, 1933.

---

6 "Congress Elects Nahum Sokolow President of World Zionist Organization; Coalition Executive Without R," *Jewish Telegraphic Agency*, July 15, 1931, http://www.jta.org/1931/07/15/archive/congress-elects-nahum-sokolow-president-of-world-zionist-organization-coalition-executive-without-r.

7 "Britain Reassures Zionist Body Here; Cunliffe-Lister in Cable to Fete for Sokolow Pledges Nation to Balfour Declaration. Policy Constant, He Says: Head of World Organization Asserts at Reception Jews in This Country Must Aid in Palestine Crisis," *New York Times*, January 8, 1932.

The Eighteenth Zionist Congress, held in Prague during August 1933, was in a quandary over how to deal with Germany's persecution of its Jewish citizens. It was risky for the congress to debate their maltreatment – the Nazis implied retaliation – but in Sokolow's view it was still more dangerous to remain silent.

For him, Germany was an example par excellence of the fact that assimilation had not solved the Jewish problem. "The Jews are no enemies of Germany. They are friends and admirers of its culture," he noted.[8]

Sokolow pleaded with Britain to open the doors of Palestine, which it had partially shuttered under Arab pressure: "Shall this people eternally tramp the world? Shall this people be robbed of its own land and be driven from country to country, living in *perpetuum mobile*?" he asked.

He went on: "The time for deeds has come. If it is impossible for the fugitives to return to the countries whence they fled or to be accepted by other countries, then they must be led back to the land of their forefathers."[9]

At the same time, Sokolow opposed demands by Jabotinsky's Revisionists for an all-out economic boycott of Germany. On August 25, 1933, the Zionist Congress not only rejected such an approach, but created the Haavara program for the transfer of Jewish property from Nazi Germany to Palestine.

In those early days, the Nazis wanted, first and foremost, to rid Germany of its Jews and were willing to facilitate emigration to Palestine in a scheme that allowed the transfer of Jews and their capital – in the form of German export goods. The double-edged sword arrangement undermined the boycott of German goods, but eased the arrival of some sixty thousand German Jews to Palestine (1933–1939) and boosted Palestine's economic development.[10] This contentious Haavara scheme remained in place until the outbreak of World War II in September 1939.

Sokolow continued to travel throughout 1934, visiting South Africa and

---

8   "End Jewish Problem by Making Land of Fulfillment Instead of Promise, Urges Dr. S," *Jewish Telegraphic Agency,* August 23, 1933, accessed June 23, 2017, http://archive.jta.org/1933/08/23/archive/end-jewish-problem-by-making-spanpalspan-land-of-fulfillment-instead-of-promise-urges-dr-s.

9   "World Jewish Plea Urged on Zionists; Sokolow, Opening 18th Congress, Asks Issue Be Pushed in View of Persecutions. Denies Enmity to Reich, Says Palestine Must Be Made a Refuge for the Fugitives – Jabotinsky Urges Fight," *New York Times,* August 22, 1933, https://timesmachine.nytimes.com/timesmachine/1933/08/22/99919127.html?pageNumber=13.

10   Germany limited how much cash Jews leaving the Reich could take. Mandate authorities restricted Jewish immigration though made it easier for those eligible under an immigrant investor program. See Patai, *Encyclopedia of Zionism*, vol. 1, 437.

spending extensive periods of time in Palestine. He also worked to shore up international support for the Balfour Declaration.

In January 1935, he obtained the backing of the anti-Jewish Romanian government for the establishment of a Jewish National Home in Palestine. He also lobbied this line with British foreign minister John Simon and Colonial Minister Cunliffe-Lister. In the coming months he would meet with French president Albert François Lebrun and mark the eighty-fifth birthday of Czechoslovak president Tomas Masaryk.

And amidst all this, Sokolow still managed to bring out a new book titled *Hibbath Zion* – The Love of Zion.

In the face of Weizmann's determination to return to the leadership, Sokolow opted not to seek reelection. In September 1935, the Nineteenth World Zionist Congress, meeting in Lucerne, Switzerland, elected Weizmann president and Sokolow became honorary president of the World Zionist Organization.

For the man who many considered to be the "roving ambassador of Zionism," invitations to speak before Jewish and Zionist organizations worldwide continued to roll in.

However, Sokolow's health gave out at last, and he died of an apparent heart attack in London on May 17, 1936, at the age of seventy-six.

On the news of his death, Zionist offices in New York, London, and Buenos Aires closed. In Palestine, the blue-and-white Zionist flag flew at half-mast; cinemas shut their doors. In Vienna, Hebrew schools closed as a mark of respect. At London's Willesden cemetery, Britain's chief rabbi Joseph Hertz conducted the funeral service. With Jabotinsky standing near-by, Weizmann himself recited the Kaddish memorial prayer over Sokolow's flag-draped coffin.

Sokolow's blend of nationalism and progressivism was very much a product of his milieu. For all his level-headedness his outlook contained no small measure of idealism. He had hoped, for instance, that the League of Nations would one day be headquartered in Jerusalem.

Sokolow's intellectual curiosity, linguistic facility, and diplomatic skills were of the first order. His *History of Zionism* remains a key resource on the subject. And yet it is worth recalling that his earliest passion was, like that of Chaim Weizmann and Walter Rothschild, science.

Throughout his career Sokolow was a prolific writer in a variety of languages on a range of subjects. He contributed a unique, comfortable style to Hebrew newspaper writing; his journalistic legacy is recognized in the annual journalism prize in his name that is awarded by the Tel Aviv municipality, and in Beit Sokolow, the home of the Israel Journalists Association, which was dedicated in 1957.

In Israel, streets and a kibbutz – Sde Nahum – are named in his memory. In 1956, Nahum Sokolow's remains were reinterred on Mount Herzl in Jerusalem in the pantheon of other Zionists greats.

Chapter 14

WARTIME PRIME MINISTER: DAVID LLOYD GEORGE

I t could just as easily have been called the Lloyd George Declaration for
David Lloyd George (1863–1945) was the leader of the Liberal Party and
prime minister in the wartime coalition government between 1916 and
1922 under whose rule the 1917 Balfour Declaration – committing Britain
to supporting a national home for the Jewish people in Palestine – was approved. Balfour served as foreign minister in Lloyd George's cabinet.

Lloyd George's support guaranteed that the Zionist case was placed on
the War Cabinet's agenda. A dynamic figure, Lloyd George was no less instrumental in ensuring that the declaration gained subsequent international
legal authority.

He played an essential role every step of the way. The Versailles Peace
Conference after World War I led to the founding of the League of Nations
and to a mandate system that would oversee former German and Turkish
territories. Britain's Mandate for Palestine was granted in 1920 at the San
Remo Conference and approved by the league in 1922.

Subsequent British governments and civil servants backpedaled on the
spirit of the Balfour Declaration, but throughout his life David Lloyd George
remained committed to upholding its principles.

While not devoid of "ordinary" anti-Semitism, Lloyd George was drawn
toward the idea of a homeland for the Jewish people partly by his Christian
upbringing. Recall his statement about being "taught far more about the history of the Jews than about the history of my own people" and how "thoroughly versed in the history of the Hebrews" he felt.[1]

---

1   See for example Eitan Bar-Yosef, "Christian Zionism and Victorian Culture," *Israel Studies* 8, no.
2 (2003): 18–44.

Actually, Lloyd George first came into contact with the Zionist idea in July 1903, when as a solicitor he helped lay the legal groundwork for the Uganda Plan, a scheme that would have created a refuge for persecuted Jews in British East Africa.

Eleven years later, Britain declared war against Germany on August 4, 1914. Notably, its declaration of war against Turkey did not come until November 5 of that year. And that is when Lloyd George, then chancellor of the exchequer, said in a conversation with Herbert Samuel, a Zionist, fellow Liberal Party MP, and the first non-baptized Jew to serve in the cabinet, that he "was very keen to see a Jewish State established in Palestine."[2]

When he first met the preeminent Zionist leader Chaim Weizmann in December 1914 – at the behest of his friend, fellow Liberal Party MP and *Manchester Guardian* editor C. P. Scott – Lloyd George was already receptive to Zionism.

Zionism wasn't the only impetus driving Lloyd George's post-World War I aspiration to split up the Ottoman Empire, which controlled huge swaths of the Middle East – Palestine included – along ethnic lines. He also took into account Turkish atrocities against Armenian Christians in 1915, and Assyrian and Greek Christians beginning in 1913.[3]

And while such sentiments played no small part in Lloyd George's thinking, on strictly pragmatic grounds he was also determined to make Palestine part of the British Empire, to consolidate the area between the Mediterranean and the Persian Gulf, and to secure the seaways to India.[4] Moreover, in any post-war rivalry with France for influence in the Middle East, he was unwavering that Palestine should come under British control. He further held that Britain was better suited to oversee the holy places. This stance dovetailed nicely with Chaim Weizmann's analysis, which regarded British administration of Palestine as vital to Zionist aims.

First elected in 1890 to Parliament as the member for Caernarvon in

---

2   Daniel Efron, *Encyclopaedia Judaica*, vol. 13, s.v. "Lloyd George, David," 148–49.

3   Turkish authorities ordered the expulsion from Anatolia of Christian Armenians, Greeks, and Assyrians. Columns of refugees were ambushed, robbed, and killed by Turkish soldiers and Kurdish militias.

4   India was famously known as the jewel in the crown of the British Empire and was the cornerstone of the country's foreign and colonial policy. Britain's Raj (or rule) of the Indian subcontinent spanned 1858 to 1947. When the exhausted British finally quit India the country was crudely partitioned and convulsed in atrocious bloodletting between Hindus and Muslims. Since then India and Pakistan have fought four wars. See Yasmin Khan, *The Great Partition: The Making of India and Pakistan* (New Haven: Yale University Press, 2017).

Wales, Lloyd George would stay on to represent the constituency for the next fifty-five years.

On the domestic front he was a religious nonconformist and favored the disestablishment of the Church of England. His first speech in the House of Commons was in support of temperance – abstinence from alcohol – though his primary political passion was home rule for Wales. He was uncompromising in his opposition to the Second Boer War (1899–1902), which pitted South African whites against British colonial forces.

In 1905, Lloyd George joined the cabinet as president of the Board of Trade in the government of Liberal prime minister Henry Campbell-Bannerman.

When Herbert Asquith (1852–1928) became Liberal prime minister in 1908, Lloyd George was appointed chancellor of the exchequer. As chancellor his policies at the Treasury helped the country weather wartime economic turbulence. Notably, he promoted a series of social welfare initiatives and played a huge part in founding Britain's welfare state.

For example, to cover the cost of old-age pensions (between one and five shillings a week to those aged over seventy) he proposed a "People's Budget," which called for taxing land and income. "Death is the most convenient time to tax rich people," he once said. The 1911 National Insurance Act for workers was another of his initiatives.

In May 1915, Asquith formed a coalition with the Conservatives and shifted Lloyd George to the Ministry of Munitions. There he proved adept at settling industrial disputes and taking measures that improved wartime production. He also met regularly with Weizmann, who, in addition to campaigning for the Zionist cause, was also respected in government circles as a chemist. He became Lloyd George's chemical adviser, making a considerable contribution to the war effort.

Still, according to Weizmann's biographer Jehuda Reinharz, the notion that Lloyd George rewarded Weizmann's wartime contributions by supporting Zionism – as the premier himself asserted in his memoirs – is purely mythical. Weizmann certainly didn't buy it. His retort to Lloyd George's portrayal of a straightforward quid pro quo was to remark that "history does not deal with Aladdin's lamps." In Weizmann's telling, "I almost wish that it had been as simple as that, and that I had never known the heartbreak, the drudgery and uncertainties which preceded the Declaration." What's more,

Weizmann points out, "Lloyd George's advocacy of the Jewish homeland long predated his accession to the Premiership, and we had several meetings in the intervening years."[5]

When Field Marshal Horatio Kitchener was lost at sea in June 1916 after his ship struck a German mine, Lloyd George briefly – from June 6 until December 5, 1916 – became minister for war.

Disenchanted with Asquith's leadership, Lloyd George helped prompt his departure and then succeeded him as prime minister on December 6, 1916. For Zionists, this meant crucially that they had a strong ally at Number 10 Downing Street as well as in Arthur James Balfour, newly appointed at the Foreign Office.

In the new Conservative-Liberal-Labour War Cabinet of five ministers, Lloyd George was the only Liberal.[6] Yet, he galvanized the war effort, taking an active role in military strategy, to the chagrin of the general staff. He also boosted popular morale during the darker days of the conflict. And he brought in Mark Sykes, who had become sympathetic to Zionism, as one of his advisers.

He took intense interest in and spurred on the British military campaign to take Palestine. Before Sykes left for Egypt on April 3, 1917, to become political adviser to Gen. Edmund Allenby, Lloyd George laid out his policy: Palestine had to be under British rule; no promises should be made to the Arabs regarding the country; and nothing should be done to undermine the Zionist objectives in Palestine.[7]

On October 4, 1917, the War Cabinet, with Lloyd George and Balfour in the lead, debated the latest draft – crafted by Leo Amery – of what would come to be known as the Balfour Declaration.

Inside the cabinet in the days leading up to the November 2, 1917, declaration, Lloyd George enthusiastically backed Zionist aspirations. He told Weizmann, "I know that with the issue of this declaration I shall please one group [the Zionists] and displease another [the Jewish opponents of Zionism]. I have decided to please your group because you stand for a great idea."

---

5   Weizmann, *Trial and Error*, 150.

6   The original War Cabinet included Lloyd George, Lord Curzon (Conservative), Andrew Bonar Law (Conservative), Arthur Henderson (Labour) and Lord Milner (Conservative). The group broadened and by 1917 became the Imperial War Cabinet and included, among others, the South African general Jan Smuts.

7   Daniel Efron, *Encyclopedia Judaica*, s.v. "Lloyd George, David," 148.

In his memoirs (six volumes published between 1933 and 1936) and testimony, Lloyd George explained how he understood the Balfour Declaration:

> As to the meaning of the words 'national home' to which the Zionists attach so much importance, he [Balfour] understood it to mean some form of British, American or other protectorate, under which full facilities would be given to the Jews to work out their own salvation, a real center of national culture and focus of national life…it was contemplated that when the time arrived for according representative institutions to Palestine, if the Jews had meanwhile responded to the opportunity afforded them and had become a definite majority of the inhabitants, then Palestine would thus become a Jewish Commonwealth.

> The notion that Jewish immigration would have to be artificially restricted in order that the Jews should be a permanent minority never entered the head of anyone engaged in framing the policy. That would have been regarded as unjust and as a fraud on the people to whom we were appealing.[8]

In the event, when the terrible world war finally ended on November 11, 1918, Britain did move to formalize its Jewish homeland commitment.

In April 1920, after the San Remo Conference, having been instrumental in bringing about international ratification of the Balfour Declaration, Lloyd George told Weizmann: "Now you have got your start, it all depends upon you."[9]

Next, Lloyd George appointed Herbert Samuel, strongly identified as a Zionist, as Britain's first high commissioner in Palestine, with effect from July 1, 1920. It was a controversial selection disparaged by generals and Arabist civil service mandarins alike.

By October 19, 1922, Lloyd George was out of office. He stayed on in the House of Commons until his death in 1945, but he would be Britain's last Liberal prime minister.[10]

---

8   Cited by Weizmann, *Trial and Error*, 212. See, too, "Mr. Lloyd George Explains Jewish National Home Policy: I Was Prime Minister when Balfour Declaration," *Jewish Telegraphic Agency,* April 13, 1931, accessed June 25, 2017, http://www.jta.org/1931/04/13/archive/mr-lloyd-george-explains-jewish-national-home-policy-i-was-prime-minister-when-balfour-declaration.

9   Reinharz, *The Making of a Zionist Leader,* 318.

10   The June 2017 snap British elections left the Liberal Democrats (as the party is now called) with twelve seats in Parliament (about 7% of the vote), according to the BBC (http://www.bbc.com/

Regrettably, the successive Conservative governments of Andrew Bonar Law, Stanley Baldwin, Ramsay MacDonald, and Neville Chamberlain were markedly less sympathetic toward the Zionist idea. Indeed, by the time the Second World War erupted, the gates of Palestine were effectively closed to Jewish immigration.

As a former prime minister, Lloyd George continued his support for a Jewish homeland in Palestine. In 1925, he rather extravagantly characterized himself as a Zionist "proselyte," invoking "acetone," and crediting his "conversion" to "my friend Dr. Weizmann."[11] And in 1931, he told a Jewish audience: "I was glad to take part in the Zionist declaration. It was a very remarkable member of your race who directed and guided me in that – Dr. Weizmann, whom I regard it as a great privilege to have met, one of the noblest and most unselfish men I have ever met."[12]

Of his support for Zionism during the Great War he said: "There we were, confronted with your people in every country of the world, very powerful. You may say you have been oppressed and persecuted – that has been your power! You have been hammered into fine steel.... And therefore we wanted your help. We thought it would be very useful."[13]

His rather inflated view of Jewish influence even extended to Russian

---

news/election/2017/results). The Lib-Dems are routinely critical of Israeli policies, though the party has dissociated itself from figures such as David Ward and Jenny Tonge who have crossed the line into extreme anti-Zionist rhetoric. See "David Ward Removed as a Candidate by Lib Dems," *Jewish News*, April 26, 2017, accessed July 14, 2017, http://jewishnews.timesofisrael.com/david-ward-removed-as-a-candidate-by-lib-dems/.

11   R. H. S. Crossman, "Gentile Zionism and the Balfour Declaration," *Commentary*, June 19, 2017, https://www.commentarymagazine.com/articles/gentile-zionism-the-balfour-declaration/.

12   "I Am Very Pleased My Efforts on Behalf of Jewish People Should Be Perpetuated in Such Inspiring Manner," *Jewish Telegraphic Agency*, March 19, 1931, accessed August 7, 2017, http://www.jta.org/1931/03/19/archive/i-am-very-pleased-my-efforts-on-behalf-of-jewish-people-should-be-perpetuated-in-such-inspiring-mann. In his memoirs Herbert Samuel, a member of the cabinet, wrote: "Long before [Lloyd George] had to cope with a shortage of acetone he had taken a close interest in the Palestine question and had shown a full understanding of its significance. From the beginning, he had been unwavering in his support of the policy that was ultimately embodied in the Balfour Declaration. As Prime Minister, his approval ensured its adoption. Afterwards, at the Peace Conference in Paris and subsequently, his tenacity was to carry it through many difficulties and over many obstacles. And it was Weizmann the enthusiast, Weizmann the diplomatist who is entitled to high credit whenever the story is told; Weizmann the chemist only in a very minor degree." Indeed, Rufus Daniel Isaacs (Marquess of Reading) wrote to Samuel on February 5, 1915, reporting that he'd spoken to Lloyd George about Samuel's idea of Palestine for the Jews and that he was sympathetic. "Your proposal appeals to the poetic and imaginative as well as to the romantic and religious qualities of his mind." Herbert Louis Samuel, *Memoirs* (London: Cresset Press, 1945), 143–47.

13   Abraham E. Millgram, *Jerusalem Curiosities* (Philadelphia: Jewish Publication Society, 1990), 259.

Jewish Bolsheviks whose motivations were, in fact, quite antithetical to Jewish nationalism.

In the face of official British backtracking on Zionism, Lloyd George did not waver. He argued passionately against the 1930 White Paper that came in the wake of the murderous Arab riots of 1929, and which restricted Jewish settlement in Palestine. He asserted that halting Jewish immigration to Palestine would be "a fraud."[14]

Again in 1939, he spoke out against the way that Prime Minister Neville Chamberlain had responded to Palestinian Arab violence – which was to issue an anti-Zionist White Paper intended to severely restrict Jewish immigration.

As post-WWI prime minister, he had taken an uncompromising stance against Germany and went to the Versailles Peace Conference intent on making Germany pay for the Great War.

His subsequent misgivings over Versailles led to a brief flirtation with Hitler's Germany. In 1936, Lloyd George visited the Nazi dictator at his estate in the Bavarian Alps. He came back believing that "the Germans have definitely made up their minds never to quarrel with us again."[15] This led him to urge that Hitler's diplomatic overtures be taken at face value.

But by May 1939, he saw the situation more clearly and dropped appeasement. He would have wanted Britain to have Russia as an ally before taking on the Nazis. His May 1940 speech in the House of Commons was instrumental in pressuring Chamberlain to resign, thus setting the stage for Winston Churchill to take over.[16]

He could look back on a full life.

David Lloyd George was born on January 17, 1863, outside Manchester to Welsh parents. His father, William George, died when he was an infant and David was raised by his mother, Elizabeth, the daughter of a Baptist minister. He was taken to Wales when he was only two months old; his maternal uncle, Richard Lloyd, took him under his wing. In his teens – and now known as David Lloyd George – he trained as a solicitor and was articled at age sixteen to a firm of solicitors in Wales. In 1884, he received a law degree and soon established his own office. At the age of twenty-five he married

---

14 Daniel Efron, *Encyclopaedia Judaica*, vol. 13, s.v. "Lloyd George, David," 148.

15 "Lloyd George and Hitler," Cymdeithas Lloyd George – Lloyd George Society, accessed June 25, 2017, https://lloydgeorgesociety.org.uk/en/article/2008/0130361/lloyd-george-and-hitler.

16 *Encyclopedia of World Biography* (Detroit: Gale Research, 1998), s.v. "Lloyd George, David," link.galegroup.com/apps/doc/K1631004007/BIC1?u=huji&xid=13628ee5, accessed August 7, 2017.

Margaret Owen, the daughter of a well-to-do farmer, with whom he had four children.

Two years after Margaret died in 1941, he married Frances Louise Stevenson, his personal secretary of thirty years. Margaret had never moved to London, and it was an open secret in his inner circle that Lloyd George was a womanizer.

He returned to Wales in 1944, stricken by cancer, and toward the end of the year was elevated to the peerage. He died aged eighty-two on March 26, 1945, one month and twelve days short of VE Day.

There is a mountain and a school in Canada named after David Lloyd George, as well as an avenue in Cardiff. Both Jerusalem and Tel Aviv have named streets after him.

But his lasting legacy is the Jewish homeland itself, which he championed when it most mattered.

Chapter 15

THE OTHER BALFOUR "AUTHOR": LEO AMERY

A Conservative politician and diplomat, Leo Amery (1873–1955) was a Zionism supporter who as assistant secretary to the War Cabinet (1917–1918) crucially drafted the penultimate Balfour Declaration text. In the cabinet, Parliament, and the government, Amery showed himself steadfast in his support for Jewish rights.

Just before the War Cabinet met on October 4, 1917, as Amery recalled in his diary, Lord Alfred Milner – Amery's mentor, an influential force in the cabinet, and himself a pro-Zionist – asked him to draft "something which would go a reasonable distance to meeting the objections both Jewish and pro-Arab without impairing the substance of the proposed declaration."[1]

The resultant Milner-Amery draft, written under extreme time pressure, contained the essential points of the final draft though it referred to the Jewish "race" instead of "people" and had a slightly drawn-out formula regarding "the rights and political status enjoyed in any other country by such Jews who are fully contented with their existing nationality (and citizenship)" and would not move to Palestine.[2]

Also in 1917, Amery had facilitated Ze'ev Jabotinsky, the Zionist leader, in gaining official British approval for the formation of the Jewish Legion. Jabotinsky recalled in *The Story of the Jewish Legion* that Amery managed to lay before the War Cabinet his petition. The War Cabinet approved the Jewish Legion idea in principle and instructed Lord Derby (Edward Stanley), the secretary of state for war, to work out the details. Amery's support for Jabotinsky's campaign did not flag despite bureaucratic foot-dragging.

---

1   Stein, *Balfour Declaration*, 520. See also, S. J. Goldsmith, "The Last-Minute Drama That Made Leo Amery the Brains behind the Balfour Declaration," *Times*, November 2, 1977.
2   Stein, *Balfour Declaration*, 521.

Amery started out on the editorial staff of the *Times* (1899–1909) having been a correspondent for the paper during the Boer War (1899–1900). Later, as a hard-nosed Conservative parliamentarian, he held Birmingham's Sparkbrook constituency (1911–1945) for thirty-four years. After WWI, he opposed the League of Nations because it gave all states equal voting rights, which he felt was injudicious.

Amery frequently played the role of political powerbroker: he reportedly maneuvered the exits of three prime ministers – Herbert Asquith, David Lloyd George, and Neville Chamberlain. As Chamberlain, a Conservative, dithered over Hitler's September 1, 1939, invasion of Poland, Amery led the criticism from within the party. And in a House of Commons speech in May 1940, Amery helped to bring Winston Churchill to power.

His political resume included first lord of the admiralty (1922–1924) during the Washington Naval Conference; and secretary of state for dominions and colonies (1924–1929), which included jurisdiction over Palestine. In Parliament, he worked against the anti-Zionist policies of successive British governments and opposed the 1929 White Paper.

For much of World War II (1940–1945), he served Prime Minister Winston Churchill as secretary of state for India. Throughout the war, he remained opposed to cooperation with the Soviet Union because of a visceral disdain for communism.

In 1946, Amery took a pro-Zionist view in testimony before the Anglo-American Committee of Inquiry on Palestine. And fittingly, in 1950, Amery was one of the first senior British figures to visit the new State of Israel.[3]

Amery was born on November 22, 1873, in Gorakhpur, India. He attended Harrow along with Winston Churchill, and then Oxford. He saw action during the Great War at Flanders. Together with his wife Florence, known as Bryddie, the Amerys ran an influential political salon at their Eaton Square home in London.

What almost none of his contemporaries knew was that on his mother's side he was of Jewish ancestry.

After Amery's death in 1955 at the age of eighty-two, researchers discovered that his mother Elisabeth Leitner was Jewish and part of a well-known Hungarian family. Her father was Leopold Saphir or Sapier and her mother

---

3   Oskar K. Rabinowicz, *Encyclopaedia Judaica*, 2nd ed., vol. 2, s.v. "Amery, Leopold Charles Maurice Stennett," 66, go.galegroup.com/ps/i.do?p=GVRL&sw=w&u=huji&v=2.1&id=GALE%7CCX2 587500980&it=r&asid=0265f038a9f956cf0b78077cf2a81064, accessed August 7, 2017.

Marie Henriette Herzberg; the family name became Leitner after Marie re-married. Various relatives had converted to Protestantism around 1840 and later immigrated to Britain, starting in the 1850s.

Amery hid his Jewish lineage during his lifetime even as he championed Zionism against both Jewish and non-Jewish foes.

In a bizarre twist to the revelations about Amery's Jewish heritage, his eldest son, John (1912–1945) was an anti-Semite and fascist who resided in Germany during WWII as a Nazi propagandist broadcasting to Britain. Despite his father's efforts to save him, John Amery was hanged for treason in 1945.

Another son, Julian (1919–1996), was a Conservative member of Parliament from 1950 until 1992.

Chapter 16

ZE'EV JABOTINSKY: THE JEWISH LEGION-BALFOUR DECLARATION CONNECTION

BY YISRAEL MEDAD

There are few non-academics around today who are more knowledgeable about Vladimir Ze'ev Jabotinsky (1880–1940) than Yisrael Medad, and I am obliged that he was able to answer my call to flesh out Jabotinsky's role in the lead-up to the Balfour Declaration. Medad, a journalist-activist, is the director of education and information resources at the Menachem Begin Heritage Center in Jerusalem and he is a member of an editorial board now working on a new edition of the collected writings of Jabotinsky.

The legendary Jabotinsky was born in Odessa, studied law in Switzerland and Italy and then turned to journalism, writing, and translating. The Kishinev pogroms of 1903 transformed him into a leading personality in Russian Zionist circles and a renowned advocate of Jewish self-defense. In the Great War, after some hesitation, he pushed for Zionist backing of Britain.[1]

He lobbied vigorously for the establishment of a Jewish Legion as part of the British Army. Beginning with a nucleus of Jewish immigrants

---

1   To recap the chronology of the Great War: It was the assassination of Archduke Franz Ferdinand of Austria by a Bosnian Serb on June 28, 1914 that led to a chain of events igniting World War I. Between July 28 and August 1, Austria-Hungary declared war on Serbia and Germany declared war on Russia (Serbia's ally). By August 3, Germany and France were at war; on August 4, Britain and Germany were at war. So by the end of August much of Europe was engulfed while the United States remained neutral. It was not until November 5 that Britain and France declared war on the Turkish Ottoman Empire (which was in possession of Palestine).

to Palestine who had been deported by the Turks to Alexandria, Egypt, the Jewish Legion came together on March 5, 1915, under the leadership of Joseph Trumpeldor, a Jewish officer who had served in the Tsarist army. The unit put itself at the disposal of the British war effort.

Chaim Weizmann, and in the United States, Louis Brandeis, backed Jabotinsky's idea of a Jewish fighting force but most Zionist leaders were opposed or ambivalent.

Initially, British military headquarters in Egypt permitted the formation of a mule corps to offer logistical support. Lt. Col. John Henry Patterson, a Christian philo-Semite led the unit. Jabotinsky himself went to London to lobby for a bigger Jewish role in the war. The Zion Mule Corps operated valiantly for eight months in Gallipoli where British forces were devastatingly routed.[2] The Jews' willingness to fight and die had a profound symbolic and practical impact.

As Medad shows, creating a Jewish Legion was an uphill campaign, but by February 1917 Jabotinsky won British authorization for a larger fighting force. Its creation was announced in August 1917 and by February 1918 enlistees in the legion were on their way to Palestine. The legion eventually consisted of five battalions made up of 5,000 men: the 38th Battalion of the Royal Fusiliers, the remnant of the Zion Mule Corps and the 39th, 40th, 41st and 42nd battalions.

The fighters operated in the broiling Jordan Valley and elsewhere. Patterson proudly noted that "the sons of Israel were once again fighting the enemy not far from the spot where their forefathers had crossed the Jordan under Joshua."[3]

Later, as the British backtracked on the Balfour Declaration, Jabotinsky demanded that the Zionist organization declare explicitly that the aim of the movement was the establishment of a Jewish state on both sides of the Jordan River based on a Jewish majority.

He founded the Revisionist party, created the Betar youth movement and, though exiled from Palestine, was the honorary commander of the Irgun Zva'i Le'umi underground. Jabotinsky, a Renaissance man was a classical liberal. To learn more about this extraordinary figure, I recommend

---

2   Gallipoli is a peninsula between the Aegean Sea and the Dardanelles in western Turkey.

3   John H. Patterson, *With the Judaeans in the Palestine Campaign* (New York: Macmillan, 1922), 130. See, too, Colin Shindler, "The Road to Balfour," *Jewish Renaissance*, July 2017; and Joseph Schechtman, *Encyclopedia of Zionism*, s.v. "Jewish Legion," 624–26.

Shmuel Katz's comprehensive biography *Lone Wolf* and Hillel Halkin's concise and accessible *Jabotinsky: A Life*.[4]

* * *

Vladimir Ze'ev Jabotinsky is remembered as "a gifted orator, a writer of some genius and a magnetic personality," in the words of Israeli historian Israel Kolatt.[5] In 1914, with over a decade of involvement in Zionist activity, Jabotinsky was on assignment for the *Russkie Vedomosti* (Russian News), which was aligned with the liberal-right Constitutional Democratic Party. Arriving in Stockholm at the end of August, he conferred with two senior Zionist figures, Yechiel Tschlenow and Israel Rosoff.

The Great War had already broken out and Jabotinsky at first wanted the Zionist Organization, then based in Berlin, to transfer its headquarters to a neutral country. In this way the Zionists could be positioned to make their voices heard in any future peace talks no matter how the war played out.[6]

However, within weeks he reversed himself on the issue of neutrality. And from that point on, he engaged in a herculean effort, almost singlehandedly, to create the first Jewish fighting force in two thousand years; one that would join with Great Britain to liberate the historic Jewish homeland.

That he had practically no help was dictated in great part by the decision taken later in 1914 by the World Zionist executive to declare the Zionist movement impartial in the war and moving its headquarters from Berlin to neutral Copenhagen.[7] Neutrality meant that Jabotinsky's idea of actively helping England win the war over Turkey could not be promoted officially.

Traveling through the Western Front, Jabotinsky learned while in Bordeaux, France, that Turkey had entered the war as an ally of Germany. Britain formally declared war on Turkey on November 5, 1917. He wrote in

---

4   Shmuel Katz, *Lone Wolf: A Biography of Vladimir Jabotinsky* (New York: Barricade Books, 1996); Hillel Halkin, *Jabotinsky: A Life* (New Haven, CT: Yale University Press, 2014). See, too, Elliot Jager, "Like Lincoln for the Republicans, Jabotinsky has Become the Likud's Mascot," *Jerusalem Report*, September 25, 2016, http://www.jpost.com/Jerusalem-Report/A-LEGACY-BORN-OF-COURTESY-NOT-AFFINITY-464459.

5   Israel Kolatt, "Jabotinsky's Place in the National Pantheon," in *Essays on Ze'ev Jabotinsky*, eds. Avi Bareli Pinhas Ginossar (Sede Boqer: Ben-Gurion University of the Negev, 2004), http://in.bgu.ac.il/bgi/iyunim/DocLib3/abstracts.pdf. http://in.bgu.ac.il/bgi/iyunim/DocLib3/content.pdf.

6   Elias Gilner, *War and Hope: A History of the Jewish Legion* (New York: Herzl Press, 1969), 18.

7   When WWI broke out, two members of the Zionist executive were German citizens, three Russian, and one Austrian. The movement's dilemma was plain and its decision for neutrality is summarized by Walter Laqueur, *History of Zionism*, 171–77.

The History of the Jewish Legion that he'd concluded already in 1909 when he was based in Constantinople that the "only hope for the restoration of Palestine – the revolution in Jewish national life – lay in the dismemberment of the Ottoman Empire."[8]

On September 17, now in London, he conferred with British-based Zionists figures including Ahad Ha'Am, Israel Friedlander, Leon Simon, and Norman Bentwich and corresponded with Chaim Weizmann who was in Manchester.

In a letter sent from Madrid on November 3, after discussing his Jewish fighting force idea with Zionist luminary Max Nordau living in exile there, Jabotinsky informed his friend Israel Rosoff in St. Petersburg that he had come to the conclusion that the Zionist movement needed to offer England, or England and France, to establish a Jewish military corps of volunteers that would assist in the conquest of Eretz Yisrael in exchange for well-defined promises.[9]

In Alexandria, Egypt, by early February 1915, Jabotinsky was in contact with Jews expelled from Palestine by the Turkish authorities. In addition to his journalistic obligations, he was helping these refugees, and conferring with Zionist leaders about diplomacy and strategy.

In was in Alexandria on March 3 that the decision was taken, in a meeting of several hundreds of Jews, including the Zionist activist Joseph Trumpeldor, to establish a Jewish Brigade which would join England's fighting forces and help liberate Eretz Yisrael.

The local British commander could only offer the formation of a transport mule corps. For Jabotinsky, that was not enough and he left for London to make the case for a larger role. Trumpeldor accepted the mule corps proposal and eventually 650 men were recruited and 562 served in the Gallipoli Campaign in Turkey later that year. The corps was disbanded on May 26, 1916, having suffered thirteen killed in action.

On August 23, 1917, thanks to Jabotinsky's efforts, the formation of a Jewish battalion was officially announced. It was later joined by the 39th Battalion raised at Fort Edward, Nova Scotia, which was made up almost

---

8   Vladimir Jabotinsky, *The Story of the Jewish Legion* (New York: B. Ackerman, 1946), 30. He wrote, "I never doubted that once Turkey entered the war, she would be defeated and sliced to pieces...I am at a loss to understand how anyone could ever have had any doubts on this subject." Yet, "The old sage," as Jabotinsky referred to Nordau, was skeptical about the Jewish Legion idea.
9   Katz, *Lone Wolf*, 149. See, too, Ze'ev Jabotinsky, *Letters*, vol. 2, September 1914–November 1918 (Jerusalem: Jabotinsky Institute in Israel and *Hasifriya Hatziyonit*, 1995), letter 3, 6 (Hebrew).

entirely of US and Canadian Jews. By the spring of 1918, more than one thousand Palestinian Jews had also enlisted in the battalion.

The Jewish fighting force saw action in June 1918, near Shiloh, close to the Arab village of Abuein, and then in the Jordan Valley. The Jewish Legionnaires also participated in the Battle of Megiddo in mid-September, 1918, crossing the Jordan River and chasing Turkish troops to Es-Salt. Jabotinsky himself took part in the effort. Later, he was decorated and the Jewish troops were informed by British Major-General Edward Chaytor: "By forcing the Jordan fords, you helped in no small measure to win the great victory gained at Damascus."[10]

John Henry Patterson, the unit's commander would later write in *With the Judeans in the Palestine Campaign* that "it was well for Jewry that Jabotinsky was a chosen instrument, because, if no Jewish troops had fought in Palestine, and no Jewish graves could be seen in the cemetery on the Mount of Olives…it would have been, for all time, a reproach unto Israel, and I have grave doubts whether the [post-WWI Paris] Peace Conference would have considered the time ripe for the Jewish people to be restored to their ancient land."[11]

Patterson added: "I know that Dr. Weizmann had vision enough to foresee the strength which such a Legion would give to his diplomacy, but unfortunately his colleagues on the Zionist Council did not see eye to eye with him in this matter until it was too late."[12]

He drew a connection between the military and political, noting that Jabotinsky's vigorous efforts "resulted in the creation of a Jewish Battalion in August, 1917, followed a little later by the famous Balfour Declaration in favor of a national home for the Jewish people in Palestine."[13]

Weizmann and Jabotinsky were knocking on some of the same doors. And for a brief moment, their activities dovetailed to create a united front

---

10   "Jewish Legion," *Wikipedia*, modified July 13, 2017, https://en.wikipedia.org/wiki/Jewish_Legion. See Patterson's forward in Jabotinsky, *The Story of the Jewish Legion*, 21. In a March 9, 1920 letter to Patterson, Chaytor wrote: "So few people have heard of the battalion's work…that in the operations that we hope have finally reopened Palestine to the Jews a Jewish force was fighting on the Jordan…. I shall always be grateful to you and your battalion for your good work while with me in the Jordan Valley. The way you smashed up the Turkish rearguard when it tried to counter-attack across the Jordan made our subsequent advance up the hills of Moab an easy matter." See, too, John Henry Patterson, *With the Judeans in the Palestine Campaign* (New York: Macmillan, 1922), 192.
11   Ibid., 16.
12   Ibid., 16.
13   Ibid., 3.

that impressed, influenced, and convinced government officials, ministry staff, the press, and the Jewish leadership just how determined the Zionists were.

In his *The Jewish Legion and the First World War*, Martin Watts refers to the lobbying as "cross-pollination" – a twofold pressure on Prime Minister David Lloyd George, the decision maker who would ultimately decide the fate of both the declaration and the legion. "Without Lloyd George there would have been no Balfour Declaration or Jewish Legion: his motivation coming from personal beliefs, sympathies and an overwhelming desire to achieve strategic success."[14] He was being pressed by the Zionists: allow us to fight and allow us our country. The two messages likely merged into one from the prime minister's perspective.

Consequently, as he and his ministers were receiving missives and memoranda during late 1916 and throughout 1917, both for the legion and a declaration, the two issues became one. Both were promoted by the Zionists, both were intended to assist in the war effort, both would garner support from important sections of world Jewry and both would prove to be advantageous. And both would be just and true.

The dual Weizmann-Jabotinsky campaign saw both figures walking down the same corridors, sitting in the same wood-paneled rooms, meeting with the same decision makers, one following the other. The positive effect was multiplied.

Moreover, for several months, Jabotinsky lodged at Vera and Chaim Weizmann's flat at 3 Justice Walk in Chelsea. They conferred, argued, and exchanged ideas on both projects. Weizmann had committed himself to the legion idea in April 1915 when he met Jabotinsky in Paris. Both men agreed on the supreme importance of political work in English circles to counter what they saw as the do-nothing neutral position of the official Zionist establishment.

Jabotinsky and Weizmann took part in meetings, including one on August 8, 1917, at the War Office, with high-ranking British officials that included both Jewish opponents and supporters of Zionism and a Jewish fighting force.[15]

---

14 Martin Watts, *The Jewish Legion During the First World War* (Basingstoke, UK: Palgrave Macmillan, 2014), 9.

15 Among the roughly twenty present were: Lord Rothschild, Lionel de Rothschild, military man and diplomat Neill Primrose (later mortally wounded in the Palestine fighting against the Turks), William Ormsby Gore of the Arab bureau, MP Edmund Sebag Montefiore, who, like Lionel

Patterson, who was present and addressed the group, was taken aback by the sharp differences on the Jewish side. He would later recall: "The bitterness and hostility shown were quite a revelation to me. I could not understand how any Jew could fail to grasp this heaven-sent opportunity and to do all in his power to further the efforts of the British government on behalf of the Jewish people."[16] Patterson, who was Irish, was shocked that the formation of a Jewish fighting force had been "vigorously denounced" and "damned" along with the aspirations of the Zionists.[17]

The British needed tangible Jewish involvement in the war which the legion provided. It paved the way and broke down the barriers that allowed the statement of political policy – in the form of the Balfour Declaration – to be made.

Jabotinsky was convinced that there was great political significance in creating the legion, in its record of service, and in the lobbying process that led to its establishment.

The Jewish opponents of Zionism who were defeated on the fighting force were, by and large, the same people attempting to combat the Balfour Declaration. As Zionism's opponents were being weakened, those seeking British support for an independent Jewish commonwealth in Palestine were being strengthened.

"Half of the Balfour Declaration belongs to the legion," Jabotinsky wrote at the end of *The Jewish Legion*.[18] "Balfour Declarations," he emphasized, "are not given to individuals. They can only be given to Movements." Neutrality had paralyzed the official Zionist movement during the Great War and left it "completely outside the narrow horizons of a warring world."[19] Thus, the greatest manifestation of Zionism's readiness to sacrifice, one that compelled "ministers, ambassadors and – most important of all – journalists, to treat the striving of the Jewish people for its country as a matter of urgent reality" was the Jewish Legion movement.[20]

Rothschild, worked to recruit Jews to the British war effort but opposed the Legion, Weizmann, Joseph Cowen, C. J. Greenberg, Rev. S. Lipson (senior Jewish army chaplain in England), Jabotinsky, Sykes, and Amery.

16   Patterson, *With the Judeans*, 7.
17   Ibid., 8.
18   Jabotinsky, *The Jewish Legion*, 182.
19   Ibid.
20   Ibid.

Chapter 17

GETTING BEYOND PICOT: THE MARK SYKES STORY

N ot quite age forty, Sir Mark Sykes (1879–1919) was already a member of Parliament, a retired military officer, an established Middle East authority, a seasoned diplomat, and an intrepid traveler. His contemporaries thought that his career was destined for even greater things.

Sadly, Sykes died of influenza at the Lotti Hotel in Paris on February 16, 1919, while attending the Peace Conference. He was felled by the influenza pandemic that claimed more lives – between twenty and forty million – than the catastrophically costly world war that had just ended.

Entrusted with key British diplomatic and military missions during the Great War, Sykes has gone down in history for having crafted a secret agreement with François Picot (1870–1951) of France concerning the disposition of Greater Syria and Mesopotamia – territories Ottoman Turkey was expected to lose when defeated.

In point of fact, Sykes soon became disenchanted with the deal and in the years that followed, worked assiduously to walk it back.

He'd begun his career as a soldier in the 1902 Boer War in Southern Africa. Afterward, he trekked through Syria, Mesopotamia, and Kurdistan. He met Prime Minister Arthur Balfour in 1904–1905 when Sykes was parliamentary secretary to George Wyndham, chief secretary for Ireland. Balfour sent him to Constantinople as honorary attaché to the British embassy, a posting which further catalyzed his interest in the region.

In 1915, appointed as one of the two assistant secretaries to Prime Minister Herbert Asquith's cabinet, he was responsible for providing the cabinet with intelligence summaries on the Middle East.

Also, during the First World War, Sykes served briefly on the Western

Front before being attached to the general staff of Lord Kitchener, the secretary of state for war (1914–1916). With communications poor, Kitchener sent his protégé to the Middle East and India instructing him to come back with a first-hand report about the situation on the ground.

Upon his return to London in 1916, Sykes helped set up the Arab Bureau in Cairo in preparation for Britain's post-war Middle East policy. The Bureau brought together the resources of the India Office and military and naval intelligence under the auspices of the Foreign Office.

As for the agreement with which his name has ever since been associated, this is the background:

Sykes took part in secret Anglo-French negotiations held in London that culminated in the so-called Sykes-Picot Agreement. In January 1916, London and Paris agreed in principle on a proposed division of Turkish territories. The arrangement was outlined in a May 9, 1916, letter prepared for French Ambassador to Britain Paul Cambon and British Foreign Secretary Sir Edward Grey, and ratified on May 16, 1916.

Regarding Palestine – seen as part of Greater Syria – the agreement would have established zones of French, British, and international jurisdiction. France and Britain agreed to create Arab protectorates within their zones. Besides France and Britain, the 1916 Sykes-Picot agreement assigned a sphere of Mideast interest to Tsarist Russia.

However, Britain promptly reconsidered the idea of splitting Palestine with France. After all, its soldiers – and not those of France – were nearing Palestine. The French were bogged down in the European land war (having suffered some one million killed), and Russia, for its part, was in the throes of a revolution. Moreover, London's key regional interest was the Suez Canal and a Jewish Palestine could well serve as a strategic bulwark to secure this vital waterway between Europe and India.

A committee authorized by Asquith's government made clear on June 30, 1915, that "Palestine must be recognized as a country whose destiny must be the subject of special negotiations in which both belligerents and neutrals alike are interested."[1]

In the last two years of the war, Sykes was assigned to the War Cabinet Secretariat where he wrote communiqués lauding the principle of self-

---

1   Stein, *Balfour Declaration*, 247. The committee was headed by Sir Maurice de Bunsen and was tasked with developing policy about what to do with any territory captured from the Ottoman Empire in the course of the war.

determination – having the Arabs, Jews, and Armenians in mind. Sykes read, in January 1916, a memorandum Herbert Samuel, the first Jewish person to serve in the cabinet, had sent to all its members the year before recommending that Britain become a champion of Zionist aspirations. At Samuel's initiative Moses Gaster, the Sephardic chief rabbi, began to engage Sykes on Zionism.

On February 7, 1917, Sykes met in London with nine pro-Zionist leaders including Nahum Sokolow and Chaim Weizmann. In part this was to foster the view that the Jewish people preferred British rather than French suzerainty over Palestine. By this point, Sykes had become most sympathetic toward Zionism and had basically dissociated himself from the deal he had struck with Picot the year before. He had also come to believe that were Britain to show support for the Zionist cause it could more easily disentangle itself from Sykes-Picot.

All the while, his Zionist interlocutors were unaware of Sykes-Picot.

Chaim Weizmann learned of the deal from *Manchester Guardian* editor C. P. Scott only on April 16, 1917. His response was to tell British officials that the Zionists favored a Palestine solely under British protection. This is what they wanted to hear. By this time, London was seeking world Jewish support for its control over the Holy Land.

Sykes's vision was that the Zionists, Arabs, and Armenians would work together in a post-Ottoman Middle East; such cooperation being of mutual benefit while also serving British interests.

As a well-placed Catholic layman, Sykes used his influence in Rome in 1917, making the Zionist case to the Vatican authorities especially in connection with Palestine's holy places. He played a leading role in the final Zionist draft of a proposed British statement on Zionism submitted to Foreign Secretary Arthur Balfour on July 18, 1917, and ultimately issued on November 2 of that year.

Afterwards, Sykes told a Zionist gathering on December 2, 1917: "It might be the destiny of the Jewish race to be the bridge between Asia and Europe, and to bring the spirituality of Asia to Europe and the vitality of Europe to Asia."[2]

Born in London, Sykes was raised a Roman Catholic and educated in Monaco, Brussels, and Cambridge. As a child, he traveled extensively with

---

2   Isaiah Friedman, *Encyclopaedia Judaica*, vol. 19, s.v. "Sykes, Sir Mark."

his father, Sir Tatton Sykes, to Turkey and its environs. He paid his first visit to Palestine when he was around eight years old, according to Nahum Sokolow's *History of Zionism*.

He married Edith Gorst, a fellow Roman Catholic whose father was active in Conservative politics. The couple had six children.

His passion for travel led him to write, among other works, *Through Five Turkish Provinces* (1900) and *The Caliph's Last Heritage* (1915).

At his untimely death he was a Conservative MP for Hull, which he had represented since 1911.

Writing in April 1919, Sokolow predicted that Sykes would be immortalized in the annals of the Zionists: "His life was as a song, almost as a Psalm. He was a man who has won a monument in the future Pantheon of the Jewish people and of whom legends will be told in Palestine, Arabia, and Armenia."[3]

---

3   Sokolow, *History of Zionism*, xxxvi.

Chapter 18

THE RABBIS BREAK WITH TRADITION

Like their religiously progressive counterparts, Britain's Orthodox rabbinate was by and large dubious about political Zionism.

Rabbi Hermann Adler who served as chief rabbi in Britain (1891–1911) described Zionism as "an egregious blunder."[1] He worried that rather than solve the Jewish Question, Zionism was actually exacerbating it. This put Adler on the same page as Claude Montefiore, founder of Liberal Judaism.[2]

The arrival on the scene of rabbis Joseph Herman Hertz and Moses Gaster significantly shifted attitudes within British Orthodoxy toward a more favorable view of Zionism.

Gaster (1856–1939), the haham of the Spanish and Portuguese Jewish congregation in the United Kingdom, took part in the initial meetings that laid the groundwork for the Balfour Declaration. An Oxford linguist and historian, he discreetly cultivated an interest in Zionism among British officials.

Hertz (1872–1946), chief rabbi of the United Hebrew Congregations of the British Commonwealth, lent his prestige and support to the Zionist cause thereby strengthening the movement among both his coreligionists and government officials.

The start of his crucial tenure as the spiritual leader of Ashkenazic British Jewry began shortly before WWI and ended just after WWII.

---

1 Cecil Roth, *Encyclopaedia Judaica*, vol. 1, s.v. "Adler, Hermann."
2 For a Montefiore family tree during the Balfour-era see JewishEncyclopedia.com, s.v. "Montefiore," accessed July 27, 2017, http://www.jewishencyclopedia.com/articles/10960-montefiore.

On February 7, 1917, Moses Gaster hosted a gathering at his home for Sir Mark Sykes, the British strategist and diplomat. Present were Zionist leaders Herbert Samuel (a government minister), Chaim Weizmann, Nahum Sokolow, Lord Rothschild, James de Rothschild, Joseph Cowen, Harry Sacher, and Herbert Bentwich. This and other meetings in which Gaster took a leading role helped set the stage for the November 2, 1917, Balfour Declaration.

Expelled from Romania for protesting anti-Jewish persecutions, Gaster arrived in England in 1885 and mastered the language with alacrity. By 1887, he had obtained a lectureship at Oxford and become haham (or religious leader) of the Sephardic community, a position he retained until 1919 when failing eyesight necessitated his stepping down.

Gaster established himself as a Romanian expert, linguist, historian, and folklorist; he was also a sought-after orator. By this point, Romanian authorities were delighted to welcome him back as an honored guest. He declined an offer of citizenship, however.

Among his numerous writings – he was also a halachic expert – is a history of Bevis Marks, the oldest synagogue in the UK. Gaster even played a role in perfecting the first Hebrew typewriter.

Gaster joined the Zionist movement early on, becoming a vice president of the first Zionist Congress in Basel, Switzerland, in 1897. He helped establish the settlements of Zichron Ya'akov and Rosh Pina. He was president of the English Zionist Federation for two years and was elected as vice president of the second, third, fourth, and seventh Zionist Congresses.[3] But he conducted his Zionist work in a private capacity because it did not have the imprimatur of the organized Sephardic community.

He tactfully encouraged Herbert Samuel, a Jewish cabinet member, to broaden his Zionism education. Subsequently, Samuel was able to open doors to British officialdom.

Gaster had first met Mark Sykes on May 2, 1916, at Samuel's suggestion to present his concerns about Jewish life in Europe, thereby initiating a relationship that would benefit the Zionist case.

So it was only fitting on December 2, 1917 – one month after the Balfour Declaration – that Sykes told a celebratory London gathering:

"I should like to say, before I say one other word, that the reason I am

---

3   *The YIVO Encyclopedia of Jews in Eastern Europe Online*, s.v. "Gaster, Moses," accessed July 3, 2017, http://www.yivoencyclopedia.org/article.aspx/Gaster_Moses.

interested in this Movement is that I met someone two years ago who is now upon this platform and who opened my eyes as to what the Movement meant.... I mean Dr. Gaster."[4]

Moses Gaster was born in Bucharest on September 16, 1856. He graduated from the University of Breslau (Poland) and the Jewish Theological Seminary of Breslau. Within five years of his arrival in London in 1885, he married Lucy Friedlander. The couple had seven sons and six daughters.

Lucy Gaster was a vice president of the Women's World Zionist Organization and a president of B'nai B'rith Women's Lodge.

Gaster died in 1939 at the age of eighty-two on his way to deliver a speech. To the very end he was an opinionated individual, calling for the boycott of Germany because of its anti-Jewish policies. While no one doubted his brilliance, he was variously described as having a "stubborn," "combative" and autocratic temperament.[5]

Their personal frictions notwithstanding, Chaim Weizmann spoke at Gaster's memorial service, which followed his funeral in London's Golders Green. Weizmann's gloom fitted the occasion, as history would justify: "We all need comfort in these difficult times, but I am afraid we may have to pass through more difficulties in the future."[6]

Among those in the funeral procession was Gaster's son-in-law Neville Laski, president of the Board of Deputies of British Jews.

Joseph Hertz was a robust champion of the cause, while many in the Orthodox world stood aloof from Zionism. In answer to leaders of the organized community who were opposed, Hertz brought the prestige of his office to bear on the side of Zionism.

On May 28, 1917, he wrote a letter to the *Times* in which he rejected the notion that the recent attack in the newspaper on Zionism by Claude Montefiore of the Anglo-Jewish Association and David Alexander of the Board of Deputies reflected "the views held by Anglo-Jewry as a whole or by the Jewries of the overseas dominions."[7]

Fatefully, on October 6, 1917, the War Cabinet led by Prime Minister David Lloyd George decided to send out the draft of a planned government

---

4   Sokolow, *History of Zionism*, 106.

5   Cecil Roth, *Encyclopaedia Judaica*, vol. 7, "Gaster, Moses."

6   "Throngs Attend Services for Dr. Gaster in London," *Jewish Telegraphic Agency*, March 10, 1939, accessed June 26, 2017, http://www.jta.org/1939/03/10/archive/throngs-attend-services-for-dr-gaster-in-london.

7   J. H. Hertz, "Letter to the Times," *Times*, May 28, 1917.

statement about a Jewish homeland in Palestine to eight Jews – four anti-Zionists and four Zionists – for comment.

Chief Rabbi Hertz along with Lord Rothschild and Zionist statesmen Nahum Sokolow and Chaim Weizmann all submitted supporting letters. Hertz wrote:

"It is with feelings of the profoundest gratification that I learn of the intention of His Majesty's Government to lend its powerful support to the re-establishment in Palestine of a national home for the Jewish people. The proposed declaration of His Majesty's Government that it 'will use its best endeavours to facilitate the achievement of this object' will mark an epoch in Jewish history. To millions of my brethren throughout the world it will mean the realization of Israel's undying hope of a restoration – a hope that has been the spiritual loadstar of Israel's wanderings for the last 1,800 years."[8]

Hertz was also associated with the Mizrachi Orthodox stream of Zionism which saw the return of the Jewish people to Palestine as part of a Divine plan. In the years ahead, he criticized the British Government's Mandatory policies as a reversal of the spirit of the Balfour Declaration.

A frequent visitor to Palestine, Hertz took part in the 1925 opening of the Hebrew University of Jerusalem on Mount Scopus. He went on to serve on the university's Board of Governors. In the wake of the 1929 Arab riots in Palestine – ostensibly ignited over Jews praying at Jerusalem's Western Wall – Hertz delivered on behalf of the English Zionist Federation an address on the significance of the holy place to Jewish civilization.

A prolific author, Hertz edited and translated the Authorized Daily Prayer Book (1942–1945), which followed his earlier translation and commentary on the Pentateuch (1929–1936). In both instances his purpose was to make Scripture and prayer accessible. His Modern Orthodox outlook took cognizance of contemporary Bible criticism while faithfully adhering to Jewish tradition. Within the community he defended Orthodoxy against dissent from Liberal Judaism.

He took his first pulpit in upstate Syracuse, N.Y. (1894–1896). Leaving New York, he became rabbi of Johannesburg in South Africa. Expelled (1899–1901) by President Paul Kruger for his British sympathies during the Boer War, he was later permitted to return.

In 1911, Hertz took the pulpit of Orah Hayyim, an Orthodox congrega-

---

8   Paul Goodman, ed., *The Jewish National Home: The Second November 1917–1942* (London: J. M. Dent and Sons, 1943), xviii.

tion on Manhattan's Upper East Side. He left for London in 1913 when he was selected as Chief Rabbi.

Hertz was born in the central European country of Slovakia. In 1884, when he was twelve, his family moved to New York City.

He became the first graduate of the Conservative Movement's flagship Jewish Theological Seminary (1894).[9] He also found a bride in New York, marrying Rose Freed. The couple went on to have two sons and three daughters.

Over the years, Hertz became a public intellectual and a sought-after speaker with a towering communal presence.

In 1943, he became the first British rabbi to be made a Companion of Honour, one of the highest signs of respect the monarch can bestow upon a British citizen.

During World War II, Hertz sought to mobilize Christian support on behalf of European Jews suffering Nazi tyranny.

When news of his death in London at the age of seventy-three reached Palestine, the quasi-governmental Jewish Agency declared that his demise was "a severe blow to Jewish scholarship and a formidable loss to Zionism, for at every critical period in Zionist history he took a leading part with characteristic and dauntless courage, never hesitant to speak frankly and passionately when he believed his people were not getting a fair deal."[10]

---

9 The seminary located in New York City was founded in 1887 with a charter that called for the preservation of historical Judaism. Orthodox rabbinical students were drawn to JTS and Conservatives of the day thought of themselves as part of the "not Reform" bloc.

10 "Chief Rabbi Joseph H. Hertz of Britain Dies in London, Was Educated in New York," *Jewish Telegraphic Agency*, January 15, 1946, accessed June 26, 2017, http://www.jta.org/1946/01/15/archive/chief-rabbi-joseph-h-hertz-of-britain-dies-in-london-was-educated-in-new-york.

Chapter 19

THE BALFOUR WOMEN AND ROTHSCHILD LEGACY

When the Balfour Declaration was issued in 1917, Britain's women did not have the right to vote or serve in Parliament.[1] The Jewish women who helped bring about the declaration tended to exert their influence in more subtle ways.

For instance, on November 15, 1916, Emma Rothschild, widow of Nathaniel Mayer de Rothschild, the first Baron, hosted a reconciliation luncheon during which James Rothschild, son of Baron Edmond Rothschild of the French branch, tried – unsuccessfully – to bridge the gap between Chaim Weizmann's Zionist camp and the anti-Zionists within the British Jewish community. (James Rothschild served in the British Army in Palestine and became an MP.)

James's wife, Dorothy, was very much his collaborator, in part because James had been temporarily sidelined by war-related injuries. She was also Chaim Weizmann's intermediary, not just with James but also with his father Edmond. She opened up any number of doors through which Weizmann could make his case to the right people in British society.

The Balfour Declaration was addressed to Lionel Walter Rothschild. His sister-in-law Rózsika Edle (Charles Rothschild's wife) also provided Weizmann entrée to British decision-making circles.

And it was thanks to Providence and Vera Weizmann that her husband Chaim met Charles Prestwich Scott, editor of the *Manchester Guardian*.

As Vera wrote toward the end of 1913:

---

1 Women in the United States got the vote in 1920. Some women in Britain got the vote in 1918, but universal suffrage was granted only in 1928. The first woman to take her seat in Parliament was Nancy Astor in 1918.

> Chaim and I were invited to another afternoon [tea] ritual this time in the home of Mr. and Mrs. Eckhard. She was the chairman of the clinic for mothers in which I served as medical officer.... Chaim and I went to this tea without an inkling that it would mark a momentous turning point in Chaim's political career and, indeed, in the fortunes of the Zionist movement.[2]

Tsarist policy required Russian Jews to live in a "Pale of Settlement." Vera Chatzman's family, however, was given the privilege of living in Rostov-on-Don (outside the designated territory) because her father had been conscripted into the Russian army for twenty-five years. The family was comparatively well off and socially acculturated. Jewish holidays were observed and Vera's two brothers were given some religious instruction, but Vera and her four sisters had only a rudimentary familiarity with Judaism and no Hebrew or Yiddish. However, Vera received a first-rate Russian education, which included French and Latin. She graduated from the University of Geneva with a medical degree (later completing her medical studies in England).

At the University of Geneva's Zionist Club Vera happened to be in the audience for a lecture by a young scientist named Chaim Weizmann. Six years later, in 1906, Chaim and Vera were married in a synagogue ceremony in Germany.

Zionism had to be a key element in the couple's partnership. They spent part of their honeymoon in Cologne where Chaim participated in a Zionist Executive conference.

Vera Weizmann moved to Manchester where her husband already had a lectureship in chemistry. She arrived speaking no English. By 1911 or so, she had mastered English and German (the common language of many of Weizmann's Zionist colleagues) and become a British citizen.

She was certified to practice medicine in Britain in 1913 and began working as a public health physician in the Manchester slums specializing in women's and infant care.

Her husband's scientific contributions to Britain's World War I effort necessitated a move in 1916 to London where they lived in Addison Crescent.

After WWI, Vera Weizmann made her first trip to Palestine in 1919 together with Rebecca Sieff and Edith Eder, members of the British Zionist Federation Ladies Committee. Together with Olga Ginsburg, Romana

---

2   Vera Weizmann, *Memoirs,* 52.

Goodman, and Henrietta Irwell, among others, they established the Women's International Zionist Organization, or WIZO.

Weizmann made her second trip to Palestine in 1925, joining Chaim for the opening ceremony of the Hebrew University in Jerusalem. As WIZO treasurer Vera raised monies to train and educate women settling in Palestine.

From about 1937 until 1944, the couple stayed mostly in London rather than at their home in Rehovot. In February 1940, their son Michael's plane went down while on a World War II mission for the Royal Air Force. Their other son, Benjamin, also served in the British Army.

Vera contributed to the WWII effort as a physician-volunteer for the Red Cross in London's poor neighborhoods.

After the Second World War, Chaim's duties required the couple to travel back and forth between London and Rehovot. In Palestine, Vera became a head of the Youth Aliyah movement bringing traumatized youngsters to Palestine. She traveled widely to raise money on behalf of a variety of Zionist causes.

When the State of Israel was proclaimed in 1948 and Chaim was elected its first president, Vera became First Lady.

In that capacity her medical training drew her to public health issues. She devoted huge energies to developing Magen David Adom, Israel's combination Red Cross and emergency ambulance service. Together with Dr. Chaim Sheba she made a major contribution to the establishment of Tel Hashomer Hospital in metropolitan Tel Aviv and its project to rehabilitate disabled soldiers. Among other responsibilities she was president of the Israel and British Commonwealth Association.

Vera Weizmann died aged eighty-seven on September 24, 1966, while on a private visit to London. She was buried next to her husband (who had died in 1952) in Rehovot, near the grounds of what is today the Weizmann Institute for Science.

Prime Minister Levi Eshkol noted in his order for a state funeral that at nearly every step of the way Vera's life was intertwined with the Zionist movement's quest – first to establish and then to nurture the Jewish homeland.[3]

Dorothy (Dolly) Mathilde de Rothschild (1895–1988) learned about

---

3   "Israel to Conduct State Funeral for Mrs. Weizmann at Rehovot Today," *Jewish Telegraphic Agency*, September 27, 1966, accessed June 26, 2017, http://www.jta.org/1966/09/27/archive/israel-to-conduct-state-funeral-for-mrs-weizmann-at-rehovot-today.

Zionism first hand from her father-in-law Baron Edmond de Rothschild (1845–1934). She soon became a skillful political facilitator who regularly filled in for her husband James when he went off to war or was convalescing from his war-related injuries.

Dorothy arranged meetings and forged important contacts for Chaim Weizmann and his circle, thus enabling them to press Britain to support a Jewish homeland in Palestine.

Years later, after the birth of Israel, her discreet philanthropic generosity helped to develop the Jewish state's civil society, build some of its most important institutional edifices, and unleash the human potential of a new generation of Israelis through a vast array of educational initiatives.

All the while, Dorothy maintained a profound commitment to the family's civic responsibilities in British society, including overseeing the initial stages of the handover of the family's six thousand-acre Waddesdon estate in Buckinghamshire to the National Trust for Historic Preservation. Under the leadership of the current Lord Rothschild, the Rothschild Foundation underpins all of Waddesdon's activities on behalf of the National Trust.

She was born Dorothy Pinto into an Anglo-Jewish London family on March 7, 1895. On February 25, 1913, just short of her eighteenth birthday, she married James, then age thirty-five, at Waddesdon Manor. Thus, while still just a teenager she was to play a critical role in introducing Weizmann to the Rothschild family and the broader Jewish and general communities.

The family name Pinto is often traced to Sephardic Jews, descendants of the Jews expelled from Portugal during the Inquisition, some of whom moved to the Arab world. Dorothy's family on her father's side had roots in Egypt. Her maternal grandfather, Levi Cohen, was a founder of the Liberal Synagogue in London.

Even while James served as an MP, she became a local alderman and Justice of the Peace.

Dorothy's father-in-law, Baron Edmond de Rothschild of France, began making philanthropic investments in Palestine in the late 1880s, having visited Jerusalem with his wife Baroness Adelheid in 1887. He helped establish some of the first settlements in Eretz Yisrael (Land of Israel) and went on to join forces with the Palestine Jewish Colonization Association (PICA). Indeed, in doing so, he massively bolstered PICA's ongoing work.

Under Baron Edmond's leadership, PICA's many activities included the establishment of over forty agricultural settlements as well as key industries such as the flour mills in Haifa, the salt works in Atlit, and Haifa's fertilizer and chemical plants. Likewise, cuttings from the Rothschild vineyards in France were used to help establish Carmel's Rishon LeZion Wine Cellars – thus laying the foundations for the country's wine industry, which today comprises dozens of commercial firms producing world class wine.

During the Great War, Dorothy's husband James – French born and Cambridge educated – was mobilized into the French army, leaving the London-born Dorothy to replace him as the intermediary between her husband, his father, and the London-based Zionist leaders headed by Weizmann and Nahum Sokolow. In addition to serving in the French army during the Great War (WWI), James A. 'Jimmy' Rothschild served as an officer in the Royal Canadian Dragoons and, later, as part of the British-sponsored Jewish Legion in Palestine.

As a result of James's war-related injuries and prolonged convalescence, Dorothy became Weizmann's "resourceful collaborator," according to historian Simon Schama. "Young as she was," he writes in *Two Rothschilds and the Land of Israel*, "she combined charm, intelligence, and more than a hint of steely resolution in just the right mixture to coax commitment from the equivocal, enthusiasm from the lukewarm, and sympathy from the indifferent."[4]

In *Chaim Weizmann: The Making of a Statesman*, biographer Jehuda Reinharz describes Dorothy as Weizmann's "trusted collaborator,"[5] crediting her with making the connection between Weizmann and the families of both Walter and Charles Rothschild. Or as Schama puts it: "Through tireless but prudent social diplomacy she had managed to open avenues of influence and persuasion at a time when they were badly needed."[6]

Very early on, writes Schama, Weizmann enlisted Dorothy "as a vital link between himself and the higher echelons of the Anglo-Jewish and British non-Jewish notability."[7] In this way, Dorothy was delivered into the maelstrom of Zionist politics.

Dorothy joined James in helping to press the British government for a commitment to work toward establishing a Jewish homeland in Palestine

---

4   Simon Schama, *Two Rothschilds and the Land of Israel* (New York: Alfred A. Knopf, 1978), 197–98.
5   Reinharz, *The Making of a Statesman*, 29.
6   Schama, *Two Rothschilds*, 198.
7   Ibid., 188.

once it was wrested from the Ottoman Empire. The couple used their considerable contacts to expand entrée to British decision makers for Weizmann, Nahum Sokolow, and their Zionist circle. These efforts were instrumental in bringing about the famous November 2, 1917, letter from Foreign Secretary Arthur Balfour to Lord Rothschild (Lionel Walter), head of the British branch of the family.

In 1920, James became a naturalized British citizen. From 1924, he nominally headed PICA and, on his father Edmond's death in 1934, he formally assumed the entirety of the family's responsibilities. From 1929 to 1945 he also served as a Liberal member of Parliament.

In 1957, James felt that PICA's task had been fulfilled. He declared that he was turning over all the remaining PICA lands to Israel's national institutions and asked that the state and the people, supported by world Jewry, carry on with the work. He died that same year at age seventy-eight.

Dorothy made philanthropy her life's work. In 1958, in reflection of her philanthropic giving, her resolute Zionism and her desire to honor the wishes of her late husband and his father, she founded Yad Hanadiv. Her cousin Lord Rothschild (Jacob) continues to uphold her precious philanthropic legacy.

Following through on a pledge that James had made to Israel's first prime minister David Ben-Gurion, Dorothy de Rothschild and her family funded the construction of Israel's parliament – the Knesset – in Jerusalem. The cornerstone was laid in 1958. The building, dedicated in 1966, marked its fiftieth anniversary in the summer of 2016.

In part to fulfil James's wishes, as well as to commemorate the approaching centenary of her father-in-law Edmond's birth, Dorothy endowed and oversaw the construction of Israel's new Supreme Court building.[8] The government granted the court a site that is adjacent to the Knesset and government quarter and Dorothy took an active interest in every aspect of the project.

The Supreme Court compound opened in 1992, four years after Dorothy's death. In line with the philanthropic ethos of the Rothschild family, which regards philanthropy as a privilege and responsibility rather than a form of public relations, Dorothy requested that publicity regarding the role of Yad Hanadiv in the project be kept to a minimum.

---

8   The building was designed by brother and sister architects Ram Karmi and Ada Karmi-Melamede. Israel's Supreme Court has across the board appellate jurisdiction and as the High Court of Justice (Bagatz), rules on issues of constitutionality.

Currently, Lord Rothschild and Yad Hanadiv are supporting and actively involved in the renewal of the National Library of Israel, including the construction of a magnificent new home for the library on a plot of land facing the Knesset.

A driving force of Yad Hanadiv, Dorothy helped create a vast and enduring array of good works in Israel, including practical programs aimed at improving the lives of ordinary Jewish and Arab citizens of the country; backing for the Jerusalem Foundation, founded by Mayor Teddy Kollek in 1966; and fellowships and academic awards for gifted scholars.

Under her stewardship, Yad Hanadiv helped establish the Jerusalem Music Centre at Mishkenot Sha'ananim and the Institute for Advanced Studies at the Hebrew University of Jerusalem. It has supported scientific work at the Technion and the Weizmann Institute of Science, established educational television in Israel (thus introducing television to the country), and created the Open University whose campus in Ra'anana is uncharacteristically named for Dorothy de Rothschild. All this is in addition to her efforts on behalf of the rights of Jews in the Soviet Union during the communist era.

James and Dorothy had no children of their own, yet they left a lasting legacy. In effect, they even became the surrogate parents to thirty German-Jewish boys (aged six to fourteen) to whom they gave refuge on the family's Waddesdon estate for over five years. In 1939, on the eve of the Second World War, Dorothy arranged for the boys who were pupils at a Jewish school in Frankfurt to be granted asylum in Britain. Tragically, most of their families and classmates who remained behind in Europe were engulfed by Hitler's war against the Jews.

When she was eighty-eight, some of the "old boys" returned for an emotional reunion with their benefactress. "How delighted my husband would have been to see you make your way in life so well. It must have taken courage and resolution," she said. "Although you are very much grown up, you will always remain boys to me," she told them, adding "It's been such a very long time since you've been here with me."[9]

The boys went on to careers in business, the professions, and academia. One even returned to Britain as an Israeli diplomat.

Dorothy's death in London on December 10, 1988, at the age of nine-

---

9 "15 Who Fled Nazis as Boys Hold a Reunion," *New York Times*, July 27, 1983, http://www.nytimes.com/1983/07/28/world/15-who-fled-nazis-as-boys-hold-a-reunion.html.

ty-three, brought to an end seventy-five years of prolific work on behalf of Zionism and humanism. She is buried at Willesden Jewish cemetery in the Rothschild family compound and close to Walter Rothschild to whom the Balfour Declaration was addressed.

Dorothy bequeathed her estate as well as responsibility for Yad Hanadiv to her cousin Jacob, today Lord Rothschild, who over the years had become actively involved in the foundation's philanthropic work. Alongside his successful career as an investment banker, Lord Rothschild has served as a dedicated steward and visionary chair of Yad Hanadiv since 1989 – growing the foundation's assets and guiding its activity.

In addition to the Open University's Dorothy de Rothschild campus, Dorothy is memorialized by Shadmot Dvora (in the image of Dorothy), an agricultural moshav, or cooperative farm, in the Lower Galilee that was founded by German Jewish settlers in 1939 and named in her honor.

Chapter 20

CONSCIENTIOUS OBJECTOR: LUCIEN WOLF

I n 2013, David Duke's website carried an article by one Patrick Slattery that grappled with a quandary that old line white supremacist and anti-Semites, such as Duke, find themselves in: How should people who despise Jews relate to Jews who despise Zionism and Israel. "Countless Jews do very important work exposing certain aspects of Zionism regarding Israel, yet at the same time defend, or at least draw attention away from, Jewish domination of the United States and other Western countries," Slattery opined.

He cited Max Blumenthal, Norman Finkelstein, Noam Chomsky, Amy Goodman, and Naomi Klein as "sincere" in being opposed to Israel's existence. But at the end of the day, he surmised "their priority is to preserve Jewish power and privilege in the United States."[1]

Now, I mention this to bang home a point. While there's no shortage of anti-Zionist Jews, today's strain have almost nothing in common with the Jewish opponents of Zionism during the period of the Balfour Declaration.[2]

The leading anti-Zionists of the Balfour era were mostly individu-

---

1   Dr. Patrick Slattery, "What do to about anti-Zionist Zionists?" [*sic*] David Duke.com: For Human Freedom and Diversity, October 8, 2013, http://davidduke.com/what-do-to-about-anti-zionist-zionists/.

2   Today's anti-Zionists come in a variety of hues. Arab and Muslim anti-Zionism need not detain us here. But on the hard left, Jewish and non-Jewish anti-Zionists tend to espouse an economic and military boycott of Israel, an imposed Israeli withdrawal to the 1949 armistice lines, and the right of Palestinian Arab refugees from the 1948 War – plus millions of their descendants – to "return" to a truncated Israel. While hard-left Jewish campaigners are often Jewishly-illiterate, as often as not, they claim to be motivated by Jewish values. On the hard right, opposition to the Jewish state is rooted in a racial hatred of Jews. Then there are the outliers such as the risible Neturei Karta Jewish sect who dress in traditional Hasidic garb and are a ubiquitous presence at anti-Israel gatherings from London to Teheran.

als deeply committed to Jewish civil rights. Most were, at the very least, Jewishly-literate.

Take the case of Lucien Wolf (1857–1930). A British-Jewish journalist, community activist, and historian of Anglo-Jewry, Wolf was an indefatigable campaigner for oppressed Jewry. He was also an outspoken opponent of political Zionism. He believed that the Zionists were wrong to give up on the idea that European Jews would ultimately secure full citizenship rights.

Wolf became the voice of Jewish opposition to Zionism even though he was not unsympathetic to elements of the Jewish homeland idea.

In December 1915, Wolf wrote a memo to the British Foreign Office on the question of how US Jewish opinion could be harnessed to advocate for an American entry into World War I. Recognizing that Britain was looking for leverage to end Washington's neutrality, Wolf frankly acknowledged that American Jews, largely opposed to entry into the war, were sympathetic to the Zionist idea. If Britain made it clear that were Palestine to come under its jurisdiction, it would back "a liberal scheme of self-government" for the Jews that might dampen the Jews' predisposition to neutrality.[3]

Philosophically, Wolf rejected the view that the Jews "constitute a separate political nationality."[4] Despite his opposition to Zionism, which stemmed from a genuine conviction that it would be bad for Jews, Wolf sufficiently appreciated Zionism that he was called upon to write an *Encyclopedia Britannica* entry on the topic. He also contributed a piece on the history of anti-Semitism for the encyclopedia's eleventh edition.

Unlike the Zionists, Wolf did not want to "negate the diaspora."[5] Indeed, he had high hopes for an ever more tolerant Europe.[6] On August 17, 1916, Wolf and Zionist leader Chaim Weizmann met at the home of James de Rothschild in a failed attempt to achieve a modus vivendi.

Jewish opposition to the Balfour Declaration was usually accompanied by a genuine concern for Jews qua Jews. The Russian pogroms of 1881 had greatly affected Wolf's psyche, leading him to devote much of his life to campaigning for Jewish rights in eastern Europe. He developed an expertise

---

3   Schneer, *The Balfour Declaration*, 157.

4   Vivian David Lipman, *A History of the Jews in Britain Since 1858* (Teaneck, NJ: Holmes and Meier, 1990), 132. See, too, Stein, *Balfour Declaration*, 566.

5   "Negation of Diaspora Urged by Nahum Sokolow in Farewell Address," *Jewish Telegraphic Agency*, March 15, 1926, http://www.jta.org/1926/03/15/archive/negation-of-diaspora-urged-by-nahum-sokolow-in-farewell-address.

6   At the time, he could not have possibly foreseen the rise of Nazism and the subsequent destruction of European Jewry in the Shoah.

in minority issues, including the Catholic position in Britain. Wolf's open hostility toward the anti-Semitic Tsarist regime impelled him to leave the world of advocacy-journalism and become the top official at Conjoint, the joint foreign committee of the Anglo-Jewish Association and the Board of Deputies of British Jews. In effect, he became the foreign minister of the organized Jewish community – a role for which he was admirably suited. He was well traveled, had the benefit of a cosmopolitan education, and was fluent in French and German.

Furthermore, the anti-Zionists didn't oppose Jewish immigration to Palestine; and they fully accepted Palestine's special significance to the Jewish people.

Wolf's position on Palestine was articulated in March 1916 while the country was in Turkish hands: Should Palestine come under British control, London ought to take into account the "historic interest that country possesses for the Jewish community."[7] He advocated for Jewish civil and religious liberty as well as equal political rights with the rest of the population. He also favored "reasonable" facilitation of Jewish immigration and colonization.[8]

In April 1917, Wolf complained that the Zionists "declare that where emancipation does not exist it is not worth striving for and where it does exist it is no remedy."[9] Ultimately, his anti-Zionist sails were trimmed when on June 17, 1917, the Board of Deputies in a policy shift criticized him for taking his opposition to political Zionism into the pages of *the Times*.

After WWI, he took part in the Versailles Conference in Paris as a spokesperson for the ad hoc National Union for Jewish Rights. He helped draft the Minorities Treaties, which were aimed at protecting the civil and religious rights of Jewish communities in Poland, Romania, Czechoslovakia, Greece, Yugoslavia, and beyond. He even briefly chaired the League of Nations committee on refugees. At home, he lobbied against Sunday closing laws which barred Jewish-owned concerns from doing business on the Christian Sabbath.

---

7   Schneer, 158.

8   Isaiah Friedman, *The Question of Palestine, 1914–1918: British-Jewish-Arab Relations* (New York: Schocken Books, 1973), 52.

9   Isaiah Friedman, *The Rise of Israel: Britain Enters into a Compact with Zionism, 1917, Part 1* (New York: Garland, 1987), 451. See, too, Leon Simon, *The Case of the Anti-Zionists: A Reply,"* (Charleston, SC: Nabu Press, 2011), 17. Simon writes: "This is a gross travesty of the Zionist view that emancipation has not solved and cannot solve the Jewish problem. Zionists do not maintain anything so absurd as that emancipation is not worth striving for."

Lucien Wolf was born in London on January 20, 1857. He turned to journalism at age seventeen, joining the *Jewish World* in 1874. He worked as a sub-editor and leader writer at the *Daily Graphic*, starting in 1890, and as London correspondent for the Paris-based *Le Journal* between 1893 and 1897. The *New York Times* often reported on his newspaper commentaries on international relations.

He married Francis Moses in 1880 and the couple had four sons and three daughters. He died in 1930 at the age of seventy-three. He was survived by his second wife, Margaret, whom he had married in 1923.

This is a good point at which to reintroduce Edwin Montagu, the most persistent opponent of political Zionism inside the David Lloyd George government. Even so, on August 23, 1917, he advised: "That the government will be prepared to do everything in their power to obtain for Jews in Palestine complete liberty of settlement and life on an equality with the inhabitants of that country who profess other religious beliefs."[10]

Montagu had recently been appointed secretary of state for India. In addition to his anti-Zionist views as an English Jew, he also worried how any declaration would affect his standing as an authority of the British Raj.

With the aim of blocking what came to be known as the Balfour Declaration and head off political Zionism, on September 14, 1917, Montagu offered yet another idea for the government to consider: "His Majesty's Government accepts the principle that every opportunity should be afforded for the establishment in Palestine for those Jews who cannot or will not remain in the lands in which they live at present, will use its best endeavours to facilitate the achievement of this object, and will be ready to consider any suggestions on the subject which any Jewish or Zionist organizations may desire to lay before it."[11]

Yet another prominent opponent of Zionism was Claude Montefiore (1858–1938) great nephew of Sir Moses Montefiore. Claude was greatly influenced by Benjamin Jowett, a leading Christian thinker. But Montefiore applied himself to the study of Judaism, even engaging Solomon Schechter as his private tutor. He helped sponsor the traditional Singer Jewish prayer book though ultimately he facilitated the establishment of Liberal Judaism in

10   "Memorandum of Edwin Montagu on the Anti-Semitism of the Present (British) Government," The Balfour Project, accessed June 27, 2017, http://www.balfourproject.org/edwin-montagu-and-zionism-1917/.

11   Friedman, *The Rise of Israel*, 262.

Britain, theologically to the left of Reform. A believer in Jewish universalism he maintained, "We have come forth from the ghetto to be worldwide and free. We cannot again be cribbed and confined by geographical limitations."[12] Today let it be noted that while its clergy may be critical of certain Israeli policies, Britain's Liberal Judaism stream has affirmed a love for the Land of Israel and a strong commitment to the State of Israel.

Like their Zionist adversaries, the anti-Zionists were products of their milieu. They worried – among other things – that hard-won Jewish rights in western Europe would be withdrawn if Jews had their own national home. They did not argue against immigration to Palestine or deny its special place in Jewish civilization.

---

12   "Dr. Claude Montefiore, Scholar, Philanthropist, Dead at 80; Exponent of Liberal Judaism," *Jewish Telegraphic Agency*, July 11, 1938, accessed August 1, 2017, http://www.jta.org/1938/07/11/archive/dr-claude-montefiore-scholar-philanthropist-dead-at-80-exponent-of-liberal-judaism.

Chapter 21

WHAT WENT WRONG?
BRITISH BACKTRACKING AND
ARAB REJECTIONISM

So, what went wrong? Why did Britain backpedal on its solemn promise to facilitate a national home for the Jewish people in Palestine?

There are two main reasons.

There's a Bible verse that comes to mind to explain part of what happened: "Now there arose up a new king over Egypt, who knew not Joseph" (Exodus 1:8). With the end of the Great War, Lloyd George's philo-Semitic government gave way to a new unsympathetic administration.

Secondly, Arab opposition became vociferous and violent. And when the going got tough the British…capitulated – not all at once, but incrementally and inexorably.

Arab reaction to the Balfour Declaration was initially mixed.[1] Zionist leaders had hoped to win Arab support for the restoration of the Jews to Palestine; they saw a win-win situation that would benefit Jews and Arabs alike. Two Arab representatives even attended a Zionist celebratory meeting in London's Covent Garden on December 2, 1917. That said, it is also worth noting that on November 10, 1917, Amir Ali, an India-born Muslim barrister and London-based communal leader, wrote to British diplomat Lord Hardinge: "Your Lordship will readily realize how offensive the idea must be to [Muslims] that their holiest places in Palestine should be placed under Jewish control."[2] Of course, the Balfour Declaration did no such thing.

---

1   There were to be sure initiatives by British Muslims under the auspices of the Islamic Society in June 1917 to oppose the idea of a Jewish homeland in Palestine, see Schneer, *The Balfour Declaration*, 245.

2   Ibid., 373. For more on Ali see "Syed Ameer Ali," *Wikipedia*, last modified July 26, 2017, https://en.wikipedia.org/wiki/Syed_Ameer_Ali.

In May 1918, under British tutelage, Chaim Weizmann met Emir Feisal, a son of Hussein bin Ali, Sharif of Mecca (1854–1931), in the Red Sea port of Aqaba where they exchanged letters of mutual support. With T. E. Lawrence as a middleman the two continued with a series of meetings that led to a January 3, 1919, memorandum in which Feisal endorsed the Balfour Declaration.[3]

On March 3, 1919, Feisal wrote to Felix Frankfurter expressing sympathy for the Zionist movement.[4] "We are working together for a reformed and revived Middle East, and our two movements complete one another. The Jewish movement is national not imperialist, and there is room in Syria [conceiving of Palestine as part of a Greater Syria where for a short time he would rule as monarch] for us both."

Added Feisal: "I think that neither can be a real success without the other."[5]

Tragically for future generations, advocates of Arab-Zionist collaboration such as Feisal would in due course be silenced, shunted aside, and branded as traitors. Sometimes, they were assassinated.[6]

There was also the matter of how the British authorities implemented the mandate. Lord Curzon (1859–1925), who had replaced Balfour at the Foreign Office and would remain there until January 1924, had never been overly sympathetic to the Zionist enterprise.

With the appointment of Ronald Storrs as Jerusalem's military governor in 1917 the die was cast. "I am not for either, but for both," Storrs asserted. "Two hours of Arab grievances drive me into the synagogue, while after an

---

3   "The Weizmann-Feisal Agreement," Israel Ministry of Foreign Affairs, January 3, 1919, accessed August 1, 2017, http://www.mfa.gov.il/mfa/foreignpolicy/peace/mfadocuments/pages/the%20 weizmann-feisal%20agreement%203-jan-1919.aspx.

4   At the time, Frankfurter (1882–1965) was a member of the American Zionist delegation to the post WWI Versailles Peace Conference, a Harvard law professor, and later from 1939 a justice of the US Supreme Court. To recapitulate, WWI ended on November 11, 1918. The peace conference began in January 1919 and closed in January 1920 with the inaugural General Assembly of the League of Nations.

5   Weizmann, *Trial and Error*, 246. The letter went on: "People less informed and less responsible than our leaders, ignoring the need for cooperation of the Arabs and the Zionists, have been trying to exploit the local differences that must necessarily arise in Palestine in the early stages of our movements. Some of them have, I am afraid, misrepresented your aims to the Arab peasantry, and our aims to the Jewish peasantry, with the result that interested parties have been able to make capital out of what they call our differences. I wish to give you my firm conviction that these differences are not on questions of principle, but on matters of detail, such as must inevitably occur in every contact with neighbouring peoples, and as are easily dissipated by mutual goodwill."

6   On the tribulations of being an Arab moderate see Elliot Jager "Where the Moderates Are," *Jagerfile*, http://elliotjager.blogspot.co.il/2008/03/where-moderates-are.html.

intense course of Zionist propaganda I am prepared to embrace Islam."[7] But Zionists certainly perceived him to be unsympathetic to their cause. Storrs made sure that, for example, Jerusalem's Jewish majority was not reflected in the distribution of municipal power. Even though Jews comprised most of the taxpayers and a majority of the population, the British always appointed a Muslim mayor and two deputy mayors, one Jewish and one Christian.[8]

General Sir Arthur Money, who replaced General Edmund Allenby in 1919, was also no great friend of Zionism. Other mandate figures such as Vivian Gabriel and Lt. Col. J. E. Hubbard were decidedly cold to Jewish sensibilities.

For Palestine to become a national homeland for the Jewish people, the gates of the country needed to be open to Jewish immigration. Arab opposition to Jewish immigration began to manifest in violent ways, and British officials, even those perhaps initially sympathetic toward Zionist aspirations, acknowledged that Jewish immigration was a catalyst of Arab violence.

As Jerusalem's Jewish population became bigger, British efforts to mollify Arab rage invariably fell short. Anything could set off the violence. Typically, it was the unfounded rumor that the Jews planned to destroy the Dome of the Rock or the Aksa Mosque, the Muslim holy places atop the Temple Mount.[9]

The atmosphere went from bad to worse. In 1921, British High Commissioner Sir Herbert Samuel appointed Haj Amin al-Husseini as Mufti or spiritual leader of Palestinian Arab Muslims (almost all of whom are Sunni). He would remain at the epicenter of anti-Zionist incitement un-

---

7   Tom Segev, *One Palestine, Complete: Jews and Arabs under the British Mandate* (New York: Henry Holt and Co., 2001), 92. British Arabists such as the legendary Gertrude Bell were, shall we say, not sympathetic to Zionism. Daniel Johnson, "Putting the Dons on their Mettle," *The Telegraph*, September 3, 2006, http://www.telegraph.co.uk/culture/books/3655036/Putting-the-dons-on-their-mettle.html.

8   For how Zionists viewed Storrs, see Rory Miller, "Sir Ronald Storrs and Zion: The Dream That Turned into a Nightmare," *Middle Eastern Studies*, 36, no. 3 (2000): 114–44. For population figures see "Demographics of Israel: Population of Jerusalem," (1844–2009), Jewish Virtual Library, accessed July 17, 2017, http://www.jewishvirtuallibrary.org/population-of-jerusalem-1844-2009.

9   This falsehood has been a constant phobia among Muslims due to a disinformation campaign hammered home by Arab media outlets. Thus, a December 2015 survey conducted by the EU-funded Palestinian Center for Policy and Survey Research found that an overwhelming majority of Palestinian Arabs believe that al Haram al Sharif (or the Temple Mount) is in grave danger from Israel (accessed July 27, 2017, http://www.pcpsr.org/en/node/625). Though no Israeli government has ever entertained the notion, one poll of Israeli grassroots opinion found some support for erecting a third temple. Nir Hasson, "One third of Israeli Jews Want Temple Rebuilt in Jerusalem, Poll Finds," *Haaretz*, October 30, 2014, http://www.haaretz.com/israel-news/.premium-1.535336.

til he fled to Adolf Hitler's Berlin during World War II. He died in Beirut, Lebanon in 1974.[10]

On September 16, 1922, the British divided Mandatory Palestine into two administrative areas with 77 percent earmarked for the Arabs.

The sequence of events is worth recalling even though I wrote about it earlier. The Hashemite Emir Feisal, who had been made king of Syria in March 1920, was dethroned in July of that year by France. Britain, which had the mandate for Iraq, offered Feisal the Baghdad throne. But the Iraqi throne had been pledged to Feisal's brother Abdullah who anyway turned down the offer because Feisal had been thrown out of Damascus. The men were the sons of the Hussein bin Ali, Sharif of Mecca.

Abdullah organized a ragtag force to march on Damascus. He set up camp in Transjordan, the eastern side of the River Jordan and part of the Palestine Mandate.

Colonial Secretary Winston Churchill headed for Cairo to handle the crisis and brokered an arrangement whereby eastern Palestine would be transformed into Jordan with Abdullah made sovereign. Feisal would become king in Iraq.

This was technically possible because the League of Nations had not yet ratified Britain's Palestine Mandate. The draft was now altered so that Britain had the right to "withhold" the Jewish homeland provisions of the mandate "in the territories lying between the Jordan and the eastern boundary of Palestine."[11]

T. E. Lawrence wrote that creating Transjordan "honorably fulfils the whole of the promises we made to the Arabs in so far as the so-called British spheres are concerned."[12]

Thus, out of the blue, the Jewish national home provisions of the mandate were rendered inoperative as they applied to eastern Palestine; the

---

10   "Haj Amin el-Husseini Dies; Ex-Palestine Grand Mufti," *New York Times*, July 5, 1974, http://www.nytimes.com/1974/07/05/archives/haj-amin-elhusseini-dies-expalestine-grand-mufti-headed-dissident.html?_r=0.

11   The text of the Mandate is available here: The Avalon Project, "The Palestine Mandate," accessed June 27, 2017, http://avalon.law.yale.edu/20th_century/palmanda.asp. The decision to separate eastern Palestine from Britain's commitment to foster a Jewish homeland in Palestine and the function of Article 25 is summarized in Patai, *Encyclopedia of Zionism and Israel*, vol. 2, 751. For a fuller description see "Mandate for Palestine: The Legal Aspects of Jewish Rights," accessed June 27, 2017, http://www.mythsandfacts.org/conflict/mandate_for_palestine/mandate_for_palestine.htm.

12   For Lawrence's view, see, T. E. Lawrence Studies, accessed August 7, 2017, http://www.telstudies.org/writings/letters/1929/291022_yale.shtml.

space for a Jewish national home became dramatically smaller. Not until 1946 would this eastern chunk of territory become officially known as the Hashemite Kingdom of Transjordan. Britain also ceded the Golan Heights, situated overlooking the Galilee, to be included in the French Mandate of Syria.

Some Zionist leaders led by Vladimir Ze'ev Jabotinsky (1880–1940) were never reconciled to the loss of eastern Palestine. Most others, however, came to accept it as a fait accompli.

By 1925, the Hashemite family had been elbowed out of Arabia by the Saud clan (hence the name "Saudi Arabia," which was proclaimed in 1932).[13] So the Hashemite clan had lost the Syrian throne in 1920 after a brief reign. They would be forced out of Iraq in a military coup after ruling that country from 1921 to 1958. The one remaining twenty-first-century Hashemite royal is Jordan's King Abdullah II. The legitimacy of the family's rule hinges, partly, on assertions that it is descended from Islam's founding prophet.

Meanwhile, Arab opposition to Jewish immigration continued to harden. By 1922, the Arab population in the Middle East was some ten million. In Palestine, out of an estimated population of 757,182, there were 590,890 Arabs and 84,000 Jews. Christians numbered 73,024 and Druze 7,028.[14]

Violent Arab opposition to a Jewish homeland was first manifested on a large scale on Passover in April 1920 with the Nebi Musa riots in Jerusalem. A month earlier, in March 1920, Arab irregulars comprised of Shi'ites from Syria and local Sunni Bedouin attacked the Galilean settlement of Tel Hai killing its Jewish commander, Joseph Trumpeldor. A comrade of Jabotinsky, he had been instrumental in founding the WWI Jewish Legion. The Tel Hai settlement was overrun and destroyed, but Trumpeldor became a Zionist national hero.

In May 1921, riots broke out in Jaffa. Among the killed was Yosef Haim Brenner, one of the pioneers of Modern Hebrew literature.

In 1922, British policymakers led by Churchill – though he was personally supportive of the Zionist enterprise – announced (in the Churchill

---

13   Ibn Saud had been an ineffective British ally against the Turks during WWI. Some Arab scholars contend that the British turned against Hashemite rule in Arabia and boosted the Saud clan because Hussein bin Ali, Sharif of Mecca, unlike his sons, rejected the idea of Palestine becoming a Jewish homeland. Today's Jordanian view is that Hussein's objective in undertaking the Great Arab Revolt was to establish a single unified Muslim Arab state stretching from Syria to Aden, Yemen.

14   The Israeli-Palestinian Conflict: An Interactive Database, "1922 Census of Palestine," Economic Cooperation Foundation, accessed July 27, 2017, https://ecf.org.il/issues/issue/1087.

White Paper) that Jewish immigration to Palestine would be restricted to "economic absorptive capacity."[15]

On April 1, 1925, Balfour aged seventy-seven, visited Palestine for the first time.[16] The occasion was the official opening of the Hebrew University of Jerusalem. Palestinian Jews were delighted he had made the journey. Present to greet him on Mount Scopus were scores of dignitaries, among them Chaim Weizmann and Palestine's Chief Rabbi Avraham Yitzhak Kook.

But Arab shop owners closed in protest.

Later, after driving to Damascus, Balfour was confronted by six thousand hostile Arabs demonstrating outside his hotel.

With the Mufti in the vanguard, violence became a reality of life in Jerusalem and throughout Palestine. In 1925, the spark was a general strike. In 1926, it was a protest against the French presence in Syria. In 1928, the catalyst was the installation of a flimsy gender partition at Jerusalem's Old City Western Wall to separate Orthodox Jewish men and women during the Yom Kippur prayer service.

And yet, materially, the British Mandate was improving life day by day. By 1928, electricity had become readily available. Jerusalem had a reservoir but lacked an infrastructure for efficient water distribution; the British made headway in solving that perennial problem as well and, by 1935, had drawn a pipeline that brought drinking water up to Jerusalem from the coastal plain. Many people, though, continued to use rooftop cisterns to capture rainwater.

The face of Jerusalem, Tel Aviv, and Haifa changed in large measure thanks to a British-inspired construction boom which brought Bauhaus and other international architectural styles to the country. Of course, Tel Aviv was unique as the first solely Jewish-built city – a testimony to Zionist innovation.

The mandate authorities took city planning seriously and laid down ascetic policies – the rule that all building façades in Jerusalem needed to be of pale Jerusalem limestone, for example.[17] The expansive construction in Jerusalem alone included Government House, a mansion atop the Hill of Evil Counsel on the south side of the city; a YMCA designed by the architect of New York's Empire State Building; and, across the street, the regal King

---

15   The Avalon Project, "British White Paper of June 1922," accessed June 27, 2017, http://avalon.law.yale.edu/20th_century/brwh1922.asp.

16   At the time, Joseph Chamberlain, half-brother of Neville Chamberlain, was foreign minister.

17   Segev, *One Palestine*, 61.

David Hotel. Then there was the Rockefeller archeological museum near the Damascus Gate of the Old City, and King George Avenue which became the heart of modern Jerusalem.

But aesthetic and across-the-board quality of life improvements notwithstanding, the Arabs would not be reconciled to the Jewish homeland idea. Jerusalem's population continued to increase so that by 1931 there were 51,222 Jews, 19,894 Muslims and 19,335 Christians.[18]

Tisha B'Av 1929 fell on Wednesday night and Thursday August 14–15 and saw thousands of Jerusalem Jews gathering at the Western Wall and young people arriving from throughout the country. After Friday prayers, Muslims began attacking Jews in Jerusalem. That heralded a week of countrywide rioting spurred on by the Mufti which left 116 Jewish killed (many horribly mutilated) – 67 in Hebron alone. Jews were forced to abandon the city. The Hebrew newspaper *Davar* reported that the toll would have been higher still had not some Hebron Arabs shielded their Jewish neighbors.[19] Jewish shop owners also began abandoning Jerusalem's Old City.

In an attempt to mollify the Arabs, the British authorities took one measure after another that backtracked on the 1917 Balfour Declaration. The Shaw Inquiry, the Hope-Simpson Report, and the Passfield White Paper (all issued during 1930) represented this trend of rowing back from the Balfour Declaration.

In 1933, in a variation on the theme, the rioting targeted the British as much as the Jews. This was also the year Hitler came to power in Germany.

In April 1936, the Mufti instigated yet more rioting, this time under the auspices of the Arab Higher Committee comprised of clan and political party leaders under his chairmanship. The violence was ultimately put down thanks to a surge in British forces.

The British Government's Peel Commission of 1936 recommended, in its report the following year, the division of the remaining territory of

---

18 For an historic overview and analysis of demographic trends see Yaakov Feitelson, "Jerusalem: The Eternally Jewish Capital?" *Mida*, 29 May, 2014, http://mida.org.il/2014/05/29/jerusalem-eternally-jewish-capital/.

19 For a summary of these events see Colin Shindler, *The Triumph of Military Zionism: Nationalism and the Origins of the Israeli Right* (London: I.B. Tauris, 2010), 100–103 and "Gruesome Atrocities Committed by Fanatical Moslem Arabs on Jewish Victims," *Jewish Telegraphic Agency*, August 28, 1929, accessed July 17, 2017, http://www.jta.org/1929/08/28/archive/gruesome-atrocities-committed-by-fanatical-moslem-arabs-on-jewish-victims, as well as "7 Jews in Hebron Were Saved by Arabs from Massacre," *Jewish Telegraphic Agency*, October 3, 1929, accessed July 17, 2017, http://www.jta.org/1929/10/03/archive/7-jews-in-hebron-were-saved-by-arabs-from-massacre.

western Palestine into two states. But the Arabs rejected any territorial compromise with the Jews – even though they would have received the bulk of the land. The idea was not popular among the Zionist factions led by Jabotinsky's Revisionists, religious Zionists, and part of the labor Zionist movement – Golda Meir for example.

At some point, most likely in 1937, Arab violence devolved into organized attacks on civilians – in plain words, terrorism. Arab gangs bombed public transport and shot at Jewish vehicles along the winding, single lane Tel Aviv-Jerusalem road.

Finally, in May 1939, just months before World War II was to engulf Europe's Jews, Britain officially reneged on the Balfour Declaration. As it prepared to confront Nazi Germany, London needed to placate the Middle East Arabs. To that end it issued a White Paper, essentially closing the gates of Palestine to Jews and basically barring land purchases by Jews. The plan suggested fifteen thousand Jews a year be admitted for five years then the Arabs would decide what would happen next. The Mufti rejected the move as insufficient.[20]

Particularly with the outbreak of World War II in September 1939, the British authorities kept Palestine's doors locked solid leaving Europe's Jews no haven. Still, the main Zionist camps – the followers of Chaim Weizmann and those of Vladimir Ze'ev Jabotinsky – largely supported Britain's war effort. Zionist leader David Ben-Gurion famously declared: "We must assist the British in the war as if there were no White Paper and we must resist the White Paper as if there were no war."[21]

Only the small, radical, Freedom Fighters for Israel or Stern Gang (also known as Lehi) continued to attack the British throughout World War II.

Not until February 1, 1944, did Menachem Begin's Irgun (which identified with Jabotinsky, who had died in 1940) declare an end to the ceasefire against the British and launch attacks against immigration offices in Palestine. In announcing the change, the Irgun stated: "Over the last four years of the war we have lost millions of the best of our people; millions more are in danger of eradication. And the Land of Israel is closed off and quarantined because the British rule it."[22]

---

20   See "Decision to Reject 1939 White Paper," Center for Israel Education, accessed July 18, 2017, https://israeled.org/7534-2/.
21   "David Ben-Gurion: Select Quotations," Jewish Virtual Library, accessed June 27, 2017, http://www.jewishvirtuallibrary.org/select-quotations-of-david-ben-gurion.
22   Menachem Begin, Samuel Katz, and Ivan M. Greenberg, *The Revolt* (Jerusalem: Steimatzky,

World War II ended in May 1945; but Palestine still found no peace.

In Britain, the Labour Party's Clement Attlee was now prime minister, having replaced Winston Churchill. Attlee and his foreign secretary Ernest Bevin rejected a request by US president Harry Truman to allow one hundred thousand Holocaust survivors into Palestine. Militant Jewish opposition to British rule in Palestine intensified, as did British reprisals.

Relentless Palestinian Arab antagonism to a national Jewish homeland resurrected anew the idea of a second partition of Western Palestine into two states: one Jewish and one Arab. Eastern Palestine was already Arab Transjordan.

In May 1947, a special committee of the UN General Assembly recommended that Palestine be partitioned into Arab and Jewish states. And on November 29, 1947, by a vote of thirty-three to thirteen, with ten abstentions, the General Assembly voted in favor of partition.[23]

As the 1947 UN Partition Plan map was drawn, the Jewish state with its roughly six hundred thousand Jews would also be home to four hundred thousand Arabs – demographically a bi-national state. The borders themselves were pretty much indefensible. Jerusalem was to be under international auspices. Nonetheless, the Zionist leadership grudgingly accepted partition.[24]

For its part, Britain made clear that it would not cooperate with the plan and announced that its forces would pull out on May 15, 1948. The Arab side also rejected the two-state solution. The UN vote set off a new wave of violence that was countered by a more assertive Zionist defense spearheaded by the Haganah, Irgun, and Lehi.

On Friday May 14, 1948, the Zionist leadership under David Ben-Gurion gathered in Tel Aviv to proclaim the birth of the State of Israel. Notably, Israel's Declaration of Independence invoked Arthur James Balfour:

1951), 42. See, too, "The Irgun: Revolt is Proclaimed," Jewish Virtual Library, accessed June 27, 2017, http://www.jewishvirtuallibrary.org/revolt-is-proclaimed-by-the-irgun.

23   UN members voting in favor: Australia, Belgium, Bolivia, Brazil, Byelorussian SSR, Canada, Costa Rica, Czechoslovakia, Denmark, Dominican Republic, Ecuador, France, Guatemala, Haiti, Iceland, Liberia, Luxembourg, Netherlands, Nicaragua, Norway, Panama, Paraguay, Peru, Philippines, Poland, South Africa, Sweden, Ukrainian SSR, Soviet Union, United States, Uruguay, Venezuela, and New Zealand. That's thirty-three countries, 72 percent of those voting. Opposed: Afghanistan, Cuba, Egypt, Greece, India, Iran, Iraq, Lebanon, Pakistan, Saudi Arabia, Syria, Turkey, and Yemen (thirteen countries). Abstentions: Argentina, Chile, China, Colombia, Ethiopia, Honduras, Mexico, Salvador, Britain, and Yugoslavia (ten countries).

24   "The Partition Plan: Background and Overview," Map of the U.N. Partition Plan, Jewish Virtual Library, accessed July 17, 2017, http://www.jewishvirtuallibrary.org/map-of-the-u-n-partition-plan.

The right of the Jewish people to national rebirth in its own country [had been] recognized in the Balfour Declaration of the 2nd
November, 1917, and re-affirmed in the mandate of the League of
Nations which, in particular, gave international sanction to the historic connection between the Jewish people and Eretz Yisrael [Land
of Israel] and to the right of the Jewish people to rebuild its National
Home.[25]

The Balfour Declaration had come to fruition – though, sadly, not in the way
that its author had envisioned.

The new state was recognized that night by the United States and three
days later by the USSR.

The Jewish population stood at about 650,000, ranged against some 1.1
million Palestinian Arabs.

Bloody urban riots and attacks on Jewish civilians had long been under
way. Arab irregular forces had infiltrated into Palestine months earlier. The
day after independence was declared Egypt, Transjordan, Syria, Iraq, and
Lebanon – alongside the Palestinian Arabs – sent their armies to destroy
Israel.

The Egyptian secretary general of the Arab League, Abdul Rahman
Hassan Azzam, minced no words as to the goal of the invasion: "This will be
a war of extermination and a momentous massacre which will be spoken of
like the Mongolian massacres and the Crusades."[26]

The fledgling Israel Defense Forces fielded 65,000 soldiers (some 13 percent of the population) by mid-July 1948. This rose to 108,000 by January
1949.[27] The invasion force from the surrounding Arab countries consisted
of 20,000 combat troops. These were augmented by 40,000–50,000 troops

---

25   "Proclamation of Independence," Knesset.gov.il, accessed June 27, 2017, https://www.knesset.
gov.il/docs/eng/megilat_eng.htm.
26   Larry Collins and Dominique Lapierre, *O Jerusalem!* (New York: Simon and Schuster, 1972), 420.
The Arab League was founded expressly "to prevent the creation of a Jewish state in Palestine and
to conserve Palestine as a united, independent state, "ibid., 87. Historian and journalist Tom Segev,
who takes a revisionist approach to Zionist history, argues that Azzam actually made this statement
closer to October 11, 1947 and not on the eve of the Arab invasion on May 15, 1948 and that the
quote began with: "Personally, I hope the Jews do not force us into this war, because it would
be a war of extermination and momentous massacre..." Tom Segev, "The Makings of History, The
Blind Misleading the Blind," *Haaretz*, October 21, 2011, http://www.haaretz.com/israel-news/the-
makings-of-history-the-blind-misleading-the-blind-1.391260.
27   Benny Morris, *1948: A History of the First Arab-Israeli War* (New Haven, CT: Yale University
Press, 2009), 205.

from Yemen, Morocco, Saudi Arabia, and the Sudan. And this figure rose to 68,000 by October 1948.[28]

The highly motivated Jewish forces successfully pushed back the Arab onslaught. The effort to destroy the State of Israel at its birth was overcome.

The Israeli forces went on the offensive and gained strategically vital territory formerly granted to the Palestinian Arabs under the United Nations Partition Plan of 1947. Still, strategic Jewish settlements had to be abandoned; Jerusalem's Old City was lost. Some six thousand Israelis (one percent of the population) were killed; fifteen thousand were wounded.[29]

No Arab country was willing to sign an actual peace treaty, but in 1949, the UN brokered an armistice. The parties promised not to launch or permit the launching of attacks from their territory against each other. This pledge was not honored.[30] They furthermore agreed that the armistice lines were not a political border.

Israel's post-armistice line encompassed about 78 percent of the territory allocated the Jewish homeland under the mandate.

The pre-1947 Partition Plan boundaries with Egypt, Syria, and Lebanon were restored. Egypt had taken control of the Gaza Strip, which was to have been part of Arab Palestine. Jordan annexed Judea and Samaria, or the West Bank (contrary to the desires of Palestinian Arab nationalists and the Mufti). Thus, the West Bank and Gaza were under Arab control between 1949 and the 1967 Six-Day War. Jordan also ruled over the Old City of Jerusalem and its environs.

As a result of the war, two massive refugee problems ensued.

Arab policy was that Palestinian Arabs, made homeless by the war, would be kept permanently in refugee camps rather than be absorbed. The

28   Martin Van Creveld, *The Sword and the Olive: A Critical History of the Israeli Defense Force* (New York: Public Affairs, 1998), 78. Van Creveld, also a Zionist revisionist, writes, "Thus, even though the Arab countries outnumbered the Yishuv by better than forty-to-one, in terms of military manpower available for combat in Palestine the two sides were fairly evenly matches." But he does not deny that "the Arab armies were better organized and equipped..." (page 95).

29   "Israeli War of Independence: Background and Overview," Jewish Virtual Library, accessed July 17, 2017, http://www.jewishvirtuallibrary.org/background-and-overview-israel-war-of-independence.

30   From 1949 to 1956 alone about five hundred Israelis were killed in Arab fedayeen attacks. See "Major Arab Terrorist Attacks Against Israelis Prior to the 1967 Six-Day War," Israel Ministry of Foreign Affairs, accessed August 1, 2017, http://mfa.gov.il/MFA/ForeignPolicy/Terrorism/Palestinian/Pages/Which%20Came%20First-%20Terrorism%20or%20Occupation%20-%20Major.aspx; and "List of Attacks Against Israeli Civilians Before 1967," *Wikipedia*, modified June 23, 2017, https://en.wikipedia.org/wiki/List_of_attacks_against_Israeli_civilians_before_1967#Border_conflict.2C_1957-1967.

Arab states and the Palestinian Arabs refused to create a Palestinian state in the West Bank and Gaza because doing so might be seen as implying acceptance of Israel's right to exist.

According to UN figures, about 750,000 Palestinian Arabs fled, though, in a few instances, were forced out of Jewish-held areas.[31] In time, at least as many Jewish refugees fled Algeria, Egypt, Iraq, Libya, Morocco, Syria, Tunisia, and Yemen. Later in Iran, the 1979 Islamic Revolution led to the departure of most – some sixty thousand – of that country's Jews.[32]

---

31 "Palestine Refugees," UNRWA, accessed July 17, 2017, https://www.unrwa.org/palestine-refugees. Since both the Palestinian Arab leadership and the Arab League reject permanent resettlement of the refugees today, the descendants of the 1948 refugees number some five million souls, all permanently wards of UNRWA. For an unsentimental look at this issue, see Benny Morris, *The Birth of the Palestinian Refugee Problem Revisited* (Cambridge, UK: Cambridge University Press, 1988).

32 Ofer Aderet, "Israel Marks First-Ever National Day Remembering Jewish Exodus from Muslim lands," *Haaretz*, December 14, 2014, http://www.haaretz.com/jewish/.premium-1.629226. The article places the figure of displaced Jews at 850,000, all of whom have been permanently resettled.

Chapter 22

SOME FINAL WORDS

Historian E. H. Carr makes the point that what history is *not* – is the facts speaking for themselves.[1]

My purpose in writing this book is to help the curious reader make sense of the Balfour Declaration. I have provided context, surveyed the issues and sketched the key players. You'll also find a chronology in the appendix.

Like the US Constitution in 1787, the Balfour Declaration was the product of a unique set of circumstances. Providence brought together James Madison, Thomas Jefferson, and Alexander Hamilton in the same place, at the same time, and impelled them to work in concert.

Likewise, the Zionist cause was blessed with people of extraordinary caliber pulling in the same direction at a pivotal point in Jewish history. The Zionists were led by men – and backed by women – who were both visionary and wise with Chaim Weizmann, Nahum Sokolow, and Walter Rothschild at the helm buttressed by an astonishingly brilliant supporting cast.

Moreover, the Zionist campaign might have come to naught if not for the philo-Semites in the War Cabinet headed by David Lloyd George and Arthur James Balfour and their own supporting cast which included the likes of C. P. Scott and Mark Sykes.

And even all this brainpower and goodwill would most likely not have mattered were not a horrendous world war raging. The conflict was upending the international political system. When it ended Turkey lost the non-Turkish territories of the former Ottoman Empire including Palestine.[2]

With all that, the Balfour Declaration did not hand the Land of Israel to the Jews on a silver platter. It did, however, position them in a struggle that ultimately led to the creation of the State of Israel.

---

1 I recommend Edward Hallett Carr, *What is History?* (London: Palgrave, 2001) – a very short book that you will likely treasure for a long time. A fortieth anniversary edition is available.
2 Austria-Hungary, Germany, Russia, and Bulgaria also lost territory when the war ended.

"My personal hope," Balfour said at a luncheon in the presence of Rothschild on February 7, 1918, "is that the Jews will make good in Palestine and eventually found a Jewish State. It is up to them now; we have given them their opportunity."[3]

Balfour, Lloyd George, and the other members of the War Cabinet could not have envisaged that the declaration would be followed by unremitting Arab opposition to Zionism. After all, in reclaiming their ancestral homeland the Jews would be building on only a small sliver of Middle East territory. All of the rest would be in Muslim hands. And the Arab minority within the Jewish homeland would be guaranteed their civil rights.

Nor could Lloyd George and Balfour have foreseen how hurriedly their successors in government would work to undo their majestic commitment, notwithstanding that it was codified in international law by the San Remo Conference on April 25, 1920, and by the League of Nations on July 24, 1922.

Lamentably, Britain did not remain faithful to the Balfour Declaration. Once the unrelenting ferocity of Arab and Muslim opposition became plain, the British authorities did everything in their power to head off the establishment in Palestine of a national home for the Jewish people – or at least one that depended on a requisite Jewish majority. Already by 1921 the British authorities began limiting the number of Jews allowed to enter Palestine. At the same time, the flow of Arabs into Palestine went on unhindered.[4]

The Balfour Declaration was foremost an expression of British national interest during wartime. That imperial or colonial interests played some role in the declaration is transparently obvious. However, the Zionist enterprise was never part of any colonial "plot," and the Zionists were never privy to colonial machinations. Moreover, any fair-minded assessment of the declaration would acknowledge that it was the result of a confluence of historical factors.

Conspiracy mongers claim that Zionists acting behind the scenes manipulated the War Cabinet to obtain the Balfour Declaration at the expense of the Arabs. Actually, of all the deals made in WWI, the Balfour Declaration was singular in that it was not secret. Its pros and cons were debated in the cabinet. Once the declaration was issued it was publicly celebrated. The

---

3   Morris, *1948*, 10.
4   Joan Peters, *From Time Immemorial: The Origins of the Arab-Jewish Conflict Over Palestine* (New York: Harper and Row, 1984), 269–95.

intention to create a national home for the Jews in Palestine was not a scheme to undermine Arab interests in the Middle East. Indeed, Israel's future prime minister Menachem Begin came to suspect that, if anything, it was the Jews who were being manipulated.[5]

If the British goal was to thwart Arab self-determination, it didn't work out that way. Today, there are some twenty-two Arab states in the Middle East and one Israel. There is a Palestinian Arab majority in Jordan. Palestinian Arab citizens of Israel have all the rights and privileges of Jewish Israelis.[6] Plans by successive Israeli governments from Ehud Barak to Ariel Sharon and from Ehud Olmert to Benjamin Netanyahu to foster a demilitarized Palestinian state in the West Bank and Gaza Strip that recognizes the right of Israel to exist as a Jewish state have been repeatedly rebuffed by the Palestinian leadership.[7] Their intransigence makes a workable two-state solution ever more unlikely.

As we've seen, for present-day Balfour Declaration enemies – Abbas leading the charge – the only way for Britain to expiate its "original sin" of 1917 is to join those Arabs and their enablers who are seeking the dissolution

---

5   In Begin, Katz, and Greenberg, *The Revolt*, 32, a bitter Menachem Begin writing about the Irgun's armed struggle against the British in Palestine argues that Britain's "master plan" all along was to play "the ends against the middle" and had never been in genuine sync with Zionist interests.
6   Of course, Palestinian Arab citizens of twenty-first century Israel also have political and not just civil rights. The Joint List, an alliance of several Arab-dominated parties, holds 13 out of 120 Knesset seats making it the third largest faction in the twentieth Knesset. Palestinian Arabs in Jerusalem who are not citizens of Israel are eligible to vote in municipal elections. See Anshel Pfeffer, "After 50 years of Boycott, Palestinians Launch Party to Stand in Jerusalem Elections," *Jewish Chronicle*, July 10, 2017, https://www.thejc.com/news/israel/after-50-years-of-boycott-palestinians-launch-party-to-stand-in-jerusalem-elections-1.441224. In 2006, Arabs in the West Bank and Gaza voted in Palestinian elections and gave 76 of 132 seats in the Palestinian parliament to the Islamic Resistance Movement (Hamas). As a consequence, the Palestinian polity split violently in 2007 with Fatah controlling the West Bank and Hamas the Gaza Strip. In August 2005, Israel pulled its soldiers and civilians out of Gaza (home to 1.7 million Palestinians), see "The World Factbook: Gaza Strip," Central Intelligence Agency, June 21, 2017, accessed July 17, 2017, https://www.cia.gov/library/publications/the-world-factbook/geos/gz.html. While the future of the West Bank or Judea and Samaria remains contested, most Palestinian cities and towns there are governed by the Palestinian Authority. There are 2.7 million Arabs and 600,000 Jews living beyond the 1949 armistice lines in the West Bank and Jerusalem, see "The World Factbook: West Bank," Central Intelligence Agency, accessed July 17, 2017, https://www.cia.gov/library/publications/the-world-factbook/geos/we.html. Finally, there are 6.4 million Jewish and 1.8 million Arab (Muslim and Christian) citizens of Israel as of 2017, see Ofer Aderet, "Israel's Population Hits 8.7 Million on Eve of 69th Independence Day," *Haaretz*, May 1, 2017, http://www.haaretz.com/israel-news/1.786140.
7   Barak Ravid, "Netanyahu Tells Saban Forum: Solution Is Not One State, but a Demilitarized Palestinian State," *Haaretz*, December 6, 2015, http://www.haaretz.com/israel-news/.premium-1.690355. See, also, Head to Head, "Transcript: Saeb Erekat," *Al Jazeera English*, April 2, 2014, accessed July 17, 2017, http://www.aljazeera.com/programmes/headtohead/2014/03/transcript-dr-saeb-erekat-201432611433441126.html.

of the Jewish state by means of boycotts, divestments, lawfare and sanctions.[8]

If all the Balfour Declaration dots don't connect like the conspiracy theorists want, it's because in politics and history, just like in real life, humans are motivated by a multitude of factors, intentional and unintentional, conscious and subconscious, purposeful and contradictory. Politicians, diplomats and strategists operate in environments of uncertainty; their information is imperfect.

We know the War Cabinet had a genuine desire to help persecuted Jews. Balfour believed that the Christian world owed a moral debt to Jewish civilization over centuries of persecution and contempt.[9]

We also know that the British leadership had a rather inflated view of global Jewish influence. London wanted a tottering Russia to stay in the Great War and for America to accelerate its just-started military involvement in the European fighting. Britain hoped the declaration would encourage Jews in those countries to sway their governments. Winning the war was an absolute British national need. Moreover, Palestine straddles three continents. Its proximity to the Suez Canal alone made it vital strategically to protecting British interests in India. A Jewish homeland in Palestine provided legitimacy to a British presence there.

Besides, with World War I underway everyone appreciated that the Ottoman Empire which controlled Palestine would eventually be dismembered. This being the case, Zionist campaigners led by Weizmann (and Jabotinsky operating on a different plain) thought that Britain was best positioned to serve as a catalyst for a Jewish return to Palestine – one that would be sanctioned by the international community. And so it was. The League of Nations Mandate for Palestine was ratified by fifty-two member governments. Indeed, the mandate explicitly required Britain to implement the Balfour Declaration.

Apart from pursuing its own national interests, let's acknowledge that London also tried to act equitably. It backed the idea of the establishment in

---

8   BDS is the 1945 Arab League boycott (put in place even before Israel was established) warmed over and rebranded. For an overview, see Nancy Turck, "The Arab Boycott of Israel," *Foreign Affairs*, April 1977, https://www.foreignaffairs.com/articles/middle-east/1977-04-01/middle-east-arab-boycott-israel.

9   And let's not forget that life for Jews was hardly rosier in Muslim and Arab lands. Two books that I can recommend on this topic are: Bernard Lewis, *The Jews of Islam* (Princeton, NJ: Princeton University Press, 2014), and Martin Gilbert, *In Ishmael's House: A History of Jews in Muslim Lands* (New Haven, CT: Yale University Press, 2011).

Palestine of a national home for the Jewish people with a proviso aimed to protect Arab religious and civil rights.

What we can say is that the Balfour Declaration did indeed, in a matter of three decades, help to pave the way for a Jewish national homeland in Palestine. It did not happen in the way its framers envisioned, it required a violent shove from the Jewish underground in Palestine, and it became a reality only after much of European Jewry had been annihilated in the Shoah – yet the Balfour Declaration did come to fruition.

With all its lurches and imperfections, surely, Lloyd George, Balfour and their comrades would have been gratified to have seen Britain establish diplomatic relations with Israel as it did on April 28, 1950.

Let us end where we began – with Mahmoud Abbas's "lawsuit."

It is premised on the view that the Arabs oppose the very idea of a national homeland for the Jews anywhere in the Middle East. On the narrow question of whether the Arab-Israel conflict is about boundaries and settlements or about the visceral rejection of even the most moderate Arab leaders to the legitimacy of a Jewish state there can be no wiggle room, in my view. Abbas's threatened litigation regarding the Balfour Declaration makes this plain.

THE BALFOUR DECLARATION TIMELINE: 1897–1949

Backstory: Destruction of the Second Temple to the First Zionist Congress

1250 BCE	Conquest of Canaan under Joshua.
586 BCE	Destruction of Jerusalem and First Temple; mass deportation to Babylonia.
445 BCE	Exiles from Babylon return to rebuild Jerusalem's walls; Ezra reads the Torah.
70 CE	Romans destroy Second Temple; beginning of the exile.
638	Arabs conquer Jerusalem.
1096	Christian Crusaders capture Jerusalem.
September 27, 1791	Jews of France emancipated, heralding the possibility of Jews integrating into general community.
May 2, 1860	Theodor Herzl born in Budapest.
October 11, 1860	First Hebrew newspaper in Russian Empire *Ha-Melitz* (The Interpreter) begins publication in Odessa as a weekly.
1862	Moses Hess writes early Zionist polemic "Rome and Jerusalem."
1870	Mikveh Israel, first Jewish agricultural school in Eretz Yisrael, founded.
1874	Zvi Hirsch Kalischer, ultra-Orthodox German rabbi who advocated resettlement of Eretz Yisrael, dies. Most rabbis held that full-scale return to the Land of Israel must wait until the Messiah comes.

November 27, 1874	Chaim Weizmann born in Motol, White Russia.
1878	Petah Tikva (ten kilometers from Tel Aviv) and Gai Oni, the first two agricultural settlements, founded.
1881	Government-inspired pogroms in Russia following assassination of Tsar Alexander II.
1881	Eliezer Ben-Yehuda, considered the father of Modern Hebrew, arrives in Palestine.
July 6, 1882	First group of Bilu settlers arrives in Palestine as part of wave that becomes known as the First Aliyah. Unlike the Old Yishuv of established Orthodox Palestinian Jews who subsisted on charity, new arrivals are pioneers who want to build a new Jewish society.
1882	Zionist theoretician Leon Pinsker publishes *Auto-Emancipation*.
July 31, 1882	Rishon LeZion, the first moshava (village), founded.
October 18, 1882	Joseph Feinberg from Rishon LeZion meets Baron Edmond de Rothschild in Paris.
1884	Moshava of Gedera founded; Hadera and Rehovot founded in 1890.
November 6–8, 1884	Hovevei Zion (Lovers of Zion) hold first international Zionist convention in Kattowitz, Poland; Leon Pinsker voted to head it.
July 9, 1885	An MP since 1865, Nathaniel Mayer "Natty" de Rothschild elevated to the House of Lords, becoming the first Lord Rothschild.
1891	Jewish Colonization Association incorporated in London by Baron Maurice de Hirsch of Paris.
1894	Theodor Herzl covers the Dreyfus Affair in Paris for Viennese newspaper *Neue Freie Presse*.
January 4, 1895	Dreyfus court-martialed and publicly degraded after wrongful conviction.
June 1896	Herzl visits Constantinople for first time. Meets with Grand Vizier Khalil Rifat Pasha and other officials and proposes plan to finance Turkey's debt in return for turning Palestine over to the Jews. The grand vizier is unenthusiastic.
1896	Herzl publishes *Der Judenstaat* (The Jewish State), articulating the case for modern political Zionism and its plan for the return of the Jewish people to Eretz Yisrael; Jewish settlement conceived as managed and financed

	from London, framed under English law and under the protection of England.
August 18, 1896	Herzl sees Baron Edmond de Rothschild in Paris. The Baron unconvinced Herzl's plan is workable.
March 6, 1897	Herzl meets with Hovevei Zion representatives. Pushes for convening a Zionist congress.
June 4, 1897	First issue of Zionist newspaper *Die Welt* (The World), which will serve as Herzl's platform.
July 9, 1897	Reform rabbis meeting in Montreal issue strong statement against an independent Jewish state.
August 29–31, 1897	First Zionist Congress held in Basel, Switzerland, urges "a publicly and legally assured home in Palestine" for Jews and establishes the World Zionist Organization. Theodor Herzl elected president.

Herzl's Last Seven Years

September 10, 1897	Reform Rabbi Isaac M. Wise of Cincinnati, Ohio, writes in the *New York Times*: "a Jewish state nowadays 'impossible.'"
November 14, 1897	Anglo-Jewish writer and leader Israel Zangwill (1864–1926) defends Zionist idea in the *New York Times*.
August 28–31, 1898	Second Zionist Congress held in Basel.
October 18, 1898	Herzl meets Kaiser Wilhelm II in Constantinople.
October 1898	Kaiser Wilhelm II visits the Holy Land, dedicates three Lutheran/Protestant churches in Jerusalem.
October 28, 1898	Herzl greets Kaiser Wilhelm II at the gate of Mikveh Israel Agricultural School.
November 2, 1898	Herzl and other members of small Zionist delegation meet Kaiser Wilhelm II at his encampment in Jerusalem.
January 30, 1899	US diplomats estimate Jews comprise forty thousand out of population of two hundred thousand in Palestine, the *New York Times* reports.
March 20, 1899	Jewish Colonial Trust incorporated in London; intended to be the financial instrument of the Zionist Organization.
August 15–18, 1899	Third Zionist Congress held in Basel.
October 1899	Ottoman Turkey requires all visiting Jews to leave Palestine within ninety days after entering, according to the *New York Times*.

August 13–16, 1900	Fourth Zionist Congress held in London.
January 20, 1901	Sultan of Turkey renews decree forbidding Jews to remain in Palestine for longer than ninety days, the *New York Times* reports.
April 10, 1901	New York Jews raise money for Jewish farm laborers in Palestine, the *New York Times* reports.
May 30, 1901	Theodor Herzl has several audiences with Sultan Abdul Hamid II regarding Palestine colonization plan in return for Turkish debt relief.
December 26–30, 1901	Fifth Zionist Congress held in Basel.
December 29, 1901	Jewish National Fund established.
March 1902	Mizrachi Orthodox Zionist movement founded in Vilna.
July 4, 1902	Herzl meets Lord Rothschild (Nathaniel Mayer de) to promote Zionism.
July 7, 1902	Herzl testifies before Royal Commission on Alien Immigration to England; urges liberalization to allow refuge for persecuted Russian Jews.
August 12, 1902	Herzl back in Turkey to lobby Ottoman officials.
October 22–23, 1902	Herzl meets British colonial secretary Joseph Chamberlain; discusses Cyprus or El Arish in Sinai as safe havens.
October 30, 1902	Herzl publishes his utopian novel *Altneuland* (The Old New Land) set in Palestine.
November 10, 1902	New York Zionists collect three thousand dollars in Shekel Day campaign spearheaded by Reform Rabbi Stephen Wise.
December 30, 1902	Pro- and anti-Zionist speakers address Jewish audience on New York City's Lower East Side.
March 1903	Herzl sends study group to Sinai to explore viability of El Arish plan.
April 1903	Kishinev pogroms. Between 1903 and 1906 pogroms throughout Russian Empire kill some two thousand Jews.
April 23, 1903	Herzl meets Joseph Chamberlain in London to discuss safe haven. Chamberlain raises idea of Uganda territory. Herzl presses for Palestine area.
May 1903	Jewish National Fund takes ownership of two hundred dunams in Hadera from Yitzhak Goldberg of Vilna; it becomes the first parcel of land owned by the Zionist movement.

July 26, 1903	Anglo-Palestine Bank opens in Jaffa.
August 1903	Herzl travels in Russian Empire visiting Jewish communities and meeting tsar's interior minister, Vyacheslav Plehve, suspected of organizing pogroms.
August 24, 1903	Sixth Zionist Congress held in Basel. Uganda proposal for settlement in East Africa splits the Congress.
September 27, 1903	President Theodore Roosevelt accepts Jewish flag from the Zionists of Baltimore, according to the *New York Times*.
1904	Start of Second Aliyah, which lasts until 1914, bringing some forty thousand mostly Russian Jews into Ottoman-controlled Palestine.
January 22, 1904	Herzl meets Cardinal Merry del Val, Vatican's secretary of state.
January 23, 1904	Herzl sees Italian king Victor Emmanuel III, who is sympathetic to the Zionist idea.
January 25, 1904	Herzl meets with Pope Pius X requesting support for the Zionist enterprise. Says the pope: "As long as the Jews deny the divinity of Christ we certainly cannot make a declaration in their favor; not that we have any ill will towards them."
February 1904	Zionists send study group to Transjordan.
April 1904	Stormy Zionist meetings over Uganda refuge plan.
July 3, 1904	Theodor Herzl dies in Austria.

The Chaim Weizmann Era

July 27, 1905	Seventh Zionist Congress in Basel formally rejects Uganda project; David Wolffsohn elected president.
November 13, 1905	In a letter to English Zionist Federation, Prime Minister Balfour expresses horror over massacres of Jews in Russia.
November 1905	David Ben-Gurion and Yitzhak Ben-Zvi establish Poale Zion, Marxist-Zionist Jewish workers' union in Palestine.
1905	Aliens Act in England aimed at limiting Jewish immigration championed by Balfour despite his sympathy for persecuted Russian Jewry.
1905	Herbert Samuel becomes first Jewish Under-Secretary of State for the Home Department.

November 23, 1905	Press reports of many Jews going to Palestine because of ongoing persecution in Russia.
January 2, 1906	Hebrew high school established in Jaffa; Bezalel art school founded in March.
January 5, 1906	All Russian Congress of Zionist organizations meets in Helsingfors (Helsinki) to unify and strategize.
January 9, 1906	Weizmann, who'd arrived in England in 1904, introduced by Charles Dreyfus, chairman of the Manchester Zionist Society, to Conservative prime minister Arthur James Balfour during PM's visit to his Manchester constituency. They meet at the Queen's Hotel on Piccadilly (Balfour's campaign headquarters).
December 9, 1906	Leo Tolstoy writes against the Zionist idea; pleads for common humanity, the *New York Times* reports.
January 1, 1907	Eighth Congress meets in The Hague. Decides to open Palestine branch in Jaffa led by Arthur Ruppin to facilitate agricultural settlement and development.
January 1, 1907	First Hebrew-language weekly, *Ha'Olam*, appears in Germany under Nahum Sokolow's editorship.
January 10, 1907	David Wolffsohn, president of the Zionist movement, visits Palestine.
February 1907	David Wolffsohn visits Constantinople and meets Grand Vizier Farid Pasha.
July 2, 1907	Zionist movement plans bank whose profits will be used to develop Palestine industries, the *New York Times* reports.
August 1, 1907	David Wolffsohn is elected president of the World Zionist Organization.
August 23, 1907	Jewish banker and philanthropist Jacob H. Schiff does not believe a Jew can be a true American and a good Zionist at the same time, according to the *New York Times*. A practitioner of Reform Judaism, Schiff nonetheless comes to support cultural Zionism.
September 1907	Chaim Weizmann makes first visit to Palestine. He finds the country in a state of miserable neglect. The total population is about six hundred thousand of which eighty thousand are Jews. He returns to England on October 10, 1907.
October 1907	David Wolffsohn pays another visit to Constantinople for meetings with Turkish officials.

March 16, 1908	Violence breaks out between Arabs and Jews in Jaffa.
May 4, 1908	Joseph Cowen, a London Zionist leader and a founder of the Jewish Colonial Trust, pleads for aid to found a state in Palestine, the *New York Times* reports.
July 24, 1908	Young Turk Revolution restores constitutional era and raises Zionist hopes for cooperation.
April 11, 1909	Tel Aviv founded on sand dunes near Jaffa.
April 12, 1909	First Jewish self-defense group, Hashomer, organized in Tel Aviv. Bar Giora, secret guard society, founded in September 1907, was a founding component of Hashomer.
1909	Kibbutz Deganya, first communal settlement, founded in the Jordan Valley just south of the Sea of Galilee.
1909	Young Judaea, a Zionist youth movement, founded.
1909	Herbert Samuel becomes first Jewish cabinet minister after appointment by Prime Minister Herbert Asquith.
April 23, 1909	British Chief Rabbi Hermann Adler argues that since destruction of the Temple, Jews no longer constitute a nation and are exclusively a religious community.
June 13, 1909	Young Turk Revolution the previous year gives Zionists hope, the *New York Times* reports.
June 1909	David Wolffsohn back in Constantinople on his third visit. Also in Constantinople, Ze'ev Jabotinsky appointed editor of four Zionist journals.
July 26, 1909	A Jewish visitor to Turkey, novelist Herman Bernstein, reports: "Zionist prospects of obtaining autonomy in Palestine under the new Young Turks' constitutional regime even less hopeful than under Sultan Abdul Hamid."
December 26, 1909	Ninth Zionist Congress, held in Hamburg, promotes idea of cooperative settlements.
January 17, 1910	In Jerusalem, four-fifths of the population of one hundred thousand are Jewish, according to the *New York Times*.
August 9, 1911	Tenth Zionist Congress held in Basel; Otto Warburg elected president. Sessions conducted in Hebrew for first time. Headquarters relocated from Berlin to Cologne.
December 13, 1911	Palestinian Jews create the nucleus of a health system (Kupat Holim Clalit).
March 3, 1912	Henrietta Szold establishes women's Zionist organization Hadassah in New York.

April 11, 1912	Dedication in Haifa of what will become the Technion – Israel Institute of Technology.
May 19, 1912	Reform Rabbi Judah Leon Magnes addresses the Federation of American Zionists at Cooper Union in New York, encourages all Jews to settle in Palestine.
September 1, 1912	US Jewish philanthropist Nathan Straus embraces Zionism after visiting Palestine.
September 13, 1912	News reports suggest Turkey willing to grant Palestinian Jews autonomy.
September 28, 1912	The *Times* correspondent in Constantinople cautions against sympathy for Zionism or else goodwill of Arabs will be lost.
December 30, 1912	Writing from London in the *New York Times* Dr. Max Nordau, president of the Tenth Zionist Congress, argues that the Balkan War presaged partition of the Turkish Empire and that European powers should embrace the Zionist scheme for resettling the Jews in Palestine.
April 1, 1913	Central Union of German Citizens of the Jewish Faith issues resolution dissociating from Jewish nationalism.
September 2–9, 1913	Chaim Weizmann, speaking at the Eleventh Zionist Congress in Vienna, announces one hundred thousand dollars raised to establish a Hebrew University in Jerusalem.
1914	Nahum Sokolow arrives in England as member of Zionist Executive. He and Weizmann form strong partnership.
February 1914	Baron Edmond de Rothschild visits Palestine for the first time in fifteen years and praises Zionist achievements.
April 14, 1914	Nafik Bey Hakim, Arab nationalist writing in *Al-Muqattan*, Cairo, says Arab public opinion opposes creation of a Jewish state.
June 1914	Plans for Palestinian Jews and Arabs to hold a joint conference outside Beirut with Nahum Sokolow to lead the Zionist delegation. The meeting does not take place.

The Great War: A World Torn Asunder

June 28, 1914	Archduke Franz Ferdinand, heir presumptive to the Austro-Hungarian throne, assassinated in Sarajevo setting off a series of events that will lead to World War I.

July 12, 1914	Henry Morgenthau, US ambassador in Constantinople, makes extensive trip through Palestine escorted by Turkish officials.
August 1, 1914	Outbreak of World War I. Britain declares war on Germany. US president Woodrow Wilson declares policy of US neutrality. Jewish world geographically divided among warring parties. Zionist programs paralyzed.
August 28, 1914	Zionists celebrate victory of Hebrew language over German in Palestinian schools, the 1914–1915 *American Jewish Year Book* reports.
September 2, 1914	US Zionists organize aid relief to Palestinian Jews said to be starving as a result of Turkey's cutting financial relations with Europe.
September 8, 1914	Fate of foreign nationals in Turkey thrown into doubt, leaving Palestinian Jews fearing deportation.
September 16, 1914	Weizmann writes telling Ahad Ha'Am that *Manchester Guardian* editor C. P. Scott is willing to champion Zionism: "He carries great weight and may be useful." Weizmann's chance meeting with Scott occurs when he accompanies Vera Weizmann to afternoon tea at the home of her professional acquaintance.
October 29, 1914	Turkey enters the war on the side of the Central Powers. Mass exodus of Jews from Palestine.
November 5, 1914	Britain declares war on Turkey. Dismemberment of Turkey is a war aim, says PM Asquith on November 9.
November 9, 1914	Herbert Samuel talks to British foreign secretary Sir Edward Grey about Palestine's fate should Ottoman Empire collapse. Samuel raises idea of "fulfilling the ancient ambitions of the Jewish people and re-establishing a Jewish state."
November 22, 1914	*Manchester Guardian* editor C. P. Scott writes to Weizmann: "There are so few people who have the courage of an ideal and at the same time the insight and energy which make it possible."
November 29, 1914	C. P. Scott to Weizmann: "I saw Lloyd George on Friday (November 27) and spoke about the Palestine question. It was not new to him, as he had been reading the *New Statesman* [pro-Zionist] article and talking to Herbert Samuel."
December 3, 1914	Weizmann has interview with Chancellor of the Exchequer Lloyd George.

December 10, 1914	With C. P. Scott's help, Chaim Weizmann meets Herbert Samuel in London.
December 11, 1914	Turkey cracks down on Jews but agrees to allow relief aid raised in US Jewish community for one hundred thousand Palestinian Jews to enter the country.
December 12, 1914	Weizmann meets Arthur James Balfour.
December 14, 1914	Weizmann writes to Ahad Ha'Am about the interview with Balfour, who admired Weizmann's assertiveness on Zionism.
December 28, 1914	Chaim Weizmann meets Baron Edmond de Rothschild in Paris.
December 31, 1914	Zionist leaders Nahum Sokolow and Yechiel Tschlenow arrive in London and join forces with Weizmann.
January 1915	Herbert Samuel presents a memorandum to the British cabinet on the future of Palestine arguing the benefits of a British protectorate over Palestine and support for Jewish immigration.
January 1915	Key Zionist activists in Palestine including Joseph Trumpeldor, David Ben-Gurion, and Yitzhak Ben-Zvi are forced to leave the country by Turkish authorities.
January 2, 1915	Jewish National Fund given to understand Turkey is willing to sell land to Jews in Palestine.
January 11, 1915	Herbert Samuel to Chaim Weizmann: "Mr. Lloyd George... would be very glad if you would breakfast with him next Friday."
January 15, 1915	Weizmann and Samuel breakfast with Lloyd George. Weizmann uses talking points he gets from C. P. Scott.
January 19, 1915	Persecuted by Turkey, Palestinian Jews flee to Egypt, six thousand to Alexandria.
February 2, 1915	Turkey said to be inciting Arabs to attack Jews.
March 5, 1915	US diplomats report Jews in Palestine as "naturally inconvenienced" but perfectly safe.
March 1915	Weizmann meets Balfour.
March 1915	Herbert Samuel revamps memo; now entitled "Palestine," it is distributed to cabinet.
March 1915	Vladimir Ze'ev Jabotinsky arrives in Alexandria, Egypt, and joins Joseph Trumpeldor in planning to create a Jewish Legion to fight the Turks. The British agree only to permit

the creation of a Zion Mule Corps initially tasked with logistical duties, commanded by Colonel Henry Patterson.

March 16, 1915	Edwin Montagu, Chancellor of the Duchy of Lancaster and Herbert Samuel's cousin, writes a detailed critique of Samuel's pro-Zionist memo to PM Asquith.
March 21, 1915	Weizmann writes to Samuel about C. P. Scott's view that "events are shaping in favour of a British Palestine."
March 31, 1915	Nathaniel Mayer de Rothschild dies. Apparently, the first Lord Rothschild was converted to Zionism shortly before his death.
April-May, 1915	Avshalom Feinberg and Aaron Aaronsohn organize Palestinian Jewish NILI espionage ring to aid British war effort against Ottomans.
April 14, 1915	Zionists and Conjoint meet. Zionists fail to persuade Conjoint British Jewish leaders to back the Zionist platform.
April 26, 1915	Secret agreement between Britain, France, Russia, and Italy to divide up the Ottoman Empire.
May 7, 1915	*RMS Lusitania* on way from New York City to Britain sunk by German submarines. A British passenger ship also carrying munitions. Some 1,201 aboard drowned, including 128 Americans.
May 25, 1915	Coalition government formed by British premier Herbert Asquith as tensions rise over his handling of the war.
June 7, 1915	Lloyd George briefly interviews Weizmann for position in Ministry of Munitions; he is tasked with developing economical way to produce acetone.
September 1915	Weizmann moves to London where Ahad Ha'Am is already living. He shares a flat in Chelsea with Vladimir Jabotinsky.
October 24, 1915	Sir Henry McMahon writes to Sharif Hussein bin Ali of the Hashemite family of Mecca pledging the British government to recognize and support independence of the Arabs in return for Arab uprising against Ottoman Turks. No reference to Palestine.
November 21, 1915	US Consul in Jerusalem reports plague of locusts has devastated Palestine.
November 23, 1915	Sir Mark Sykes and François Georges-Picot begin their negotiations over post-war division of Mashriq (Middle East excluding North Africa). Parts of Palestine would be international zone.

November 26, 1915	*Manchester Guardian* leader argues friendly Palestine is in Britain's strategic interest.
December 1, 1915	Weizmann writes to C. P. Scott saying his position in Munitions Ministry becoming untenable and his experiments mishandled.
December 24, 1915	The *New York Morning Journal* reports eight members of the British cabinet favor establishment of a strong Jewish settlement in Palestine after the war.
January 23, 1916	Weizmann, Joseph Cowen, Vladimir Jabotinsky, Nahum Sokolow, Ahad Ha'Am, and other leading Zionists meet in London to plan strategy.
January 24, 1916	Reform Rabbi Stephen Wise says: "I know I can be a loyal American...and still insist I am a Jew.... Zionism is not a religion...but it is touched by the spirit of religion."
January 27, 1916	US president Woodrow Wilson endorses charity campaign to aid Jewish war sufferers, designating this "Jewish Relief Day."
January 28, 1916	President Wilson announces nomination of Louis D. Brandeis, a key Zionist leader, to the US Supreme Court.
February 6, 1916	Shipment of medicines sent to Palestine aboard US warship *Collier Sterling* by the Central Committee for the Relief of Jews Suffering through the War.
February 19, 1916	The Distribution Committee of the Jewish Relief Fund sends $142,000 for Palestine relief work.
February 26, 1916	Sir Mark Sykes writes to Herbert Samuel: "I imagine that the principal object of Zionism is the realization of the ideal of an existing centre of nationality rather than boundaries or extent of territory."
March 13, 1916	Jews plan a demand for rights after war; national union in London organized to secure the rights of Jews.
March 15, 1916	Russian foreign minister Sergei Sazonov views the settlement of the Jews in Palestine with sympathy.
March 1916	Weizmann sees Balfour at Mrs. Waldorf Astor's luncheon.
March 25, 1916	Merchants in New York give to war relief; Jewish bazaar raises $150,000 in goods.
March 26, 1916	Louis D. Brandeis addresses Philadelphia Zionist meeting on Jewish rights.
March 27, 1916	Tens of thousands participate in New York Jewish war relief fair featuring Palestine street scene. Function nets $75,000.

April 1916	Sykes-Picot Agreement: Pending approval from British Foreign Minister Edward Grey, France (François Georges-Picot) and Britain (Sir Mark Sykes) concur on division of Ottoman Empire. Eretz Yisrael (Palestine) to be divided with France controlling Galilee and Britain the Haifa area, with rest of country under international control. No British commitments to the Arabs made regarding Palestine. Deal worries Zionists (when they become aware of it).
May 1916	British disband Zion Mule Corps after the Gallipoli campaign. Jabotinsky persists in efforts to create Jewish Legion.
May 16, 1916	Sykes-Picot Agreement: Foreign Minister Grey on behalf of Britain ratifies division of Ottoman Empire. In Palestine, France controlling Galilee, Britain Haifa; Jerusalem under international control; talks had begun in October 1915.
June 1916	In a process beginning in 1915, Britain offers in the McMahon-Hussein correspondence to give Arabia to the Arabs if the Arabs fight the Turks. Palestine is excluded.
August 17, 1916	Weizmann meets British Jewish figure Lucien Wolf at the home of James de Rothschild; accepts he will not win Wolf over to the Zionist cause.
September 20, 1916	Turkish governor expels Arthur Ruppin, head of Zionist office in Palestine; he works with the British from Egypt.
September 30, 1916	Sokolow is charged by the executive of the English Zionist Federation with writing a document on Palestine which will eventually be presented to the British government.
October 9, 1916	Aaron Aaronson arrives in London and offers the British the services of NILI.
October 9, 1916	Sokolow presents "Outline of Program for the Jewish Resettlement of Palestine" to the English Zionist Federation executive.
November 18, 1916	Battle of the Somme ends; with approximately 1.5 million casualties, it will be remembered as one of the bloodiest military operations in history.
November 28, 1916	First non-zeppelin bombing of central London by a fixed-wing aircraft; German biplane drops six bombs near Victoria station.
December 1916	Sharif of Mecca declares himself king of the Arabs.
December 7, 1916	Asquith resigns; Lloyd George becomes prime minister.
December 7, 1916	Mark Sykes begins a pro-Zionist initiative due to a more

receptive government coalition headed by Lloyd George and Balfour.

December 11, 1916   Lloyd George establishes a War Cabinet.

Fateful Year: Countdown to the Balfour Declaration

January 17, 1917   British eavesdroppers intercept secret telegram from German foreign minister Arthur Zimmerman and use it as part of elaborate operation to bring US into war on Britain's side.

January 24, 1917   Jabotinsky's plan for a Jewish military force submitted. Military echelon unenthusiastic.

January 24, 1917   James de Rothschild meets Sykes.

January 28, 1917   Weizmann meets Sykes for first time accompanied by the *Jewish Chronicle* editor Leopold Greenberg and James Malcolm, who is campaigning on behalf of the Armenians.

January 30, 1917   Moses Gaster, the haham of the Spanish and Portuguese Jewish congregation in London, records in his diary that Sykes told him the Zionists should have men on the spot when the British enter Jerusalem.

January 31, 1917   Mark Sykes given a redrafted memorandum of Zionist views.

February 7, 1917   Meeting with Sykes at home of Moses Gaster; attending are Zionist leaders Herbert Samuel, Weizmann, Sokolow, Lord Rothschild, James de Rothschild, Joseph Cowen, Harry Sacher, and Herbert Bentwich.

February 8, 1917   Sykes introduces Sokolow to Picot, who tells him the future of Palestine will have to be decided between France, Russia, and Britain.

February 10, 1917   Weizmann and Sokolow discuss the latter's meeting with Picot.

February 10, 1917   Sykes, Sokolow, and Weizmann meet at Sykes's residence to review the situation.

February 11, 1917   Weizmann elected president of English Zionist Federation. James de Rothschild pledges five hundred pounds.

February 11, 1917   C. P. Scott writes to Weizmann that Foreign Office is pessimistic about French willingness to renounce claims to Palestine.

February 12, 1917   Jewish Workmen for Peace National Committee meeting at *Forward* newspaper building in New York adopts anti-war appeal to President Wilson.

February 1917	British troops capture much of Sinai Peninsula.
March 11, 1917	British troops capture Baghdad.
March 13, 1917	Chaim Weizmann breakfasts with C. P. Scott; asks for help in getting to see Lloyd George.
March 8–15, 1917	*[Russian Calendar, February 23]* Russian Revolution (part one). Tsar Nicholas II abdicates. Kerensky becomes new political leader of a democratic state.
March 17, 1917	Discriminatory Pale of Jewish Settlement in Russia abolished by new Russian revolutionary regime.
March 20, 1917	Weizmann to C. P. Scott: "The Zionist negotiations with Sir Mark Sykes are entering upon their final stages."
March 20, 1917	Churches in England warn medications in short supply in Palestine, the *New York Times* reports.
March 22, 1917	Weizmann has serious practical talk with Balfour, now foreign minister, on Zionism and a possible French or American role in Palestine.
March 26–28, 1917	British troops make failed attempt to capture the Gaza Strip. As a result, Turks order Jews in Jaffa to evacuate northwards.
March 28, 1917	Turkish authorities expel Jews from Jaffa and Tel Aviv.
March 30, 1917	*Daily Chronicle* leader: "The project for constituting a Zionist state under British protection has much to commend it."
March 30, 1917	Battle for Gaza under way against twenty thousand Turkish troops.
April 3, 1917	Lloyd George tells Weizmann and C. P. Scott that the British Army's advance into Palestine was the one really interesting part of the war.
April 3, 1917	Lloyd George and British Conservative statesman Lord [George Nathaniel] Curzon meet Sykes on the eve of his departure for Middle East and tell him no pledges should be given to the Arabs concerning Palestine.
April 3, 1917	Weizmann meets Lloyd George for breakfast. Premier opposes arrangement with France, suggests joint control of Palestine between Britain and the United States.
April 4, 1917	British churches appeal for funds to stave off civilian starvation in Palestine.
April 4, 1917	Sykes to Weizmann: "Be ready to leave London for Egypt as soon as Gaza Strip is captured from Turks."

April 4, 1917	Weizmann writes to Sokolow that Lloyd George is "emphatic on the point of British Palestine."
April 4, 1917	Zionist view is that fall of Russian tsar simplifies Big Power contest in Palestine favoring Britain over France.
April 4, 1917	Russian Jews granted equality by Russian revolutionary Kerensky government.
April 6, 1917	The United States of America declares war on Germany. The impetus for a reluctant Woodrow Wilson was the February 1, 1917 German decision to resume unrestricted submarine warfare and revelations connected to the Zimmerman telegram.
April 6, 1917	British troops make another failed attempt to capture Gaza.
April 6, 1917	Sykes sees Picot in Paris and begins to break news that England wants suzerainty over Palestine. Picot had been slated to be appointed French high commissioner for Palestine and Syria.
April 8, 1917	Weizmann writes to Brandeis to update him on recent meetings with Balfour and Lloyd George and asks that he lobby US government to support Zionism.
April 9, 1917	Sokolow meets high-ranking French officials in Paris; reports the Zionists project is welcomed enthusiastically.
April 14, 1917	Sokolow tells Alliance Israélite (which opposes political Zionism) that the Zionists do not desire a state and would be satisfied to be subjects of the protecting power.
April 1917	Mid-month, Chaim Weizmann becomes aware of the hitherto secret Sykes-Picot agreement.
April 17, 1917	Yet another British assault on Gaza is repelled.
April 19, 1917	Sokolow writes to Weizmann about his meeting with French representatives. "I was told they accept in principle the recognition of Jewish nationality in terms of a national home, local autonomy, etc."
April 19, 1917	Sub-committee of War Cabinet meets to consider British territorial claims at the end of the war. Lord Curzon suggests that Palestine should be included in a British protectorate. General Jan Smuts states Britain needs to secure command in Palestine.
April 20, 1917	Lloyd George says the French will have to accept a British protectorate in Palestine as Britain shall be there by conquest, and shall remain.
April 20, 1917	Armenian lobbyist James Malcolm writes to Weizmann.

April 22, 1917	Balfour arrives in Washington following America's entry into the war.
April 23, 1917	British War Cabinet fatefully decides to carry on campaign to bring Palestine permanently under British control.
April 23, 1917	Weizmann sends a memorandum to Philip Henry Kerr, a member of Lloyd George's secretariat.
April 24, 1917	Pending decision on new British offensive, a gloomy Sykes cables Sokolow and Jabotinsky from Cairo.
April 25, 1917	Foreign Minister Balfour in Washington; his discussions raise Zionist hopes.
April 25, 1917	Lord Robert Cecil, under-secretary of state for foreign affairs, tells Weizmann he would like to see world Jewry speak out for British control in Palestine.
April 25, 1917	Turkish troops halt British advance in Palestine, the *New York Times* reports.
April 28, 1917	Weizmann tells Sokolow to drop talks with the French.
April 29, 1917	Sokolow in Rome (at French suggestion) is received at the Vatican by Monsignor Pacelli (uncle of the future Pope Pius XII, who led the Church during WWII) who questions him about Zionist attitudes toward the holy places.
April 30, 1917	Sokolow meets Vatican Secretary of State Cardinal Gasparri to discuss the holy places the Church plans to claim. Gasparri: "I assure you…you may count on our sympathy. We shall be glad to see the Land of Israel."
May 4, 1917	Sokolow has private audience with Pope Benedict XV. They discuss the holy places and Sokolow asks for pope's moral support for Zionist enterprise: "Yes, yes – I believe that we shall be good neighbors," the pope replies.
May 5, 1917	Lloyd George tells his aide Philip Kerr that a Jewish Legion along with a supportive declaration of Zionist interests in Palestine by the cabinet could help sway US and Russian Jews to be more supportive of British war efforts.
May 6, 1917	Balfour meets President Wilson and informs him about Lloyd George's sympathy for Zionism.
May 7 and 10, 1917	Brandeis meets Balfour twice during his visit to the United States.
May 12, 1917	Sokolow is received warmly by Italian prime minister but the Italians are non-committal on their response to Zionism.

May 1917	British forces attack Beersheba.
May 15, 1917	Sykes tells Aaron Aaronson British reinforcements are on the way to Palestine.
May 16, 1917	Claude Montefiore lobbies against Zionism, meets Lord Alfred Milner. Learns Russian Revolution and its withdrawal from war has given Turkey new staying power. Montefiore is told Palestine less immediately pressing.
May 16, 1917	Henry Morgenthau, US ambassador to Turkey, meets Secretary of State Robert Lansing to discuss the outside chance of a separate peace with Turkey,
May 17, 1917	Brandeis telegraphs Lord Rothschild: "Have had satisfactory talk with Mr. Balfour, also with our president."
May 1917	Rózsika Edle von Wertheimstein, aka Mrs. Charles Rothschild (sister-in-law of Lord Rothschild), promotes Zionist idea within her important circle of contacts.
May 24, 1917	Statement in the *Times* by Board of Deputies and the Anglo Jewish Association: "The establishment of a Jewish nationality in Palestine, founded on this theory of Jewish homelessness, must have the effect throughout the world of stamping the Jews as strangers in their native lands."
May 25, 1917	Letters from board members and others dissociating themselves from anti-Zionist statement by the board appear in the *Times*.
May 28, 1917	Lord Rothschild (Lionel Walter) publicly identifies as a Zionist in the *Times*.
May 28, 1917	Rothschild in the *Times*: "We Zionists cannot see how the establishment of an autonomous Jewish state under the aegis and protection of one of the Allied Powers can be considered in any way subversive to the position or loyalty of the very large part of the Jewish people who have identified themselves thoroughly with the citizenship of the countries in which they live."
May 28, 1917	Chief Rabbi Dr. Hertz writes to the *Times* to dispel "the misconception" that the anti-Zionist Conjoint speaks for British Jewry.
May 29, 1917	Balfour in Canada meets Zionist leaders; expresses sympathy for Zionism.
June 1, 1917	Edmund Sebag Montefiore is the lead writer of a letter to the *Times* titled "On Future of the Jews" in opposition to Zionism.

June 4, 1917	Jules Cambon, French diplomat, provides Sokolow with memo expressing French support for Zionism.
June 6, 1917	Opening of the first all-Russian Zionist Conference in St. Petersburg since February Revolution.
June 7, 1917	British air raid on Turkish positions in Gaza, the *Times* reports.
June 13, 1917	Weizmann writes to Sir Ronald Graham at the Foreign Office pressing for government declaration in support of Zionism.
June 14, 1917	Harry Sacher writes to fellow Zionist Leon Simon: "At the back of my mind there is firmly fixed the recognition that, even if all our political schemings turn out in the way we desire, the Arabs will remain our most tremendous problem. I don't want us in Palestine to deal with the Arabs as the Poles deal with the Jews, and with the lesser excuse that belongs to a numerical minority. That kind of chauvinism might poison the whole *Yishuv*. It is our business to fight against it. It is going to be extraordinarily difficult and it will give us unhappy years, but it has to be done."
June 13, 1917	Balfour accepts British claim to Palestine, yet writes in his log: "Personally, I would still prefer to associate the USA in the protectorate should we succeed in securing it."
June 8–15, 1917	Anti-Jewish disturbances in Leeds tied to anti-immigration sentiment.
June 17, 1917	Board of Deputies votes 56–51 in favor of Zionism. Board president David Alexander resigns after losing vote on Zionism, the *Times* reports. Sir Stuart Samuel, Liberal MP, nominally pro-Zionist, takes over as president. Lord Rothschild is one of two vice presidents.
June 1917	Weizmann travels to Gibraltar.
June 17, 1917	Board of Deputies criticizes Conjoint Committee and Lucien Wolf for expressing their opposition to Zionism in the *Times*. In April, Wolf wrote that the Zionists "declare that where emancipation does not exist it is not worth striving for and where it does exist it is no remedy."
June 19, 1917	Balfour asks Weizmann to submit draft of a British government declaration on Palestine that would satisfy the Zionists. Balfour promises a formal declaration of support for the Zionist venture.

June 28, 1917	General Edmund Allenby appointed commander of British forces in Palestine, replacing General Archibald Murray, and arrives at military headquarters in Egypt.
June–July 1917	Britain lobbies US against making a separate peace with Turkey.
July 1917	War Department makes arrangement for the establishment of a Jewish infantry regiment, an idea Ze'ev Jabotinsky has long been pressing for, with Weizmann's backing. In 1914 his Zion Mule Corps was engaged in Gallipoli but disbanded in 1916. A specifically Jewish Legion was opposed by the anti-Zionists but also by Ahad Ha'Am, who saw it as an "empty demonstration."
July 4–5, 1917	At Britain's behest, Weizmann clandestinely meets former US ambassador to Turkey Henry Morgenthau in Spain to dissuade him from pursuing a separate peace with Turkey.
July 12, 1917	Sokolow sends a draft of the declaration to Lord Rothschild asking that it be sent on to Mark Sykes.
July 13, 1917	Forces loyal to the Sharif of Mecca defeat Turkish forces on the Sinai border; House of Commons told.
July 14, 1917	French now convinced Zionists will not back French control over Palestine and walk back their initial support for a Jewish national home.
July 17, 1917	A small group of Zionists, including Sokolow and Sacher, meet to consider a shorter version of the declaration sent on July 12.
July 18, 1917	At Foreign Minister Balfour's request, Lord Rothschild sends him a draft declaration, primarily the work of Sokolow. Other Zionists involved in the draft discussions: Harry Sacher, Herbert Sidebotham, Ahad Ha'Am, Joseph Cowen, Akiva Yaakov Eittinger, Simon Marks, Israel Moses Sieff, Leon Simon, and Shmuel Tolkowsky. On the government's side: Sykes, Ronald Graham, and Harold Nicolson. The ultimate version is a product of back and forth between the various players to ensure it will be acceptable to Balfour.
July 22, 1917	Alexander Kerensky, from the liberal-leaning Socialist Revolutionary Party, becomes premier of Russia.
July 1917	T. E. Lawrence leads Arab force which captures Aqaba/Eilat from the Ottomans.
August 2, 1917	Balfour sends his own version of the declaration based on previous Zionists' drafts to Lord Rothschild.

August 8, 1917	The *Times* reports that Colonel Patterson is recruiting British Jews to serve in the Jewish Corps. There are forty thousand Jews from all over the world serving in the British Army, the paper reports.
August 17, 1917	Weizmann quits the English Zionist Federation annoyed over internal dissent including pacifist opposition to the Jewish Legion which he supports. Under pressure from Ahad Ha'Am, Weizmann withdraws resignation.
August 20, 1917	Field Marshall Allenby's chief political officer, General Gilbert Clayton, writes to Mark Sykes lobbying against Zionism because it would give the "Arabs yet another bone of contention."
August 23, 1917	July 18 Rothschild Declaration draft circulated to the War Cabinet members.
August 23, 1917	British government agrees to formation of 38th Battalion of Royal Fusiliers for service in Palestine.
August 1917	Turks come upon the NILI Zionist espionage ring, led by Sarah Aaronsohn, supporting the British war effort. Tortured for three days, she then commits suicide.
September 3, 1917	Draft of Declaration comes before War Cabinet. Neither Lloyd George nor Balfour can take part as both are out of London; it is decided to query Washington on its attitude toward such a declaration.
September 3, 1917	Edwin Montagu, Jewish cabinet member and opponent of Zionism, asks: How will he negotiate with the people of India on behalf of His Majesty's Government if the world has just been told that His Majesty's Government regards his national home as being in Turkish territory?
September 7, 1917	Presidential adviser "Colonel" Edward House, not known as friendly to Jews, urges President Woodrow Wilson to be wary of supporting Zionism. Wilson will make no definite statement in reply to British cabinet query, almost killing the declaration idea.
September 8, 1917	Brandeis sees House and reports a change in administration's attitude; it is now in entire sympathy with a declaration.
September 9, 1917	Anglo-Jewish Association, following a June 15, 1917 vote by Board of Deputies, calls for anti-Zionist Conjoint to be dissolved.

September 14, 1917	C. P. Scott to Weizmann: "You are the only statesman" in the Zionist hierarchy.
September 21, 1917	Weizmann meets with General Jan Smuts, War Cabinet member, who supports the Zionist cause.
September 24, 1917	Brandeis and Stephen Wise meet Colonel House at White House. Brandeis cables London that President Wilson is sympathetic to the Zionist project.
September 28, 1917	With C. P. Scott's help, Weizmann sees Lloyd George briefly. The PM agrees to place Palestine on the agenda of the next War Cabinet meeting.
October 1917	British forces capture Beersheba, control southern Eretz Yisrael and battle northwards against weakened Turkish forces.
October 4, 1917	War Cabinet discusses draft declaration supporting Zionism. Balfour reads the Cambon letter to Sokolow to the cabinet. He tells colleagues that he is in favor of "a Jewish national focus in Palestine" as well as the assimilation of those Jews who will stay in the diaspora. Lord Curzon opposes the Zionist project. He does not believe that many Jews will go to such a barren place and asks what will happen to the Muslims there.
October 4, 1917	Edwin Montagu, a leading anti-Zionist Jewish minister but not a member of the War Cabinet, writes to Lloyd George: "The country for which I have worked ever since I left university – England – the country for which my family have fought, tells me that my national home, if I desire to go there, therefore my natural home, is Palestine."
October 5, 1917	Letter from Lord Rothschild appears in the *Times* in response to anti-Zionism of Claude Montefiore and D. L. Alexander.
October 6, 1917	War Cabinet secretariat invites Jewish proponents and opponents to submit memoranda on the declaration draft. Chief Rabbi Hertz, Lord Rothschild, Nahum Sokolow, and Chaim Weizmann write in favor. Leonard Cohen, Philip Magnus, and Claude Montefiore write against. Stuart Samuel summarizes the views of British Jews but does not take a stance. Opponents do not oppose Palestine as a sanctuary but object to the "national home" idea.
October 16, 1917	War Cabinet learns President Wilson is now favorably disposed toward a declaration.
October 23, 1917	The *Times* carries story headlined "Palestine for the Jews"

reporting on a manifesto by British Jewish groups in support of Zionism.

October 24, 1917	Ronald Graham of the Foreign Office (and a Zionist sympathizer) writes Balfour that further delay by the cabinet in deciding on the Zionist question would be ill-advised.
October 26, 1917	Leader in the *Times* headlined "The Jews and Palestine" calls on government to take action.
October 26, 1917	Lord Curzon distributes memo to cabinet warning that the Arabs "will not be content either to be expropriated for Jewish immigrants, or to act merely as hewers of wood and drawers of water to the latter."
October 30, 1917	Sykes answers Curzon's October 26 memo. He argues that Palestine does have the capacity for agricultural and economic development so that Arabs and Jews alike would benefit from the Zionist enterprise.
October 31, 1917	War Cabinet approves final text (Milner-Amery version) of Balfour Declaration.
October 31, 1917	The charge of Beersheba: Australian 4th and 12th Light Horse Regiments daringly charge tenacious Turkish defenders at Beersheba.

Zionist Landmark

November 2, 1917	British forces, with Australian and New Zealand troops in the vanguard, capture Beersheba.
November 2, 1917	Balfour Declaration issued: Britain promises a national home for the Jews in Palestine.
November 2, 1917	At an impromptu dinner party at the Weizmann residence, Chaim and Vera Weizmann, Ze'ev Jabotinsky, Eliezer Margolin (then serving in the Australian army), and Weizmann's secretary Shmuel Tolkowsky do a Hassidic dance around the table in Weizmann's study.
November 5, 1917	The *Times* reports that British forces continue to advance in Palestine and aim to capture Gaza.
November 7, 1917	The *Times* leader lauds General Allenby for capture of Beersheba. Outflanked at Beersheba, Gaza is captured and Turkish resistance in southern Palestine collapses.
November 7, 1917	Bolsheviks overthrow Kerensky's Russian government and install a Communist regime under Lenin.

November 9, 1917   Declaration made public. Newspapers report on Balfour's letter to Rothschild favoring Zionism. In his *History of Zionism*, Sokolow writes: "The Press was without exception most sympathetic" followed by pages of laudatory newspaper excerpts. "The economic future of a Jewish Palestine should be bright." (*The Economist*); "We speak of Palestine as a country, but it is not a country…but it will be a country; it will be the country of the Jews…with a view to the ultimate establishment of a Jewish State." (*Manchester Guardian*)

November 10, 1917   The *Times* reports from Washington on American Jewish enthusiasm for Balfour Declaration. The newspaper says 90 percent of US Jews support Zionism.

November 1917   British-led Arab forces advance northwards up the Judean Hills toward Jerusalem defeating Ottomans at Tel el Khuweilfe, Hareira, and Sheria, and at Mughar Ridge.

November 1917   British make still another assault on Gaza Strip.

November 1917   Australian and New Zealand Army Corps Mounted Division liberates Jaffa.

November 1917   Battle of Jerusalem begins.

November 11, 1917   Montagu writes in his diary: "The government has dealt an irreparable blow at Jewish Britons and they have endeavored to set up a people which does not exist; they have alarmed unnecessarily the whole Moslem world; and in so far as they are successful, they will have a Germanized Palestine on the flank of Egypt. Why we should intern Mahomed Ali in India for Pan-Mohammedanism when we encourage Pan-Judaism, I cannot for the life of me understand."

November 14, 1917   League of British Jews founded to protect the interests of British Jews and oppose defining them as a nationality. They opposed the Balfour Declaration and also the establishment of the Hebrew University.

November 18, 1917   Board of Deputies thanks the government for their "sympathetic interest in the Jews as manifested by" the Balfour Declaration. Anglo-Jewish Association also identifies with declaration. Jews in Poland and Russia rejoice.

November 26, 1917   The *Manchester Guardian* publishes text of Sykes-Picot Agreement, leaked by Russian communists.

November 27, 1917   British government agrees to Weizmann's request to send

	a Jewish commission to Palestine to facilitate Zionist aspirations.
December 2, 1917	East End Londoners pack London Opera House for thanksgiving meeting presided over by Lord Rothschild. Lord Robert Cecil, under-secretary of state for foreign affairs, attends on behalf of government: "Our wish is that Arabian countries shall be for the Arabs, Armenia for the Armenians, and Judaea for the Jews."
December 9, 1917	British capture Jerusalem from the Turks on Hanukkah eve.
December 11, 1917	General Allenby enters Jerusalem on foot out of respect for the Holy City and quickly posts guards to protect all the sites held sacred by the Christian, Muslim, and Jewish religions.
December 12, 1917	British General Clayton, army intelligence and colonial administrator, writes Sykes: "…the Bedouin despises [the Jew] and will never do anything else, while the sedentary Arab hates the Jew, and fears his superior commercial and economic ability."
December 16, 1917	Turks hang NILI spies Naaman Belkind and Joseph Lishansky.
December 17, 1917	Vatican signals Britain its concern that the Jews might gain direct control over Palestine to the detriment of Christian interests.
December 23, 1917	Rabbi Stephen Wise at Carnegie Hall Rally in New York City: "We rejoice over nothing more than a 'scrap of paper,' but that scrap of paper is written in English. It is signed by the British government and therefore is sacred and inviolable."
December 1917– January 1918	The pro-Zionist American Jewish Congress holds founding elections. It is intended to counter-balance non-Zionist American Jewish Committee.

Balfour Enshrined in International Law

January 8, 1918	President Woodrow Wilson declares his fourteen points as the path to permanent world peace. Self-determination promised for national minorities.
January 1918	Yevkom, the Commissariat for Jewish Affairs, established by Bolsheviks in Russia to win support among the Jews.
January 26, 1918	The Zionist Commission is established by the Middle East Committee of the War Cabinet.

February 9, 1918	Prime Minister Georges Clemenceau of France meets Sokolow and issues communiqué announcing complete agreement between French and British governments concerning question of a Jewish establishment in Palestine.
March 1, 1918	Russian Communist commissar for Jewish Affairs, a former Lubavitch hassid, vows to combat Zionism.
March 2, 1918	Weizmann has audience with King George V, who appears sympathetic to Zionist aims.
March 3, 1918	Trotsky signs the Treaty of Brest-Litovsk which cedes territory to Germany and takes Russia out of the Great War.
March 4 1918	Zionist Commission en route to Palestine is in Paris; reaches Alexandria on March 20.
March 22, 1918	Ukrainian mobs massacre the Jews of Seredino Buda.
March 29, 1918	Zionist Commission members meet with Palestine Committee of Muslims and Christians.
April 1, 1918	Zionist Commission, led by Chaim Weizmann, begins to arrive piecemeal in Palestine. Weizmann discovers ranking British officers in Palestine are ignorant, or disdainful, of the Balfour Declaration.
April 5, 1918	First meeting of the Zionist Commission takes place in Jaffa.
April 11, 1918	Weizmann meets two Muslim leaders in Jerusalem, Ismail Bey al-Husseini and Grand Mufti Kamal Bey al-Husseini.
May 24, 1918	Weizmann meets General Edmund Allenby and presents him with a Torah scroll.
June 4, 1918	Chaim Weizmann meets Emir Feisal in Aqaba.
June 9, 1918	The 38th Battalion (Jewish forces) arrives in Samaria and prepares to confront Turkish forces.
June 12, 1918	Weizmann returns to Cairo to meet Lawrence of Arabia.
July 5, 1918	US Central Conference of Reform Rabbis opposes Zionist aims and Jewish nationalism in Palestine.
July 24, 1918	Chaim Weizmann and General Allenby participate in cornerstone-laying ceremony at Hebrew University on Mount Scopus in Jerusalem.
August 20, 1918	Hadassah medical relief team arrives in Jerusalem.
August 31, 1918	President Woodrow Wilson writes to Rabbi Stephen Wise: "I welcome an opportunity to express the satisfaction I have

felt in the progress of the Zionist movement in the US...
since the declaration by Mr. Balfour."

September 19, 1918	All of Palestine nearly liberated from Turks with participation of Jewish forces under British command. The 38th Battalion of the Royal Fusiliers is part of other battalions known collectively as the Jewish Legion which participates in battle of Megiddo 19–25 September 1918.
October 31, 1918	Turkey surrenders.
November 2, 1918	Zionists around the world celebrate first anniversary of Balfour Declaration.
November 11, 1918	At eleven o'clock on the eleventh day of the eleventh month of 1918, the World War ends as Germany and Allies sign an armistice.
November 12, 1918	Jabotinsky (now political officer of the Zionist Commission) writes Weizmann: "My dear friend, it will grieve you, but I must say that the whole official attitude here [of British military administrators in Palestine] is one of apologizing to the Arabs for Mr. Balfour's *lapsus linguae*, of endeavours to atone for it by putting Jews always in the background."
November 21, 1918	Polish soldiers organize a pogrom against Jews of Galicia, Poland.
December 21, 1918	Lord Rothschild tenders dinner for Feisal which is attended by senior political figures.
1919	Third Aliyah. Russian Revolution and fighting between Reds and Whites between 1919 and 1920 leaves as many as 250,000 Jews killed and triggers massive exodus of Jews, many to Palestine.
January 3, 1919	Weizmann meets Feisal in London prior to Paris Peace Conference. The leaders sign agreement on the development of an Arab state and [Jewish] Palestine. Feisal warns that the arrangement will be nullified if the Arabs are not granted the British-promised state.
January 17, 1919	Newspapers report Weizmann meeting Woodrow Wilson on sidelines of the year-long Paris Peace Conference.
February 1919	US Zionists join worldwide Jewish delegation, headed by Chaim Weizmann and Nahum Sokolow, to Paris Peace Conference at Versailles – and on February 3, present statement to the conference.

March 1919	Ben-Gurion in Palestine forms Socialist Zionist Achdut Ha'avodah Party, a precursor to today's Israeli Labor Party (in 2017 known as Zionist Union).
March 1, 1919	The *Tablet* reports Church denying pope ever expressed support for Zionism: He had offered good wishes to a Jewish home in Palestine, but opposed a state.
March 3, 1919	Feisal writes to US Zionist leader Felix Frankfurter affirming that Arab and Jewish national movements have common interests: "We will wish the Jews a hearty welcome home." British intelligence in Cairo denigrates the letter as worthless.
March 4, 1919	Wilson quoted in newspapers: "I am persuaded that the Allied nations, with the fullest concurrence of our government and people, are agreed that in Palestine shall be laid the foundations of a Jewish Commonwealth."
March 10, 1919	The pope expresses his growing concern over the Jewish ("infidels") role in Palestine.
March 12, 1919	The *Times* reports from Rome the pope saying "It would be for us and all Christians a bitter grief if unbelievers [Zionist Jews] in Palestine were put into a superior or more privileged position."
May 2, 1919	Palestine's temporary British military governor Major-General Sir Arthur Wigram Money lobbies government in London against carrying out Balfour Declaration. He is backed by General Clayton and General H. D. Watson.
June 10, 1919	King-Crane US study group visiting Palestine to gather information for Paris Peace Conference comes to anti-Zionist conclusion and advocates Palestine's incorporation into Greater Syria.
June 24, 1919	Balfour writes to US Supreme Court Justice Louis Brandeis: "We are consciously seeking to reconstitute a new community and definitely building for a numerical majority in the future."
July 1919	Christian Arab nationalists are Zionism's most implacable foes. Syrian Congress in Damascus rejects idea of Jewish commonwealth and Jewish immigration to Palestine.
July 9, 1919	Brandeis arrives in Palestine.
August 11, 1919	Balfour, not a member of the British delegation to the Paris Peace Conference but a consultant, writes memo on

sidelines of the conference. He acknowledges that "the wishes of the present inhabitants of the country" ought not to determine international policy. "I do not think Zionism will hurt the Arabs, but they will never say they want it." He goes on: "The four Great Powers are committed to Zionism. And Zionism, be it right or wrong, good or bad, is rooted in age-long traditions, in present needs, in future hopes, of far profounder import than the desires and prejudices of the seven hundred thousand Arabs who now inhabit that ancient land. In my opinion, that is right. What I have never been able to understand is how it can be harmonized with the declaration, the [League of Nations] Covenant or the Commission of Enquiry."

August 1919	Weizmann and Brandeis meet in London. Discuss and disagree about structure and operation of a Jewish agency for Palestine.
August 24, 1919	Transpires that the King-Crane group established by US government did not oppose Jewish settlement in Palestine but opposed the notion of a Jewish state. The report is not published for several years.
October 24, 1919	Lord Curzon succeeds Lord Balfour as foreign secretary.
December 11, 1919	Weizmann meets Feisal in London.
April 1920	At San Remo, France tries to torpedo Balfour Declaration saying it never officially approved it.
February 27, 1920	To counteract opposition from within British military, the British government instructs General Louis Jean Bols, chief administrator of Palestine, to state that His Majesty's Government intends to honor the Balfour Declaration. This leads to the first Arab protests and disturbances.
March 1, 1920	Arabs attack Tel Hai in Galilee. Joseph Trumpeldor and five other defenders killed.
March 7, 1920	Feisal I bin Hussein bin Ali-Hashimi proclaimed as king of Greater Syria.
April 4, 1920	Arabs attack Jews in Jerusalem following Muslim festival coinciding with Passover.
April 7, 1920	After organizing a defense force, Jabotinsky is arrested and sentenced to fifteen years of hard labor on April 19. Weizmann writes Lloyd George that British officials on the scene permitted the Arabs to riot unimpeded.

April 20, 1920	The San Remo Conference of the Allied Supreme Council in Italy endorses a Palestine Mandate based on Balfour Declaration.
June 15, 1920	The Haganah is founded.
June 20, 1920	French argue that the waters required by the Zionists in southern Lebanon should be allocated to Syria. This is eventually agreed to by the British.
June 30, 1920	Sir Herbert Samuel, a British Jewish Zionist, arrives in Palestine to take up position as high commissioner; he was actually appointed following the San Remo Conference.
August 10, 1920	The Treaty of Sevres which dissolves the Ottoman Empire and enshrines the principles of the Balfour Declaration regarding Palestine is signed in France.
December 5, 1920	Histadrut labor union formed.
December 1920	Arab-Jewish violence kills forty-seven Jews and forty-eight Arabs.

Inter-War Period: Walking Back Balfour

March 31, 1921	Disbanding of the Jewish Legion, the five battalions of Jewish volunteers in the British Army that fought against the Ottoman Empire during WWI.
April 2, 1921	Albert Einstein visits US with Chaim Weizmann on a fundraising tour for Hebrew University. Masses of New York City Jews greet them at the docks.
April 11, 1921	Transjordan established under Crown Prince Abdullah after Britain grants the Eastern part of Mandatory Palestine to the Arabs.
May 1–6, 1921	Deadly Arab riots in Jaffa, Petah Tikva, Hadera, and Rehovot claim forty-seven lives.
May 8, 1921	Haj Amin al-Husseini takes office as Mufti of Jerusalem, his selection engineered by the British. He served until 1937.
May 14, 1921	British declare moratorium on Jewish immigration.
June 14, 1921	The pope laments that the "new civil arrangement" [British Mandate] has weakened Christianity and strengthened Judaism.
1921	Brandeis-Weizmann split, nominally over the financial organization Keren Hayesod (now United Israel Appeal, the official fundraising organization for Israel), but in fact about what Zionism would mean for acculturated

American Jews. Weizmann argues the goal of a Zionist should be to settle in Israel.

September 1, 1921 — Weizmann becomes new president of the WZO at the Twelfth Zionist Congress (the first since World War I), which meets in Carlsbad, Czechoslovakia.

November 1, 1921 — *Hadoar*, the first Hebrew daily newspaper, begins publication.

December 1921 — Ben-Gurion returns to Palestine after a year in London on Zionist business.

January 9, 1922 — British establish Supreme Muslim Council with Haj Amin al-Husseini as president.

February 21, 1922 — Palestinian Arab delegation visits London to protest Balfour Declaration.

May 24, 1922 — Cardinal Gasparri, strengthened by the Patriarch of Jerusalem, Monsignor Aloysius Barlassina, denounces Jewish settlements in Palestine as boosting communism.

June 3, 1922 — Churchill White Paper calls for a limitation of Jewish immigration in order to reduce Arab resentment.

July 24, 1922 — Mandate's terms finalized and unanimously approved by League of Nations.

October 1922 — Mandatory administration conducts census in Palestine. There are 757,000 residents; 84,000 are Jews and 673,000 are Arabs and others. Jews make up 11 percent of population.

January 1923 — Jabotinsky resigns from Executive to protest Weizmann's soft line vis-a-vis British refusal to formalize Zionist national council in Palestine.

January 23, 1923 — Herzl's comrade Max Nordau dies in Paris.

August 5, 1923 — Thirteenth Zionist Congress held in Carlsbad, Czechoslovakia. Weizmann re-elected president.

September 29, 1923 — Britain cedes Golan Heights to French Mandate of Syria.

September 29, 1923 — Mandate for Palestine comes into effect.

December 27, 1923 — Betar, the Jabotinsky youth movement, formed in Riga, Latvia.

1924 — Fourth Aliyah brings some 82,000 Jews to Eretz Yisrael, a direct result of the economic crisis and anti-Jewish policies in Poland, along with the introduction of stiff immigration quotas by the United States.

1924	Weizmann opposes urban development in Palestine, apparently referring to places such as ultra-Orthodox B'nei Brak, founded in May.
1924	Palestine Jewish Colonization Association (PICA) founded.
April 1, 1925	The Hebrew University of Jerusalem officially opened by Lord Balfour, dressed in the robes of the Chancellor of Cambridge, before 2,500 guests seated in an amphitheater and thousands of spectators.
April 5, 1925	Balfour tours Palestine for three days.
April 10, 1925	Balfour arrives in Damascus to protests outside his hotel.
August 1925	Vladimir Ze'ev Jabotinsky establishes Revisionist Zionist opposition party at a meeting in Paris.
August 1925	Fourteenth Zionist Congress meets in Vienna.
August 1925	Tel Aviv's population reaches forty thousand.
May 4, 1926	Max Nordau's remains reinterred in Tel Aviv.
September 1926	Keren Hayesod moves its headquarters from London to Jerusalem.
1927	Economic depression in Palestine.
January 2, 1927	Ahad Ha'Am, founder of cultural Zionism, dies.
January 17, 1927	Chaim Weizmann and US Jewish non-Zionist leader Louis Marshall of the American Jewish Committee (AJC) meet about strengthening ties between diaspora and Zionists.
August 30, 1927	Fifteenth World Zionist Congress meets in Basel.
September 23, 1928	Muslim religious leaders seek to limit Jewish worship at Western Wall in Jerusalem.
September 24, 1928	Arab riots break out after Jews place temporary dividers near Western Wall to separate Jewish men and women during Yom Kippur prayers.
July 27, 1929	Sixteenth Zionist Congress held in Zurich.
August 1929	The Jewish Agency, a quasi-governmental body, is founded seven years after ratification of the British Mandate as per its Article IV.
August 23–29, 1929	Deadly Arab riots take 133 Jewish lives (67 killed in Hebron and Safed). Some settlements are abandoned.
October 24, 1929	British Shaw Commission sent to study reasons for Arab rioting and violence.

1929	Following a master plan developed in 1918, Sir Ronald Storrs, governor of Jerusalem, rules all buildings in the city be faced with white Jerusalem stone.
January 14, 1930	League of Nations forms commission to examine Arab-Jewish violence and rights to Jewish prayer at Western Wall.
January 1930	Mapai Labor Party formed; becomes dominant left-wing party under Ben-Gurion and a precursor of today's Israeli Labor Party.
March 19, 1930	Arthur James Balfour dies in Woking. Weizmann is among the last to see him.
August 1930	Lucien Wolf, English Jewish journalist, historian, opponent of Zionism and advocate of Jewish rights, dies.
August 22, 1930	British Hope-Simpson committee proposes moratorium on Jewish immigration and a settlement freeze.
October 20, 1930	British White Paper on Palestine, issued by Colonial Secretary Lord Passfield, limits the establishment of Jewish agricultural settlements. Weizmann protests.
January 5, 1931	Ben-Gurion camp wins 40 percent of seats to Palestinian Jewish assembly against 20 percent for supporters of Jabotinsky.
February 13, 1931	Prime Minister Ramsay MacDonald (1929–1935, Labour) writes to Zionist leader Chaim Weizmann affirming that: "His Majesty's Government will continue to administer Palestine in accordance with the terms of the mandate.... This is an international obligation from which there can be no question of receding. Under the terms of the mandate his Majesty's Government are responsible for promoting the establishment of a national home for the Jewish people, it being clearly understood that nothing shall be done which might prejudice the civil and religious rights of existing non-Jewish communities in Palestine or the rights and political status enjoyed by Jews in any other country."
1931	Haganah splits over how to respond to British backtracking on Balfour Declaration. Jabotinsky-inspired Irgun formed.
July 1931	Seventeenth Zionist Congress held in Basel. Nahum Sokolow elected president of World Zionist Organization in place of Weizmann, who is seen as too close to the British. Haim Arlosoroff heads Jewish Agency political bureau.

November 18, 1931	Jews now 17 percent of population in Palestine.
1932	Fifth Aliyah, which lasts until 1939, is primarily a result of the Nazi accession to power in Germany (1933) and later throughout Europe. Persecution and the Jews' worsening situation spur immigration from Germany to increase and from eastern Europe to continue. Nearly 250,000 Jews arrive in British-occupied Palestine during the Fifth Aliyah (20,000 of them later leave). From then on, the practice of "numbering" the waves of immigration is discontinued.
January 1933	Hitler becomes German Chancellor; beginning of anti-Jewish persecution.
June 16, 1933	Haim Arlosoroff, head of the political department of the Jewish Agency, assassinated in Tel Aviv.
July 21, 1933	Haifa harbor opened.
August 1933	The Nazis, determined that Jews emigrate from Germany, enter into Haavara Agreement with Zionist authorities in Tel Aviv whereby German Jews can take a percentage of the value of their property out of Germany. Some 60,000 German Jews arrive in Palestine between 1933 and 1939. The Nazis want to break world Jewry's economic embargo on their regime, and the Zionists are keen to rescue Jews and bring them to Palestine. Needless to say, the Germans do not favor a Jewish state and by 1937 see such a possibility as an outright threat to German interests.
August 1933	Meetings on future of Palestine between Jewish Agency head David Ben-Gurion and Palestinian Arab leaders Awni Abd al-Hadi, Musa al-Alami and George Antonius, a Lebanese-Egyptian Christian now resident in Jerusalem.
August 21, 1933	Eighteenth Zionist Congress held in Prague.
1934	Aliyah Bet: Zionist groups in Palestine organize "illegal" immigration circumventing British policies.
October 26, 1934	Ben-Gurion and Jabotinsky try unsuccessfully to iron out their differences in London.
August 10, 1935	Nineteenth Zionist Congress meets in Lucerne, Switzerland; Weizmann returns as president of WZO.
September 1935	Nuremberg Laws institutionalize anti-Semitism in German legal system.
September 12, 1935	Jabotinsky's New Zionist Organization meets in Vienna.
1935	Jews now compromise 30 percent of Palestine's population.

March 30, 1936	British establish Palestine Radio which includes first ever Hebrew-language radio broadcasts heard throughout the region.
April 1936	Arab Revolt riots and strikes in Palestine. Lebanese irregulars join fighting in Palestine. Violence will continue until 1939.
May 1936	Ad hoc group of Jewish elders tries and fails to reach an accommodation with the Arabs.
1936	Jewish Agency and Haganah continue policy of "Havlagah" or passive defense, rejecting retaliation against Arab civilians.
November 1936	Peel Commission arrives in Palestine to examine causes of Arab violence.
December 26, 1936	Palestine Symphony Orchestra established. Arturo Toscanini conducts.
April 1937	Nazis troubled that Jewish emigration out of Germany slowing because of Arab riots in Palestine. Rather than leaving, too many German Jews are adjusting to second-class status.
July 1937	Peel Commission proposes partition of western Palestine (territory between Jordan River and Mediterranean) into Jewish and Arab states. Jews are divided on offer; Arabs reject it.
1937	Settlements build watchtowers to defend against Arab infiltrators.
1937	Orde Wingate trains Jewish self-defense forces.
July 23, 1937	Sir Henry McMahon writes in the *Times*: "It was not intended by me giving this pledge to [the Sharif] to include Palestine in the area in which Arab independence was promised."
August 3, 1937	Twentieth Zionist Congress held in Zurich, Switzerland.
September 1937	Armed Arab revolt against British. Mufti flees to Lebanon.
1938	British forces recapture major Arab population centers in Palestine from Mufti's men.
May 1938	Palestinian Jews construct security barrier in Galilee to deter Arab infiltrators.
June 1938	British authorities execute Irgun member Shlomo Ben-Yosef.

November 9–10, 1938   Kristallnacht: economic ruin and rioting against Germany's Jews.

November 12, 1938   Nazis consider deporting German Jews to Madagascar.

November 15, 1938   Weizmann sees Prime Minister Neville Chamberlain at 10 Downing Street, asks that ten thousand Jewish children be allowed to enter Palestine under Youth Aliyah. PM says no, but agrees, temporarily, to permit unaccompanied children into Britain by giving rescue organizations block visas.

1938   Militant anti-Zionist ultra-Orthodox Jews in Jerusalem establish Neturei Karta, maintaining that Jews are forbidden to have their own state until the coming of the Messiah.

January 1939   United Jewish Appeal founded to raise money for Zionist settlement and development.

February 1939   British try to bring Jews and Arabs together in London. Arabs refuse to negotiate.

March 5, 1939   Death of Moses Gaster, haham of the Spanish and Portuguese Jewish congregation in London.

April 1939   Jews double down on "illegal" immigration to Palestine. New settlements created. Between 1939–1944 dozens of ships and thousands of Jewish migrants seek to break British maritime blockade of Palestine.

May 1939   MacDonald White Paper issued by Neville Chamberlain's government declares Britain will not allow a Jewish state to be created in Palestine. Limits Jewish immigration to 75,000 for five years (until 1944).

August 16, 1939   Twenty-First Zionist Congress held in Geneva. Eve of World War II.

1939   Palestinian Arabs, led by Mufti of Jerusalem, reject White Paper, which promises Arabs control over Jewish immigration.

World War II/Shoah

August 23, 1939   Nazi-Soviet Communists sign non-aggression pact.

September 1, 1939   World War II begins when Germany invades Poland.

September 2, 1939   British naval vessel off Palestine coast fires at the SS *Tiger Hill*, a ship bringing Jewish refugees to Palestine; two are killed.

September 3, 1939   Britain and France declare war on Germany.

September 12, 1939	David Ben-Gurion declares: "We shall fight the war against Hitler as if there were no White Paper and the White Paper as if there were no war." Haganah makes its forces available to the British. Irgun calls halt to revolt against British to concentrate on fighting Nazis.
September 21, 1939	Nazi Einsatzgruppen mobile killing squads active in Poland.
December 11, 1939	Weizmann meets First Lord of the Admiralty Winston Churchill in London.
1939	Between 1939 and 1944 dozens of ships and thousands of Jewish refugees seek to break British maritime blockade of Palestine.
February 1940	Imposition of White Paper against Jews buying land and against immigration.
Spring/Summer 1940	Syria/Lebanon under pro-Nazi French (Vichy) administration. Italian Fascists based in Rhodes.
May 10, 1940	Churchill becomes British prime minister.
1940	Western Europe under German occupation. Jews in Poland herded into ghettos.
July 15, 1940	Italian Fascist planes bomb Haifa; fifty dead.
August 4, 1940	Vladimir Ze'ev Jabotinsky dies in New York.
August 1940	Irgun splits. Breakaway Stern Gang (Freedom Fighters for Israel) commits to armed struggle against British policies.
September 9, 1940	Italian Fascist planes bomb Tel Aviv; one hundred dead.
November 25, 1940	In an effort to block British from returning SS *Patria* carrying 1,700 asylum seekers, Haganah sinks ship. More than 200 refugees drown in operation gone awry.
March 1941	Chaim Weizmann in US for war effort.
April 1941	Fear of Nazis invading Palestine is palpable. German General Rommel at Libyan-Egyptian border.
May 1941	Haganah organizes elite Palmach fighting unit to prepare for Nazi invasion.
May 1941	British-led Haganah sabotage team disappears at sea.
May 1941	David Raziel, a founder of the Irgun, killed in Iraq while on a commando mission for the British Army – pro-Nazi government in Iraq set up by Rashid Ali al-Gaylani. British capture Baghdad.

June 8, 1941	Britain, aided by Haganah, takes Lebanon and Syria from Vichy control.
June 10–12, 1941	Italy bombs Haifa and Tel Aviv from air in campaign that began in 1940.
June 22, 1941	Operation "Barbarossa." Nazi Germany invades the Soviet Union engulfing millions more Jews in its web of destruction.
October 1941	Germany officially forbids Jews to emigrate.
October 5, 1941	Louis Brandeis dies in Washington, DC.
November 1941	Weizmann appeals to British to create Jewish fighting force.
November 1941	Ben-Gurion in US on Zionist business.
January 20, 1942	Germany ends improvised killing of Jews and at Wannsee Conference, outside Berlin, sets stage for "Final Solution" – the systemic, industrialized genocide of European Jews.
February 12, 1942	British police kill Jewish militant Avraham Stern.
February 24, 1942	*Struma* sunk in Black Sea after Turkish authorities tow the boat out to sea and abandon it. Earlier Britain refuses to allow its 770 passengers to land in Palestine. All but one passenger killed.
May 11, 1942	Zionists adopt Biltmore program that Palestine be established as a Jewish Commonwealth.
Summer 1942	Fresh fears that Rommel will advance into Palestine. General call-up of Palestinian Jews to prepare for Nazi invasion.
October 23, 1942	General Montgomery pushes Rommel back at Battle of El Alamein and removes Nazi threat over Palestine.
November 1942	Palestinian Jews become increasingly aware of the genocide being committed against the Jews of Europe by the Nazis and their enablers.
1942	Death camps at Auschwitz, Maidanek, and Treblinka function at full capacity. Transports from ghettos to death camps run at capacity.
1943	Small units of Palestinian Jewish commandos under British command operate behind German lines in occupied Europe.
April 19-30, 1943	At Bermuda Conference, British and American representatives fail to come up with approach to save European Jews from Hitler.

November 1943	Telegram from Heinrich Himmler, Reichsführer and SS chief, to the Grand Mufti on the anniversary of the Balfour Declaration proclaims the Nazi's admiration and sympathy for the Mufti's struggle against the Jews. Mufti now based in Berlin.
1944	Both Stern Gang and Irgun now attack British targets in Palestine.
February 1944	Irgun's Menachem Begin declares Jewish Revolt against the British.
March 1, 1944	"Kill the Jews wherever you find them. It would please God, history, and religion," exhorts Haj Amin al-Husseini in Arabic broadcast on Nazi Berlin Radio.
March 15, 1944	Roosevelt administration dissociates from White Paper.
September 1944	British agree to create Jewish Brigade, which sees combat briefly in northern Italy in February 1945.
October 1944	Haganah demands Irgun end operations against the British.
November 4, 1944	Weizmann meets Churchill, who says he supports creation of Jewish state.
November 6, 1944	Lehi assassinates Lord Moyne, responsible for implementing the White Paper policy, in Cairo. A racist, Moyne believed Palestine should go to the Arabs as their race was "purer" than the "mixed" Jewish race.
March 22, 1945	Arab League of States formed in Cairo.
May 1945	WWII ends in Europe. Death camps liberated. Six million Jews exterminated by Germans and their collaborators.
May 1945	There are 554,329 Jews in Palestine (30 percent of the population).
August 25, 1945	British allow "illegal" Jewish emigrants (Holocaust survivors) who have been held on Mauritius to enter Palestine.
October 1945	The three Jewish underground branches Haganah, Irgun, and Lehi agree to pursue joint military campaign against British.
November 1945	Foreign Secretary Bevin (Labour) declares immigration of Holocaust survivors to Palestine illegal.
December 2, 1945	First branch of Muslim Brotherhood formed in Jerusalem.

Countdown to Independence

March 27, 1946	Thousands of Tel Aviv residents gather on beach to welcome an "illegal" refugee boat and clash with British security forces.
May 4, 1946	Irgun attacks Acre prison, releases dozens of British prisoners.
May 28, 1946	Egypt's King Farouk hosts the first Arab summit to create front against establishment of Jewish state.
June 1946	Combined Jewish underground destroys bridges connecting Palestine to neighboring countries.
June 29, 1946	Massive crackdown by British forces on Zionist leadership.
July 22, 1946	Irgun and Stern Gang blow up British military headquarters in wing of King David Hotel. Haganah and Jewish Agency condemn attack.
July 30, 1946	Four-day curfew on Tel Aviv as British search for those behind King David operation.
August 13, 1946	Britain redirects Holocaust survivors seeking entry to Palestine to Cyprus.
October 4, 1946	Truman administration calls for allowing one hundred thousand Jewish refugees to enter Palestine.
December 9, 1946	Twenty-Second Zionist Congress meets in Basel in the hall where the First Congress was convened in 1897. Ben-Gurion warns it may be necessary to take up arms for statehood.
February 18, 1947	Britain calls on the UN to decide Palestine's fate. Ben-Gurion returns to Palestine. Clashes with British soldiers continue.
March 19, 1947	US backtracks on support for Jewish state.
April 16, 1947	Britain hangs four captured Irgun fighters. Two others facing death sentences commit suicide.
May 15, 1947	UN Special Committee on Palestine set up.
June 11–July 9, 1947	Arabs and Jews agree on truce.
June 29, 1947	Irgun hangs three British soldiers in retaliation for the hanging of Irgun men. British soldiers in Tel Aviv respond by killing five and wounding many in Tel Aviv shooting spree.
July 18, 1947	British seize the *Exodus* carrying four thousand refugees to

	Palestine and send them back to displaced persons camps in Germany.
August 31, 1947	UN Special Committee on Palestine calls for partition into two independent states, one Arab and one Jewish.
September 26, 1947	Britain announces its intention to end the mandate.
October 1947	Arab League pledges to finance Palestinian Arab military campaign against creation of Jewish state.
November 29, 1947	UN General Assembly votes 33–13, with 10 abstentions (including Britain), to adopt a resolution requiring the establishment of Jewish and Arab states in Palestine. The Jewish Agency accepts the decision; the Palestinian Arab leadership rejects the plan insisting that all of Palestine should be an Arab state.
1947	Discovery of Dead Sea Scrolls in Judean Desert.
December 1947	Massive Arab riots; hundreds of Jews killed.
February 1, 1948	Office of the *Palestine Post*, a Zionist newspaper (now the *Jerusalem Post*) is bombed.
March 22, 1948	Road to Jerusalem cut off by Arab forces. Jewish Jerusalem besieged.
May 14, 1948	British Mandate for Palestine ends. British troops evacuate country.
May 14, 1948	At 5 o'clock in the afternoon, on Shabbat Eve, Zionist leaders led by Ben-Gurion declare in Tel Aviv the establishment of a Jewish state. (Hebrew date: 5 Iyar 5708.) Transjordan, Egypt, Syria, Iraq, and Lebanon invade and join battle on the side of Palestinian Arab irregulars. Arabs declare Israel's creation a "Nakba" or catastrophe. The Israel Declaration of Independence cites the Balfour Declaration as the first in a series of international affirmations that underpin the right of the Jewish people to rebuild its national home.
1948	Arabs flee fighting; some are expelled. Some six hundred thousand become permanent refugees. Arab world rejects absorption and resettlement of the refugees. A somewhat larger number of Jews will flee the Arab world for Israel in the years to come.
May 14, 1948	Vatican newspaper editorializes that "modern Zionism is not the true heir of Biblical Israel.... Christianity [is] the true Israel."
May 14, 1948	US grants Israel de facto recognition.

May 16, 1948	Chaim Weizmann elected chairman of the Provisional State Council of Israel. David Ben-Gurion is prime minister.
May 17, 1948	The Soviet Union recognizes Israel.
May 18, 1948	Saudi Arabia joins Arabs fighting Israel.
June 1948	Irgun chief Menachem Begin establishes Herut Party.
August 2, 1948	"Drive the Jews into the sea…and never accept the Jewish state," exhorts Muslim Brotherhood founder Hassan al-Banna, reported by the *New York Times*.
November 8, 1948	There are 782,000 Jews and 69,000 Arabs in newly declared Jewish state.
January 25, 1949	First Knesset elections held. Mapai wins first Israel elections; David Ben-Gurion is prime minister. No party gains majority needed to form government by itself.
January 28, 1949	Britain recognizes Israel.
January–July 1949	Armistice agreements signed with Egypt, Lebanon, Transjordan, and Syria under UN auspices in Rhodes. The 1967 Six-Day War begins from these boundaries.
February 14, 1949	First Knesset (parliament) opens.
February 17, 1949	Weizmann elected president.
May 11, 1949	Israel admitted into UN.
August 17, 1949	Theodor Herzl's remains reinterred in Jerusalem.
November 1949	After eighteen months of independence there are one million Jews in Israel.
December 1949	Jordan annexes West Bank.
December 13, 1949	The Knesset votes to transfer Israel's capital to Jerusalem, rejecting a UN call for the city's internationalization.

Balfour Bookshelf

If this primer has piqued your interest in the Balfour Declaration and the Arab-Israel conflict, I invite you to keep reading. Here are some suggestions on where to begin.

Overview

Sanders, Ronald. *The High Walls of Jerusalem*. New York: Holt, Rinehart and Winston, 1983.

Schneer, Jonathan. *The Balfour Declaration: The Origins of the Arab-Israeli Conflict*. New York: Random House, 2010.

Stein, Leonard. *The Balfour Declaration*. New York: Simon and Schuster, 1961.

The Great War

Gilbert, Martin. *The First World War: A Complete History*. New York: Henry Holt and Co, 1994.

Keegan, John. *The First World War*. Toronto: Key Porter Books, 1998.

Tuchman, Barbara W. *The Guns of August*. New York: The Macmillan Company, 1962.

Balfour

Adams, R. J. Q. *Balfour: The Last Grandee*. London: John Murray, 2007.

Balfour, Arthur James. *Speeches on Zionism*. Edited by Israel Cohen. London: Arrowsmith, 1928.

Dugdale, Blanche E. C. *Arthur James Balfour, First Earl of Balfour*. London: Hutchinson, 1936.

Weizmann

Reinharz, Jehuda. *Chaim Weizmann*. Vol. 1, *The Making of a Zionist Leader*. New York: Oxford University Press, 1985.

—. *Chaim Weizmann*. Vol. 2, *The Making of a Statesman*. New York: Oxford University Press, 1993.

Weizmann, Chaim. *Trial and Error*. New York: Harper, 1949.

Weizmann, Vera, and David Tutaev. *The Impossible Takes Longer: The Memoirs of Vera Weizmann*. London: Hamish Hamilton, 1967.

The Mandate

Friedman, Isaiah. *Palestine, A Twice-Promised Land?* New Brunswick, NJ: Transaction Publishers, 2000.

Makovsky, Michael. *Churchill's Promised Land: Zionism and Statecraft*. New Haven: Yale University Press, 2007.

Segev, Tom. *One Palestine, Complete: Jews and Arabs under the British Mandate*. New York: Metropolitan Books, 2000.

Zionism

Avineri, Shlomo. *The Making of Modern Zionism: The Intellectual Origins of the Jewish State*. London: Weidenfeld and Nicolson, 1981.

Hertzberg, Arthur. *The Zionist Idea*. Garden City, NY: Doubleday and Herzl Press, 1959.

Laqueur, Walter. *A History of Zionism*. New York: Holt, Rinehart and Winston, 1972.

Shindler, Colin. *A History of Modern Israel*. Cambridge, UK: Cambridge University Press, 2013.

The Conflict

Bard, Mitchell Geoffrey. *Myths and Facts: A Guide to the Arab-Israeli Conflict*. CreateSpace Publishing, 2016.

Cohen, Hillel. *Army of Shadows: Palestinian Collaboration with Zionism, 1917–1948*. Berkeley, CA: University of California Press, 2008.

Herzog, Chaim. *The Arab-Israeli Wars*. New York: Random House, 1982.

Karsh, Efraim. *Palestine Betrayed*. New Haven: Yale University Press, 2010.

Katz, Samuel. *Battleground: Fact and Fantasy in Palestine*. London: W.H. Allen, 1973.

Morris, Benny. *One State, Two States: Resolving the Israel/Palestine Conflict*. New Haven, CT: Yale University Press, 2010.

O'Brien, Conor Cruise. *The Siege: The Saga of Israel and Zionism*. London: Paladin Grafton, 1988.

Herzl

Avineri, Shlomo, and Haim Watzman. *Herzl: Theodor Herzl and the Foundation of the Jewish State*. London: Weidenfeld and Nicolson, 2013.

Elon, Amos. *Herzl*. New York: Schocken Books, 1986.

Pawel, Ernst. *The Labyrinth of Exile: A Life of Theodor Herzl*. London: Collins Harvill, 1990.

C. P. Scott

Muller, Frederick, ed. *C. P. Scott, 1846–1932: The Making of the Manchester Guardian*. London: Muller, 1946.

Wilson, Trevor, ed. *The Political Diaries of C. P. Scott, 1911–1928*. London: Collins, 1976.

British Jewish History/Rothschild

Alderman, Geoffrey. *British Jewry Since Emancipation*. Buckingham: The University of Buckingham Press, 2014.

Cowles, Virginia. *The Rothschilds: A Family of Fortune*. London: Weidenfeld and Nicolson, 1973.

Sokolow

Kling, Simcha. *Nachum Sokolow*. New York: Herzl Press, 1960.

Sokołow, Florian, and Joseph Leftwich. *Nahum Sokolow: Life and Legend*. London: Jewish Chronicle Publishing, 1975.

Lloyd George

Jones, Thomas. *Lloyd George*. Cambridge, MA: Harvard, 1951.

Leo Amery

Faber, David. *Speaking for England: Leo, Julian and John Amery; The Tragedy of a Political Family*. London: Pocket, 2007.

Mark Sykes

Adelson, Roger. *Mark Sykes: Portrait of an Amateur*. London: Cape, 1975.

Leslie, Shane. *Mark Sykes: His Life and Letters*. London: Cassell, 1923.

Lucien Wolf

Levene, Mark. *War, Jews and the New Europe: The Diplomacy of Lucien Wolf, 1914–1919*. Oxford: Littman Library of Jewish Civilization, 2010.

Christians and Zionism

Grose, Peter. *Israel in the Mind of America*. New York: Knopf, 1984.

Kaplan, Robert D. *The Arabists: The Romance of an American Elite*. New York: Free Press, 1993.

Oren, Michael B. *Power, Faith, and Fantasy: America in the Middle East, 1776 to the Present*. New York: W.W. Norton, 2007.

ACKNOWLEDGMENTS

I am indebted to the London-based Jewish Leadership Council (JLC) which offered me the opportunity to immerse myself in all things Balfour and to write the initial content for its www.balfour100.com website. I found myself engrossed by the events, personalities, and politics surrounding the Balfour Declaration. This book is a completely independent endeavor and the JLC is in no way responsible for what I have written here. Yet, I would not have been pulled to the subject if not for JLC's chief executive Simon Johnson, who set me on the path in the first place. I am no less indebted, and not for the first time, to my friend Sally Berkovic for all that she did to facilitate my Balfour role. Janine Sternberg was thoughtfully encouraging. Clare and David Raff cheered me on in London. Leonie Swaden and Leon Baum provided London hospitality. Prof. Colin Shindler saved me from several embarrassing errors and shared material from his research.

In Jerusalem, my friend and editor Judy Montagu read the first draft with her usual careful eye and worked with me to help produce the manuscript submitted to Gefen Books. At Gefen, it was shepherded initially by Lynn Douek and later by Emily Wind and made immeasurably better by editors Gayle Green and Kezia Raffel Pride. My appreciation goes to Gefen publisher Ilan Greenfield for pulling out all the stops to get this book out in time for the centenary. Kudos to Elizabeth Sandler for her work on the index.

Gratitude goes also to my venerable friend Rev. Elwood McQuaid and to the incomparable Yisrael Medad for their magnanimous contributions to this volume.

This book would not – could not – have been written without the encouragement of my life-partner Lisa Clayton. In this project and in every important milestone we commemorate our parents – my mother Yvette Jager and Lisa's mum and dad, David and Zena Clayton. They taught us *menschlichkeit*, *yiddishkeit* and to seek the golden mean.

INDEX

www.ingramcontent.com/pod-product-compliance
Lightning Source LLC
Chambersburg PA
CBHW052330100426

42737CB00055B/3287